Robert Cooke

The Visitations of Hertfordshire

Robert Cooke

The Visitations of Hertfordshire

ISBN/EAN: 9783744796156

Printed in Europe, USA, Canada, Australia, Japan

Cover: Foto ©ninafisch / pixelio.de

More available books at **www.hansebooks.com**

THE
Publications
OF
The Harleian Society.

ESTABLISHED A.D. MDCCCLXIX.

Volume XXII.

FOR THE YEAR MD.CCC.LXXXVI.

The
Visitations of Hertfordshire,

MADE BY

ROBERT COOKE, Esq., Clarencieux, in 1572,

AND

SIR RICHARD ST. GEORGE, Kt., Clarencieux, in 1634,

WITH

Hertfordshire Pedigrees

FROM HARLEIAN MSS. 6147 AND 1546.

EDITED BY

WALTER C. METCALFE, F.S.A.

LONDON:
1886.

Preface.

THE first Visitation of Hertfordshire and Middlesex was made in 1572 by COOKE, and the second in 1634 by Sir RICHARD ST. GEORGE. The original MSS. of these are G 17 and C 28 at the College of Arms.

This Volume contains so much of these two Visitations as relates to Hertfordshire.

Copies of the Hertfordshire portion of the first Visitation are to be found in Harl. MSS. 1433, 1504, 1546, and 6147; and of the second in Harl. MSS. 1504 and 1547. These MSS. contain many additions to the Visitation Pedigrees, which are not repeated in these pages. Harl. MS. 6147 also contains the additional Hertfordshire Pedigrees which are given in Appendix I.; a copy of this MS. is in the Library of Queen's College, Oxford, and has been erroneously called a Visitation of Hertfordshire in 1615 by CAMDEN.

Appendix II. contains Hertfordshire Pedigrees added to Harl. MS. 1546 by R. MUNDY.

A few explanatory notes are given in brackets.

The third and last Visitation of Hertfordshire is that of 1669 by BYSSHE, D 28 at the College of Arms, of which no copy is known to exist elsewhere.

Table of Contents.

	PAGE
ALDEN OF RICKMANSWORTH	25
ALLEY OF BERKHAMPSTEAD	1
ANDERSON OF PENDLEY	109
ANDREW OF HITCHIN	123
ANTROBUS OF ALDENHAM	123
ARNOLD OF CHILDWICK	1
BALDWIN OF REDHEATH	125
BARBER OF HERTFORD	25
BARDOLF OF HARPENDEN	2
BARDOLF OF ST. MICHAEL'S	26
BARKLEY OF EAST BARNET	26
BARLEY OF BIBSWORTH HALL	27
BARNWELL OF ST. ALBAN'S	110
BASH OF STANSTED BURY AND ST. MARGARET'S	125
BAYLY OF STANDON	27
BAYLY OF HODDESDON	27
BELFELD OF STUDHAM	3, 28
BERKHAMPSTEAD, TOWN AND BOROUGH	108
BERNERS OF THARFIELD	28
BESTNEY OF ST. ALBAN'S	126
BLAKETT OF TRING	128
BLUNT OF TITTENHANGER	29, 128
BORASTON OF ALDENHAM	110
BOTELER OF QUEEN HOO HALL	29
BOTELER OF STAPLEFORD	30
BOTELER OF WOODHALL	111
BOWLES OF WALLINGTON	112
BRADBERY OF BRAUGHIN	129
BRIGGES OF RICKMANSWORTH	30
BRISCO OF ALDENHAM	31
BRISCO OF ST. MICHAEL'S	31
BRISTOW OF SACOMB	130
BROCKETT OF WHEATHAMPSTEAD	32
BROCKETT OF CODICOT	33
BROGRAVE OF HAMMELS	33
BROGRAVE OF BRAUGHIN	131
BROMLEY OF WARE WESTMILL	34
BULL OF HERTFORD	3, 34
BULLER OF ST. ALBAN'S	35
BUSSEY OF CHESHUNT	132
CADE OF KING'S LANGLEY	133
CÆSAR OF SANDON	35
CÆSAR OF BENINGTON	133
CAGE OF HORMEAD	35

	PAGE
CAPELL OF LITTLE HADHAM	36, 113
CARTER OF GARSTON	37
CARY OF ALDENHAM	134
CASON OF ASTON BURY	37
CHAMBER OF BARKWAY	38, 137
CHAPMAN OF MARDOCKS	4
CHAUNCEY OF SAWBRIDGWORTH	4, 38
CHAUNCEY OF YARDLEY	39
CHESTER OF COCKEN HATCH	39
CHILDE OF NORTH MIMMS	138
CHUNE OF SHENLEY	40
CLARKE OF THARFIELD AND ASHWELL	41
CLARKE OF CHESFIELD	42
COCK OF BROXBOURNE	5
COGHILL OF BUSHEY	42
COLE OF SHENLEY HALL	42
COLLES OF PARKBURY	43
COLLEY OF WARE	5
COLTE OF RICKMANSWORTH	43
COMBE OF HEMEL HEMPSTEAD	6, 44
CONEY OF ST. ALBAN'S	44
CONINGSBY OF NORTH MIMMS	45
CONYERS OF BARNET	139
COPPIN OF MARKETSELL	45
COPWOOD OF TOTTERIDGE	6
COTTON OF FLAMSTEAD	46
COX OF BEAMOND	7, 46
CROSBY OF WINDBRIDGE	47
DACRES OF CHESHUNT	47
DEWHURST OF CHESHUNT	48
DIXON OF BRAUGHIN	48
DOCWRA OF PUTTERIDGE	48, 139
DOD OF BENINGTON	50
DOLMAN OF NEWNHAM	140
DREW OF BROXBOURNE	50
DYER OF WATERS PLACE	7
EAKINS OF NORTHAW	51
ELMER *alias* AYLMER OF MUCH HADHAM	141
EWER OF THE LEA AND CHESHUNT	51
FAIRCLOUGH OF FAIRCLOUGH HALL AND WESTON	52
FANSHAW OF WARE PARK	114

	PAGE
FARRAR OF GREAT AMWELL	53
FERRERS OF PUNSBORNE	141
FINCH OF ST. MICHAEL'S	142
FISHE OF HATFIELD	54
FISHE OF STEVENAGE	54
FORSTER OF HUNSDON	143
FOTHERLEY OF RICKMANSWORTH	144
FOWKE OF ST. ALBAN'S AND FLAMSTEAD	54
FRANCES OF COOKMAINES AND SALMONS	55
GAPE OF ST. ALBAN'S	144
GARDENER OF WATFORD	56
GARDINER OF JENINGSBURY	57
GARDINER OF THUNDRIDGEBURY	57
GARRARD OF WHEATHAMPSTEAD	144
GILL OF ANSTEY	58
GOODERE OF HADLEY	8
GOODERE OF HATFIELD	58
GOODMAN OF RUSHDON	145
GOURNEY OF HITCHIN	58
GRAVELEY OF GRAVELEY	8
GREENE OF EAST BARNET	59
GREVE OF SHENLEY	9
GROSVENOR OF WADESMILL	10
GRUBBE OF NORTH MIMMS	59
GULSTON OF WYDDIALL	60
HALE OF TEWIN	61
HALE OF HARMER GREEN	61
HALE OF KING'S WALDEN	62
HALSEY OF GREAT GADDESDEN	62
HALTON OF SAWBRIDGWORTH	62
HANCHETT OF BRAUGHIN	63
HARRIS OF RICKMANSWORTH	63
HARVY OF SHENLEY	10, 146
HAYDON OF THE GROVE	11
HAYDON OF WATFORD	11
HAYES OF HERTFORD	64
HERTFORD, TOWN AND BOROUGH	107
HEWETT OF RICKMANSWORTH	64
HIDE OF GREAT HADHAM	64
HILL OF WHITBOROW HILL	12
HILL OF HILL END, *see* BARNWELL	

TABLE OF CONTENTS.

	PAGE		PAGE		PAGE
Hoo of Paul's Walden	12, 65	Morrison of Sandon	76	Shirley of Hertford Town	163
Horsey of Digswell	114	Morrison of Cashiobury	116	Shotbolt of Yardley	163
Howland of St. Alban's	65	Needham of Wymondley	16	Simpson of St. Alban's	92
Humberstone of Walkarne	66	Needham of Wymondley and Welwyn	77	Skipwith of St. Alban's	20
Hurst of Sawbridgworth	66	Newce of Brickendonbury	17	Skinner of Hitchin	93
Hurst of Bishop Stortford	67	Newce of Broxbourne	17	Smithwick of Lees Langley	21
Hyde of Albury	67	Newce of Much Hadham	78	Smyth of Annables	164
Hyde of Throcking	67	Newcomen of Bishop Stortford	79	Snagg of Letchworth	21
Ibgrave of Abbot's Langley	13	Newport of Furneux Pelham	79	Snelling of St. Margaret's	164
Inkersall of Weston	68	Newport of Pelham	155	Spencer of St. Alban's	22
Ironside of Rickmansworth	68	Nodes of Stevenage	18	Spencer of Offley	165
James of Braughin	69	Nodes of Shephall	80	Sterne of Hoddesdon	93
Jennings of Sandridge	147	Norton of Marketsell	80	Sterne of Barkway	94
Joscelin of Hyde Hall	14, 69	Palmer of Shenley	18	Steward of Braughin	94
Kent of Aston	148	Pemberton of St. Alban's	81	Stratford of Meesden	95
Kimpton of Weston	69	Penne of Codicot	82, 116	Taverner of Hextonbury	95
Kingsley of Sarrat	70	Perient of Digswell	156	Taylor of Furneux Pelham	165
Kitchin of Totteridge	70	Pichford of St. Alban's	82	Thompson of Watton	97
Knight of Baldock	14	Plomer of Rodwell	83, 157	Thorogood of Tharfield	98
Knighton of Bayford	70	Potkin of Lilley and Rickmansworth	158	Thorogood of Cheshunt	117
Lake of Wilstern	71	Powell of St. Alban's	83	Tooke of Wormley	98
Lambert, see Wilson.		Pranell of Rushenwell	159	Tooke of Popes	99
Langhorne of Bedford	71	Preston of Childwick	84	Tooke of Essendon, Wormley, and Stanstead	166
Lavender of Standon	72	Puckering of Weston	160		
Lawrence of Hertingfordbury	72	Pulter of Bradfield	85	Verney of Penley	23, 168
Lee of Sopwell	149	Pulter of Wymondley	116	Vernon of Hertingfordbury	99
Leventhorpe of Shingle Hall and Albery	149	Purvey of Wormley	161		
Lewen of Hertford	115	Quarles of Cranes	161	Walter of Broxbourne	23
Litton of Knebworth	73, 115, 151	Radcliffe of Hitchin	19. 85	Warren of Colney	100
Lockey of Ridge	151	Reade of Brocket Hall	162	Warren of Harpenden	169
Lowe of St. Alban's	74	Rich of Anstey	86	Warren alias Waller of Ashwell	101
Marshall of Much Hadham	15	Robinson of Cheshunt	86		
Marston of Hemel Hempstead	74	Robotham of St. Alban's	87	Waterhouse of Berkhampstead	119
Maynard of St. Alban's	15	Rogers of Maydencroft	87	Wathe of St. Alban's	101
Mayne of Bovington	75	Rolfe of St. Alban's	88	Watts of Thundridge	102
Meautis of Hertford	75	Rotheram of Farley, co. Bedford	88	Watts of Ware	102
Mery of Hatfield	152	Sadler of Sopwell	89	Weld of Widbury Hill	103
Mildmay of Sawbridgworth	153	Sadler of Standon	89	Whitaker of Ashwell	103
Mohun of Aldenham	16	St. Alban's, Town and Borough	107	Williams of Abbot's Langley	169
Monox of Charleywood	76	Saltonstall of Barkway	90	Willimot of Kelshall	104
Moore of Hadham	153	Sapcotts of Tharfield	162	Willis of Balls	104
Morgan of Bushey Hall	76	Saunders of Beechwood	90	Wilson of Willion	105, 121
Morley of Berkhampstead	154	Scroggs of Patmore	163	Wingate of Lockleys	105
		Sedley of Digswell	91	Wrothe of Youngs	106
		Selioke of St. Alban's	91	Wyndowt of Radwell	106
		Sennoke of Layston	92	Index	171—181

The Visitation of Hertfordshire, 1572.

Alley of Berkhampstead.

ARMS.—*Azure, a pile Ermine.*

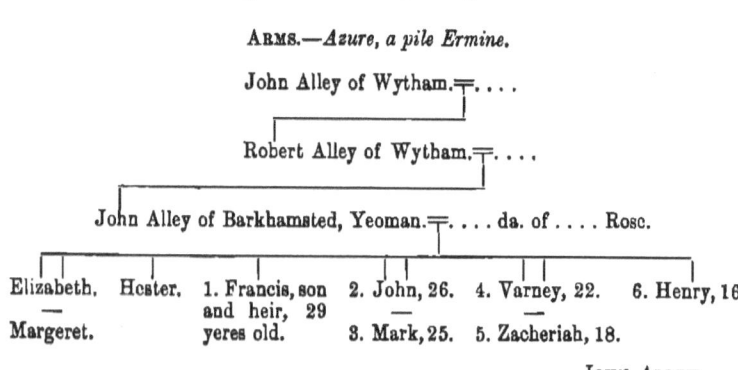

John Alley of Wytham.=. . . .

Robert Alley of Wytham.=. . . .

John Alley of Barkhamsted, Yeoman.=. . . . da. of . . . . Rose.

Elizabeth.   Hester.   1. Francis, son and heir, 29 yeres old.   2. John, 26.   4. Varney, 22.   6. Henry, 16.

Margeret.   3. Mark, 25.   5. Zacheriah, 18.

                                                                                 JOHN ALLEY.

Arnold of Childwick.

ARMS.—*Gules, a chevron quarterly Ermine and Ermines between three pheons Or.*
CREST.—*An eagle's head erased Gules, ducally gorged Argent, holding in the beak an acorn-branch, slipped leaved Vert, fructed Or.*

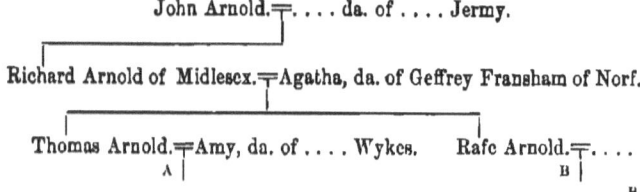

John Arnold.=. . . . da. of . . . . Jermy.

Richard Arnold of Midlesex.=Agatha, da. of Geffrey Fransham of Norf.

Thomas Arnold.=Amy, da. of . . . . Wykes.   Rafe Arnold.=. . . .
           A | B |

THE VISITATION OF HERTFORDSHIRE, 1572.

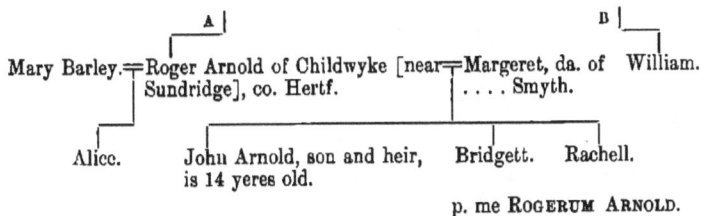

p. me ROGERUM ARNOLD.

Bardolf of Harpenden.

ARMS.—*Quarterly*—1, *Azure, a chevron between three cinquefoils pierced Or*; 2, *Argent, a lion rampant double-queued Sable*, CRESSY ; 3, *Barry of six Or and Azure, on an escutcheon a serpent* "*eating a child,*" *on a chief of the second three pallets between two gyrons of the first*, MORTIMER ; 4, *Ermine, three bars Gules*, HUSSEY.
CREST.—*Out of a coronet a dragon's head Or*.

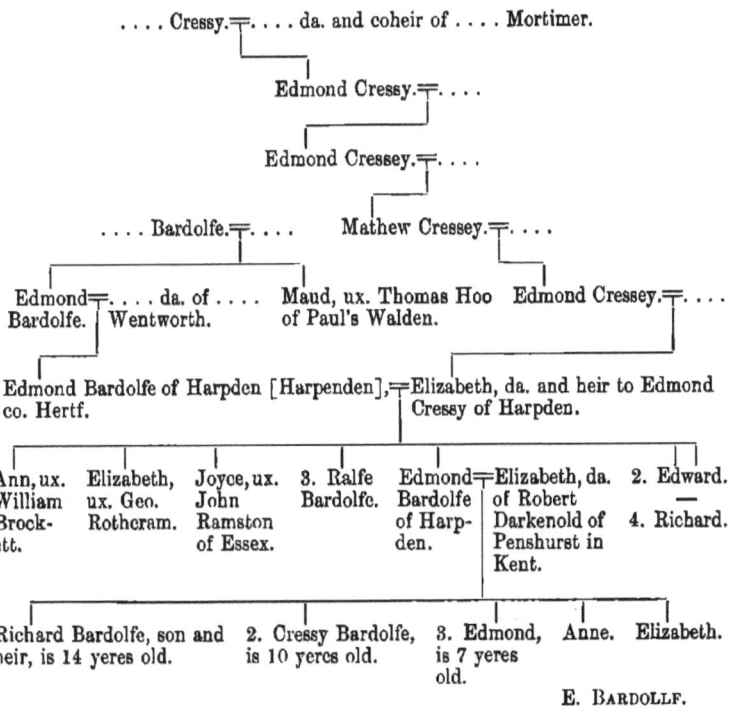

E. BARDOLLF.

Belfeld of Studham.

ARMS.—*Ermine, a mullet Gules, on a chief of the last a label of five points Argent.*
CREST.—*A demi-tiger Argent, crined Or, pierced through with a spear pennoned of the second.*

A confirmation to John Belfeld of Studham as to a third brother of Belfeld of Clegg in Rochdale in com. Lanc. to beare this coate.

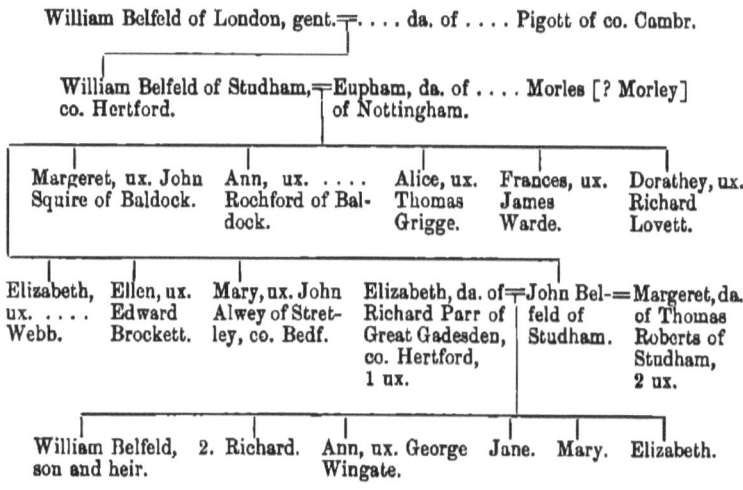

Bull of Hertford.

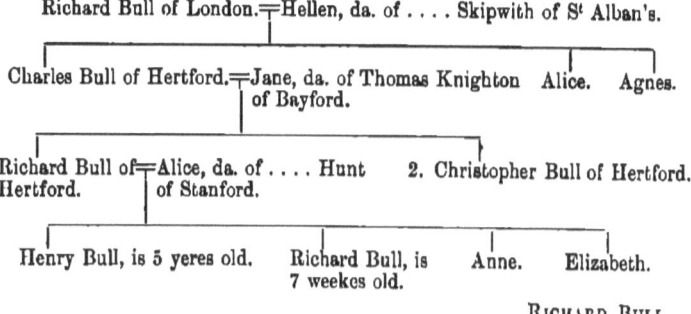

RICHARD BULL.

Chauncey of Sawbridgworth.

ARMS.—*Gules, a cross patonce Argent, on a chief Azure a lion passant Or.*
CREST.—*Out of a ducal coronet Or, a griffin's head Gules, charged with a pale Azure, between two wings displayed of the last, the inward part of the wings of the second.*
On each a crescent for difference.

William Chancy of Sawbridgeworth. =. . . . da. of . . . . Garland.

Henry Chancy of Sawbridgeworth. =Joane, da. of . . . . Tendring.

William Chancy of Sawbridgeworth. =Bridget, da. of John Raymond.

2. Alexander Chuncey. =Mary, da. of John Raymond.

George Chancy, son and heir, 13 yeres old.

2. Thomas Chancy, is 3 yeres old.

Elizabeth — Joane.

A daughter, uncrisned the 6 of Septemb. [13 Sept. 1579 —Harl. MS. 1504].

Mary. — Dorothy. — Lucey.

Henry. — Alexander. — John.

WM. CHAUNCY.

Chapman of Mardocks.

ARMS.—*Quarterly—1 and 4, Per chevron Argent and Gules, a crescent counterchanged, on a chief of the second a unicorn's head between two leopards' faces Or; 2 and 3, Or, a fret Sable,* MARDOCK.
CREST.—*A falcon Argent, beaked and legged Gules, supporting a garb Or.*

Hugh Chapman of Cambridge. =Ann, da. and heir of John Mardock.

Robert Chapman, son and heir. =Elizabeth . . . .

John Chapman of Ware, co. Hertf. =Ann, da. of Henry Mannock of Huntingdonshire.

Katherine, ux. Thomas Gardiner of London.

Henry Chapman, is 12 yeres old.

Robert, is 9 yeres old.

JOHN CHAPMAN.

Cock of Broxborne.

ARMS.—*Quarterly*—1, *Quarterly Gules and Argent;* 2, *Argent, a chevron engrailed between three mullets Sable,* HAMOND ; 3, *Vert, on a cross Or an estoile Gules,* ADAMS; 4, *Sable, a chevron engrailed Ermine between three pheons Or,* FOSTER.
CREST.—*An ostrich Or, legged Argent, holding in the beak a horseshoe of the second.*

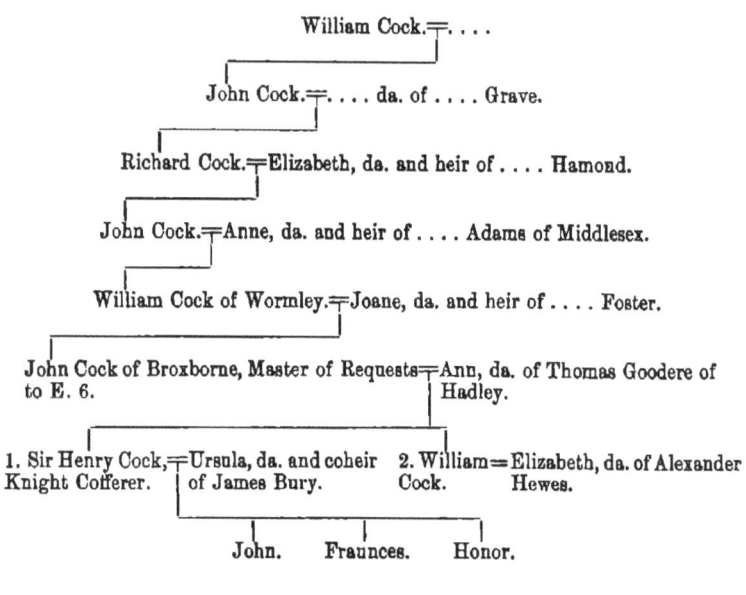

Colley of Ware.

ARMS.—*Sable, three swans' heads erased Argent beaked and within a bordure Or.*
CREST.—*An elephant's head Or, tusked and eared Gules, between two wings Sable.*

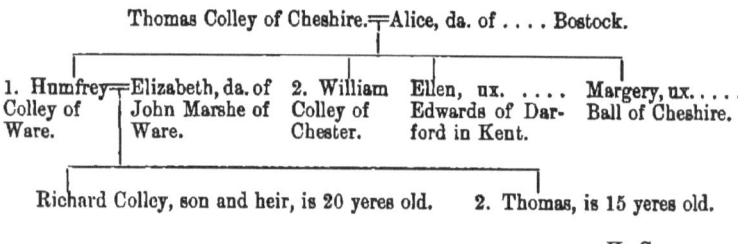

H. COLLY.

Combe of Hemel Hempstead.

ARMS.—*Ermine, three lions passant in pale Gules.*
CREST.—*An arm in armour embowed per pale Or and Sable, holding in the hand proper a broken tilting-spear of the first.*

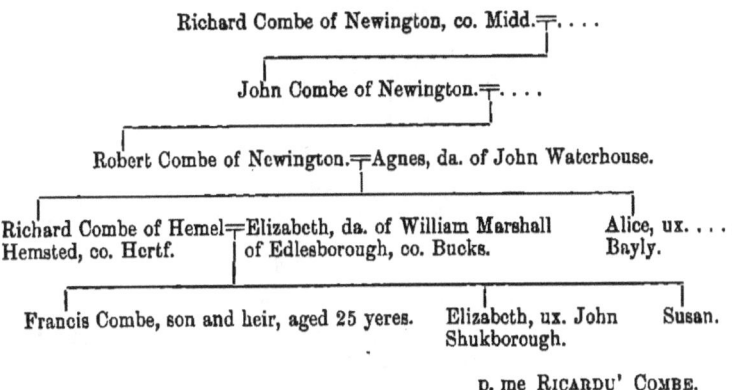

p. me RICARDU' COMBE.

Copwood of Totteridge.

ARMS.—*Argent, a pile in bend fimbriated and engrailed Gules between two eagles displayed Vert.*
CREST.—*An eagle with wings expanded Or.*

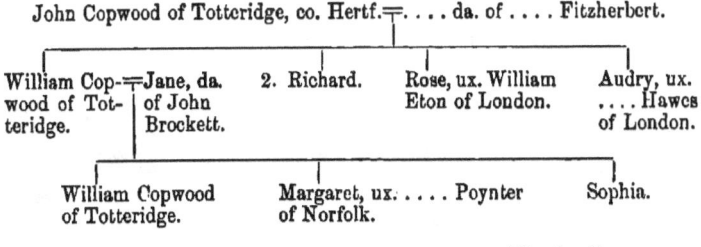

WILL'M COPWOOD.

Cox of Beamond.

ARMS.—*Or, three bars Azure, on a quarter Argent a lion's head couped Gules.*
CREST.—*An antelope's head erased Sable, horned, bearded, and pierced through the neck with an arrow Or.*

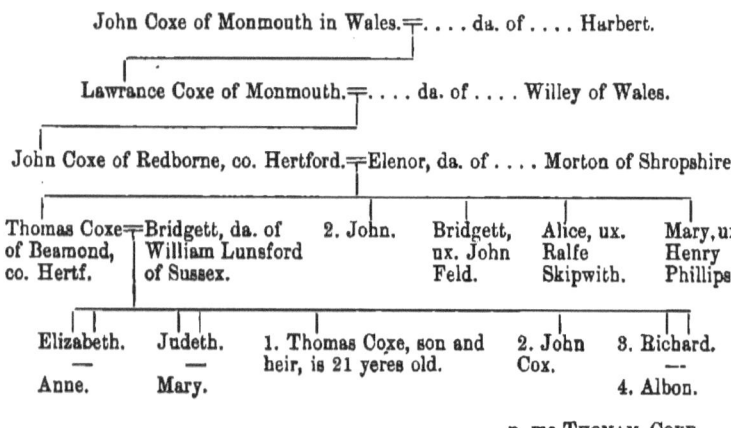

John Coxe of Monmouth in Wales.=.... da. of .... Harbert.

Lawrance Coxe of Monmouth.=.... da. of .... Willey of Wales.

John Coxe of Redborne, co. Hertford.=Elenor, da. of .... Morton of Shropshire.

Thomas Coxe=Bridgett, da. of	2. John.	Bridgett,	Alice, ux.	Mary, ux.
of Beamond, William Lunsford		ux. John	Ralfe	Henry
co. Hertf. of Sussex.		Feld.	Skipwith.	Phillips.

Elizabeth.	Judeth.	1. Thomas Coxe, son and	2. John	3. Richard.
—	—	heir, is 21 yeres old.	Cox.	—
Anne.	Mary.			4. Albon.

p. me THOMAM COXE.

Dyer of Waters Place.

ARMS.—*Sable, a fess engrailed Or between three bucks statant Argent.*
CREST.—*An old man's head sidefaced couped at the shoulders proper, vested Azure, collar Gules, his hair Sable, cap Or turned up Vairé of the first and second. Each charged with a martlet for difference.*

Thomas Dyer of Aldbury, co. Hertf.=Katherine, da. of .... Benet.

Mary, ux.	Ann, ux. .... Bowyer.	Myrabell,	1. Thomas	4. George=Joan, da.
Alexander	—	ux.	Dyer.	Dyer of and heir
Hayward	Audrey, ux. .... Ewen	Hills of	—	Waters- of ....
of Hert-	of Broxted in Essex.	Ansty, co.	2. Nicholas.	Place, co. Lacy of
ford.	—	Hertf.	—	Hertford, Essex.
	Joan, ux. .... Greene.		3. John.	gent.

p. me GEORGIU' DIER.

Goodere of Hadley.

ARMS.—*Gules, a fess between two chevrons Vair.*
CREST.—*A partridge proper, in the beak a wheat-ear Or.*
On each a crescent for difference.

John Goodere of Hadley, co. Midd., a° 20 H. 6.=. . . .

- John Goodere, son and heir. =. . . . da. of Richard Gladman, Esq. *Gules, a fauchion in fess between 3 moletts Argent.*
  - Thomas Goodere, son and heir. =. . . .
    - Francis, son and heir. =. . . .
      - Henry, son and heir.
    - William Goodere of Hadley. =Anne, da. of . . . . Cooke of London.
      - Thomas. — William.
      - Anne.
- William Goodere of Edgworth. =Ann, da. of . . . . Bostok. *Sable, a fess Argent.*
  - Henry Goodere of London. =Jane, da. of . . . .
    - Henry Goodere, son and heir, 27 yeres old.
      2. Thomas, is 19 yeres old.
      - Henry, son and heir, is 20 yeres old.
      - 2. William, is 16 yeres old.
- Richard Goodere of St. Alban's. =. . . .
  - Nicholas Goodere, son and heir. =Julian, da. of . . . . Elderington.
    - Johan, mar. to . . . . Barret of London.
    - Katheren. — Margaret. — Mary.
      - Anne, mar. to Thomas Walkden.
      - Ciceley, is unmarried.
  - Alban Goodere, s.p.

Graveley* of Graveley.

ARMS.—*Sable, a cross pointed Argent, in the dexter point a mullet of the last.*

These arms were taken out of a window in Graveley Church.

Robert Graveley, Kt. =Beatrix, da. of . . . . Ano E. filii Regis Edwardi. in a deed *sans date.* A deed of Beatrix after the decease of her husband in A° E. filii Regis Edward.

William, did give to Rafe his son. =. . . .

Rafe, the son of William, 14 E. 3. =. . . .
A

* In MS. 6147 written *Gravell* throughout.

THE VISITATION OF HERTFORDSHIRE, 1572.   9

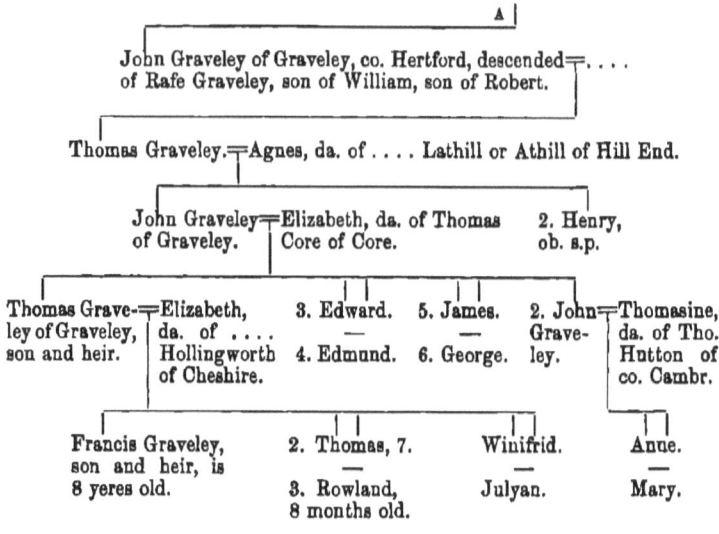

Greve of Shenley.

ARMS.—*Argent, on a fess Azure, between three pellets each charged with a lion's head erased of the field, a griffin passant between two escallops Or.*
CREST.—*A squirrel sejant Sable, charged with two bends sinister Argent, holding an escallop Or.*

A pattent granted to Thomas Greve of Rotherham in the countie of York by Garter Wriothesley and Tho. Walle *al's* Norroy, 1523, 15 H. 8.

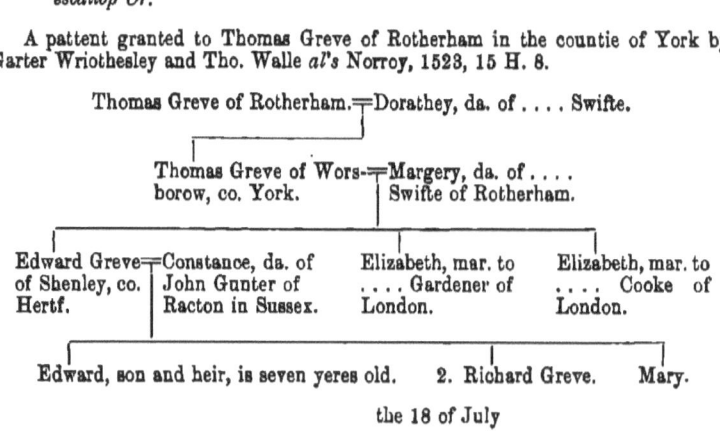

the 18 of July

By me EDWARD GREVE.

Grosvenor of Wadesmill.

ARMS.—*Quarterly*—1 *and* 4, *Azure, a garb Or between three bezants;* 2 *and* 3, *Vert, fretty Or,* WHITMORE.

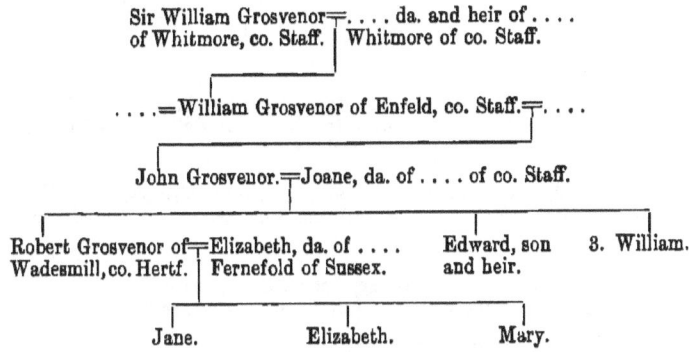

p. me ROB'TUM GROSVENOR.

Harvy of Shenley.

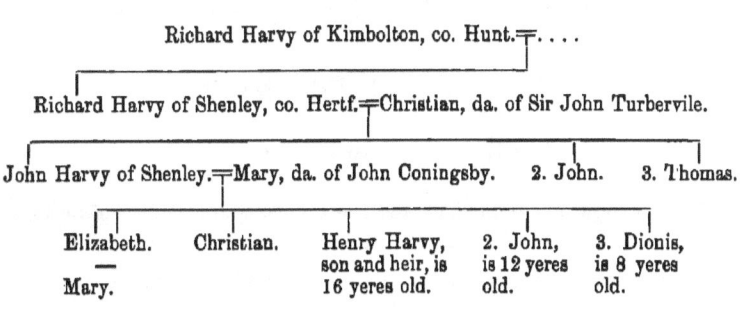

Haydon of The Grove.

ARMS.—*Quarterly*—1 *and* 4, *Quarterly Argent and Azure, a cross engrailed counterchanged;* 2, *Bendy of six Ermine and Gules,* AUBREY; 3, *Gules, a saltire between four leopards' heads erased Argent.*

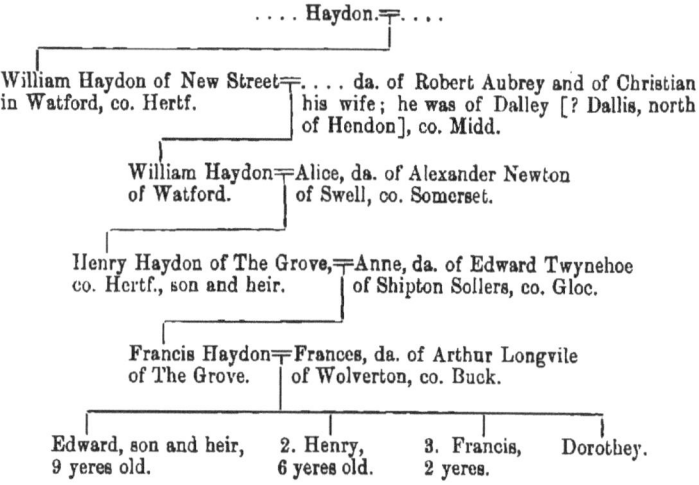

FRANCIS HAYDON.

Haydon of Watford.

ARMS.—As HAYDON of The Grove.

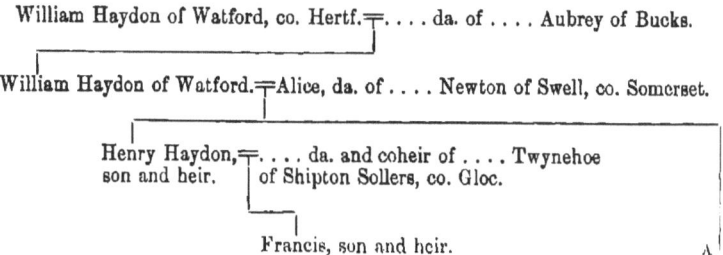

Thomas Haydon of North Cothill, mar. Margaret, da. of Simon Conder, 2 ux. =⸝= Margery, da. of .... Jacob alias Bredelaughe of Laxfeild, co. Suff., 1 ux.
2. Jerom.
3. Anthony.

Michael, son and heir, is 22 yeres old.
2. William, is 17 yeres old.
3. John, is 12 yeres old.
Winifred.

THOMAS HAYDON.

Hill of Witborow Hill.

Symon Reade.=⸝=Joan, da. and heir of Nicholas Grymbold.
ARMS.—*Argent, three bars Sable.*

Thomas Reade.=⸝= ....

.... a da., mar. to Sir Robert Litton.   .... a da.=⸝= .... Collins.

Richard Hill of London.=⸝=Lettyce, da. of .... Collins.

1. Anthony Hill. =⸝= ....
2. Gilbert Hill of Witborow Hill, co. Hertf. =⸝= Margery, da. of .... Okam of Newbery, co. Berks.

Susan, mar. to ....
1. Richard Hill, 26 yeres old.
2. Benjamin Hill, is 20 yeres old.
Phillip, mar. to Robert Edmondson of London.

Hoo of Paul's Walden.

ARMS.—*Quarterly of six*—1, *Quarterly Sable and Argent*; 2, *Azure, a fret Argent, a chief Gules*, ST. LEGER; 3, *Azure, a fess between six cross-crosslets Or*, ST. OMER; 4, *Azure, three dexter hands appaumée Argent*, MALMAYNES; 5, *Ermine, on a chief Sable three crosses patée Argent*, WICHINGHAM; 6, *Ermine, a cross engrailed Gules, over all a bend Azure*, NORWOOD.
CREST.—*A female's head and shoulders affrontée proper, crined Or, banded Gules.* On each *a crescent for difference.*

Sir Thomas Hoo, Kt.=⸝=Isabel, da. and heir of Sir John St. Leger, Kt.

Sir William Hoo, Kt.=⸝=Alison [? Ellenor], da. and heir to the Lord St. Omer, and, A | by her mother, heir to Sir Nicholas Malmaynes.

THE VISITATION OF HERTFORDSHIRE, 1572.   13

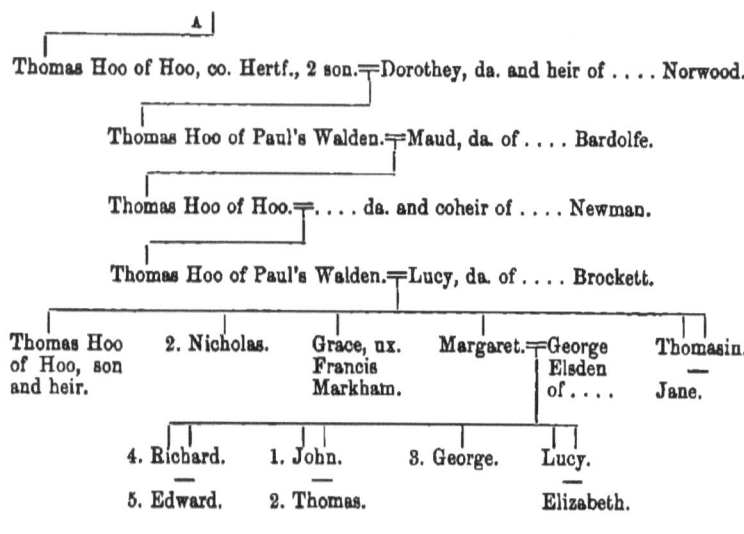

THOMAS HOO.

Ibgrave of Abbott's Langley.

ARMS.—*Quarterly*—1 and 4, *Per pale Argent and Gules, a fer-de-moline between two lozenges all counterchanged; 2, Three Catherine-wheels within a bordure engrailed; 3, Argent, a chevron engrailed between three trefoils slipped Sable.*

[Allowed to William Ibgrave of Abbott's Langley by Barker, Garter.—Harl. MS. 1546.]

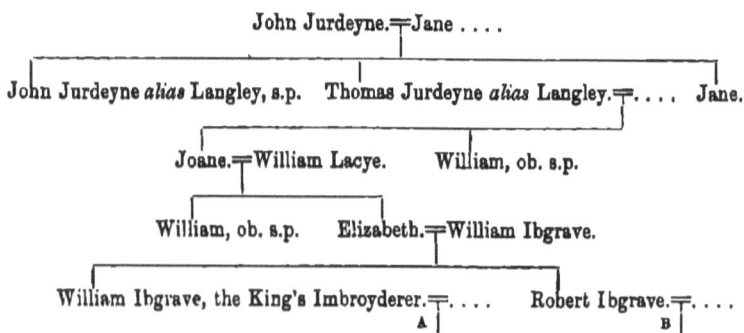

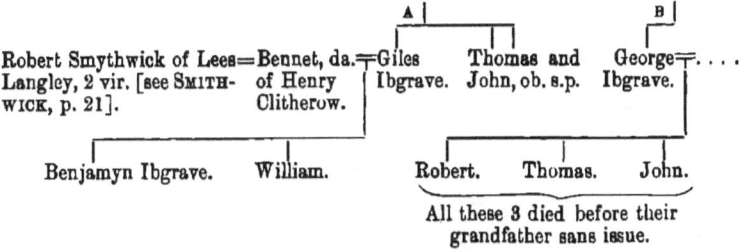

Joscelin of Hyde Hall.

Allis, 2 da. of Sir = Richard Joselyn of Sabridge- = Anne, da. of M^r
John Shelton, | worth, 1579, of Hyde Hall in | Thomas Lucas
Kt., 1 ux. | the same parish. | of Bury.

Richard Joselyn, 7 years old | Jone and Mary, borne both | Litle Wencfrid, is 12
on Bartholomew's day last | at a birth when Paul's Steple | mouthes old.
[1579]. | was burnt [1561].

Knight of Baldock and Weston.

ARMS.—*Sable, on a fess Argent three quatrefoils of the field, in chief a horse's head erased Or.*
CREST.—*A goat's head Or, erased and horned Gules, holding in its mouth an ivy-branch Vert.*

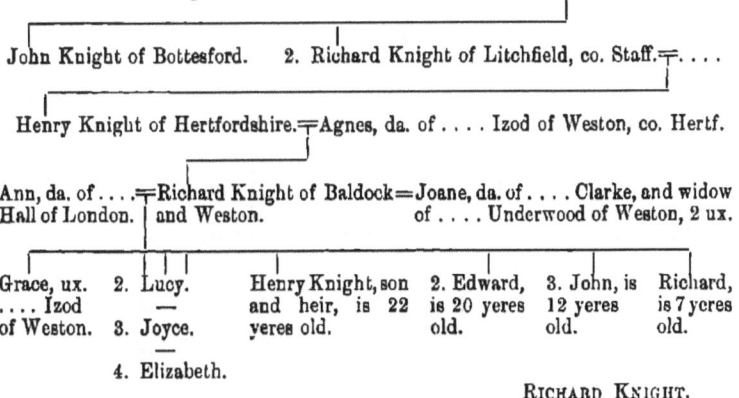

RICHARD KNIGHT.

THE VISITATION OF HERTFORDSHIRE, 1572.   15

Marshall of Much Hadham.

ARMS.—*Gules, on a fess Argent between three mascles Or as many lions' heads erased Azure.*

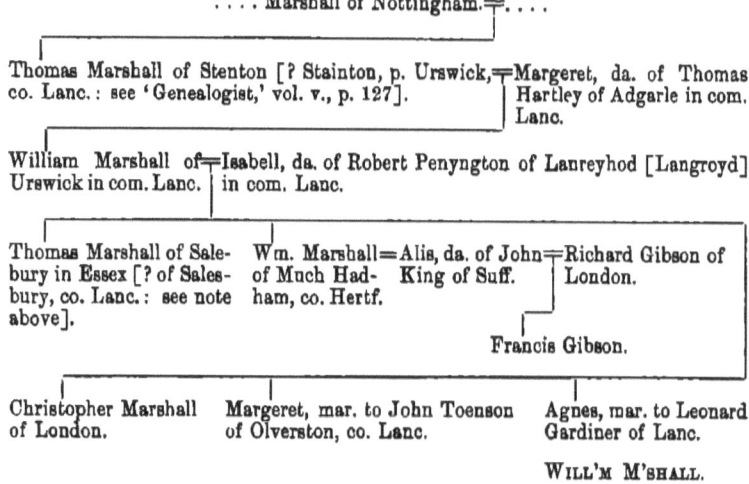

.... Marshall of Nottingham.=....

Thomas Marshall of Stenton [? Stainton, p. Urswick,=Margeret, da. of Thomas co. Lanc.: see 'Genealogist,' vol. v., p. 127]. Hartley of Adgarle in com. Lanc.

William Marshall of=Isabell, da. of Robert Penyngton of Lanreyhod [Langroyd] Urswick in com. Lanc. in com. Lanc.

Thomas Marshall of Salebury in Essex [? of Salesbury, co. Lanc.: see note above].

Wm. Marshall=Alis, da. of John=Richard Gibson of of Much Hadham, co. Hertf. King of Suff. London.

Francis Gibson.

Christopher Marshall of London.

Margeret, mar. to John Toenson of Olverston, co. Lanc.

Agnes, mar. to Leonard Gardiner of Lanc.

WILL'M M'SHALL.

Maynard of Saint Alban's.

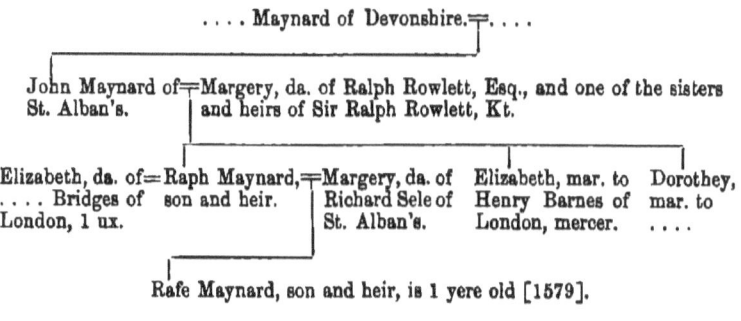

.... Maynard of Devonshire.=....

John Maynard of=Margery, da. of Ralph Rowlett, Esq., and one of the sisters St. Alban's. and heirs of Sir Ralph Rowlett, Kt.

Elizabeth, da. of=Raph Maynard,=Margery, da. of Elizabeth, mar. to Dorothey,
.... Bridges of   son and heir.   Richard Sele of Henry Barnes of mar. to
London, 1 ux.   St. Alban's.   London, mercer. ....

Rafe Maynard, son and heir, is 1 yere old [1579].

p. me RADU' MAINARD.

Mohun of Aldenham.

ARMS.—*Gules, a dexter arm proper habited with a maunch Ermine, in the hand proper a fleur-de-lis Or.*

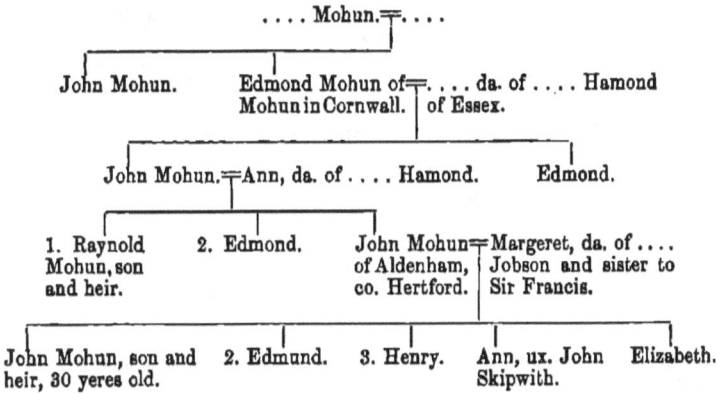

Needham of Wymondley.

ARMS.—*Azure, on a chevron between three escallops Argent as many acorns Vert, on a chief crenellée Or three martlets Gules.*
CREST.—*A dolphin naiant Or.*

Vide Cla. Cook's guift for another coat.

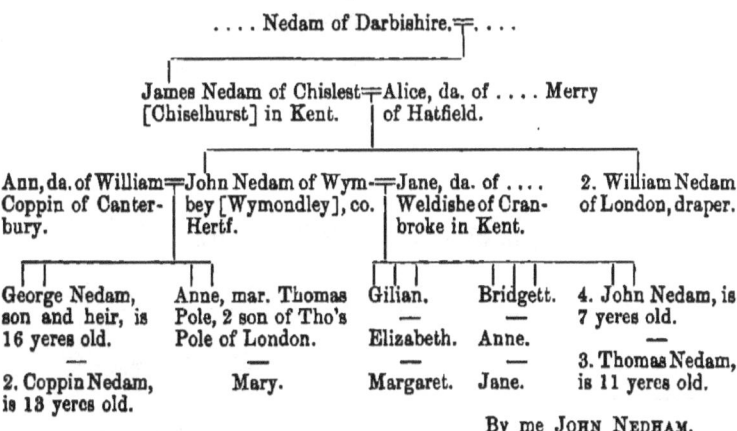

By me JOHN NEDHAM.

Newce of Brickendonbury.

ARMS.—A Patent granted to Clement Newce of London, gent., by Thomas Hawley al's Clarenceulx, aº 3 Ed'ri 6 (viz¹), *Ermins and Silver p. fesse, on a chevron Gu. under the same 2 rounds Azure, on a cheife B. a mayden's head hered and vested a cheyne about her neck between two bezants. On a wreath Gold and Azure a luyssant's or ibex's hed rased Gules, ubout his neck a crown Silver, tusked, eared, and horned Or, between two nut-branches Vert.*

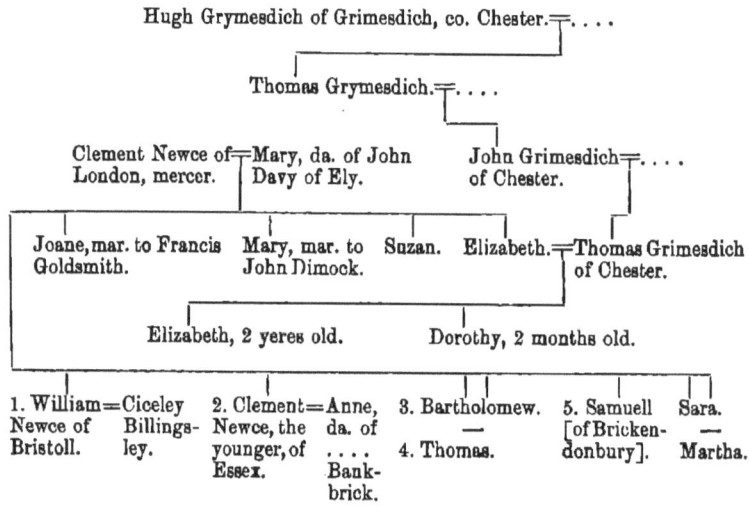

Signed 5 Septemb. 1571

By me CLEMENT NEWCE TH'ELDER.

Newce of Broxbourne.

ARMS.—*Sable, two pales Argent, on a canton Ermine a mascle Gules.*
CREST.—*On a mound Vert a garb Or, banded Gules.*

Thomas Newce of London.=Isabell, da. of .... Henage.
|
Thomas Newce of Haddam, co. Hertf.=.... da. of John Lenthorpe [Leventhorpe].
A

THE VISITATION OF HERTFORDSHIRE, 1572.

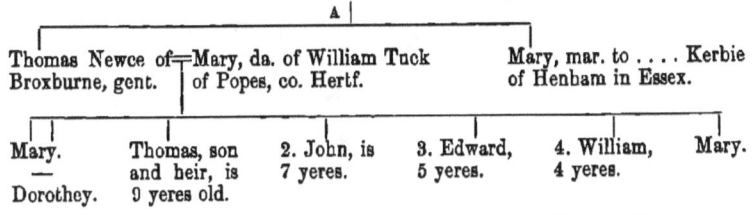

Thomas Newce of Broxburne, gent.=Mary, da. of William Tuck of Popes, co. Hertf.   Mary, mar. to .... Kerbie of Henham in Essex.

| Mary. — Dorothey. | Thomas, son and heir, is 9 yeres old. | 2. John, is 7 yeres. | 3. Edward, 5 yeres. | 4. William, 4 yeres. | Mary. |

By me THOMAS NEWCE.

Nodes of Stevenage.

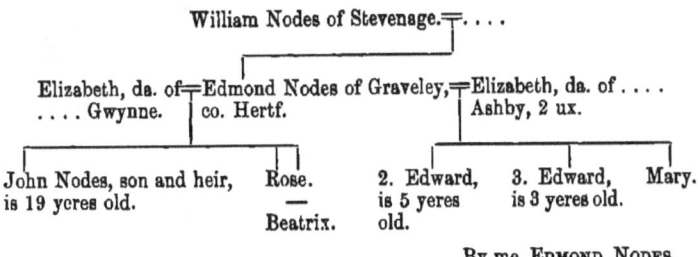

William Nodes of Stevenage.=....

Elizabeth, da. of .... Gwynne.=Edmond Nodes of Graveley, co. Hertf.=Elizabeth, da. of .... Ashby, 2 ux.

| John Nodes, son and heir, is 19 yeres old. | Rose. — Beatrix. | 2. Edward, is 5 yeres old. | 3. Edward, is 3 yeres old. | Mary. |

By me EDMOND NODES.

Palmer of Shenley.

ARMS.—*Quarterly*—1 and 4, *Azure, in chief a fleur-de-lis Or, in base two trefoils slipped Argent, within a bordure engrailed of the second*; 2, *Argent, two bars Vert,* HARTHILL ; 3, *Gules, a bend cotised between six martlets Or,* COTTON : impaling, *Per chevron embattled Sable and Argent, three mullets pierced counterchanged, within a bordure engrailed Ermine,* CHEESMAN.

CREST.—*A wyvern's head Or, collared Gules bezantée, wings expanded Vert, fretty and semée of trefoils slipped Argent.*

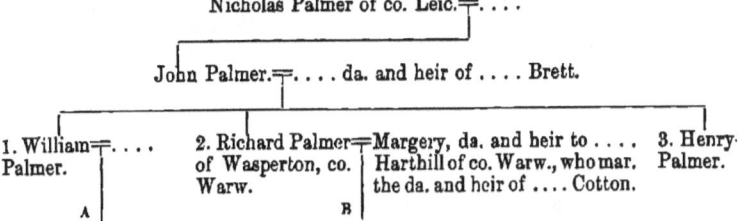

Nicholas Palmer of co. Leic.=....

John Palmer.=.... da. and heir of .... Brett.

| 1. William Palmer. A | 2. Richard Palmer of Wasperton, co. Warw. B | =Margery, da. and heir to .... Harthill of co. Warw., who mar. the da. and heir of .... Cotton. | 3. Henry Palmer. |

THE VISITATION OF HERTFORDSHIRE, 1572.   19

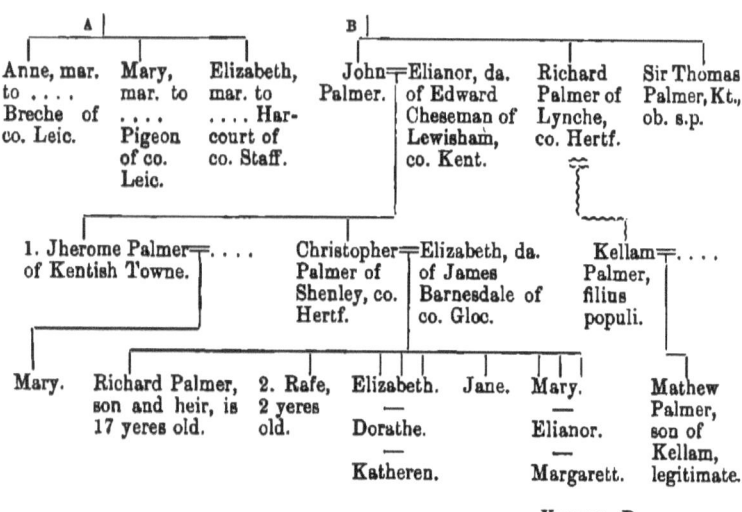

XPOFER PALMER.

Radcliffe of Hitchin.

ARMS.—*Argent, a cross-crosslet Gules between two bendlets engrailed Sable, a label of three points throughout Azure.*
CREST.—*A bull's head erased, armed Argent, tipped Or, ducally gorged and ringed of the second, charged with a cross-crosslet Gules.*

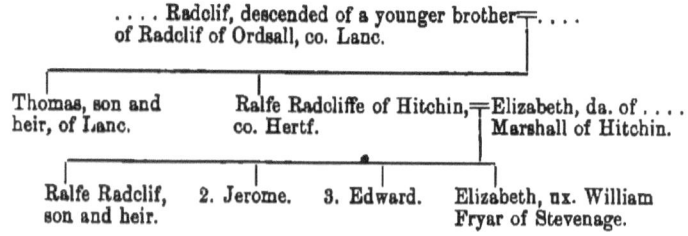

RAULFE RADCLYFFE.

Skipwith of St. Alban's.

ARMS.—*Quarterly of seven*—1, *Gules, three bars Argent, in chief a greyhound courant per pale Or and Ermine, collared Azure*, SKIPWITH ; 2, *Gules, on a chevron between two chevronels Argent three lions rampant of the field*, ROWLETT ; 3, *Paly of six Gules and Argent within a bordure engrailed, on a canton of the first a spur Or*, KNIGHT ; 4, *Quarterly per fess indented Argent and Sable, in the first and fourth quarters a bugle-horn of the second*, FORSTER ; 5, *Azure, three peacocks' heads erased Argent*, WARING ; 6, *Gules, on a fess Or, between three falcons Argent, beaked and legged Or, as many fleurs-de-lis Azure*, PENNINGTON ; 7, *Azure, a lion rampant Or within a bordure engrailed Gules, a canton of the second*, NEVILL.

CREST.—*A griffin's head erased per fess Gules and Azure, guttée d'Or, holding in his mouth a greyhound's leg Ermine.*

A Patent granted to William Skipwith of St Alban's in the com. Hertford, Esq., by Thomas Writhoesley *alias* Garter, and Roger Machado *alias* Richmond, Clarenceux King of Arms, in 1507, H. 7, 22.

MOTTO.—MEDIA SI MEA.

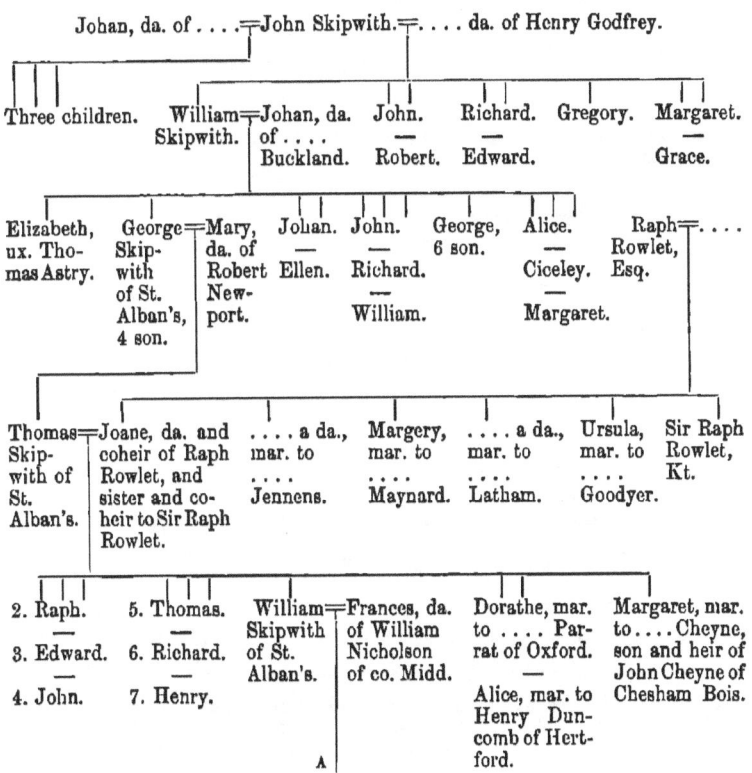

THE VISITATION OF HERTFORDSHIRE, 1572.

A
| Dorathe. — Sara. | Susan. | Margaret. — Joan. | Stephen, son and heir, is 7 yeres old. | 2. John, is 3 yeres old. | Frances. — Elizabeth. |

Smithwick of Lees Langley.

ARMS.—*Argent, a chevron engrailed Sable between three laurel-leaves Vert.*
CREST (added).—*An arm embowed, vested bendy of six Vert and Argent, cuffed of the last, in the hand a tulip all proper.*

Richard Smethwyke.=....

William Smethwyke of Cheshire, a yonger son.=.... da. of .... Bethell.

Thomas Smethwyke of Wyntonley, Chesh.=Ellen, da. of .... Furnyvall.

Robert Smethwyke of Lees Langley, co. Hertf.=Bennett, da. of .... Clytherow. 1 vir. [see IBGRAVE, p. 14].=Giles Ibgrave,   2. Thomas. — 3. Rafe.   Cicely. — Isabel.

Robert Smethwyke, son and heir, 4 yeres old.   Sence, a daughter.

ROBERT SMETHWYKE.

Snagg of Letchworth.

ARMS.—*Argent, three pheons Sable.*
CREST.—*A demi-antelope salient Ermine, attired Or.*

William Snagg of Lechworth, co. Hertf.=....

Thomas Snagg of Lechworth.=Elizabeth, da. of .... Calton of Walden in Essex.

| Alice, ux. ....Warren. | Beatrice, ux. ....Waller. | Ann, ux. Edward Dalyson of Cransley. | Margery, ux. John Sheppard. | Jane, ux. .... Downhall of Gedington. |

A

22   THE VISITATION OF HERTFORDSHIRE, 1572.

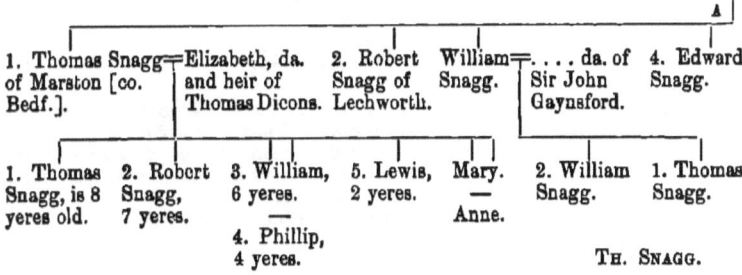

Spencer of St. Alban's.

ARMS.—*Quarterly Or and Gules, in the second and third quarters a fret of the first, over all a bend Sable charged with three fleurs-de-lis Argent.*
CREST.—*Out of a ducal coronet Argent, gemmed Gules, a demi-griffin of the first, beaked and eared of the second, collared per pale of the second and Or, winged of the third, on each wing and on the breast a fleur-de-lis Sable.*

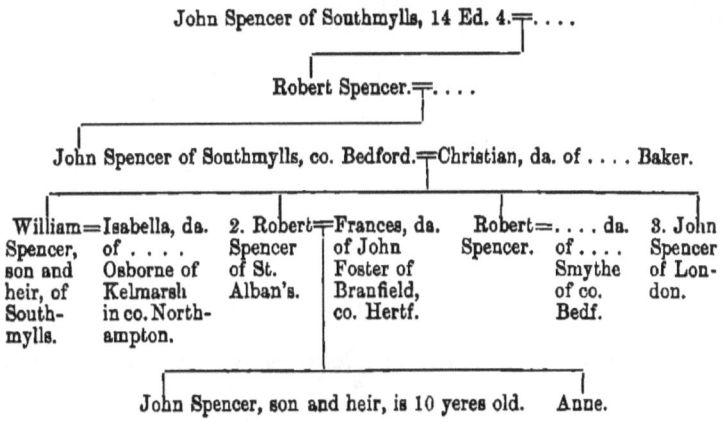

By me ROBERT SPENCER.

Verney of Penley.

ARMS.—*Quarterly*—1, *Azure, on a cross Argent five mullets pierced Gules*, VERNEY; 2, *Azure, two chevrons Or, on a canton Gules a paschal lamb Argent, holding a cross patée of the second;* 3, *Argent, a fess Vert, over all a lion rampant Gules,* WHITTINGHAM; 4, *Argent, a saltire engrailed Sable, on a chief of the second two mullets pierced of the first,* IWARDBY.
CREST.—*A demi-phœnix in flames, beholding rays of the sun, all proper.*
MOTTO.—UNG SEUL UNI SOLI.

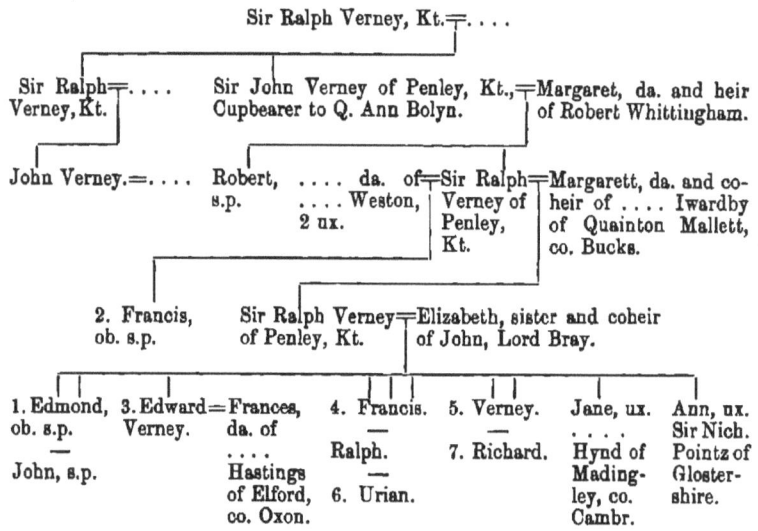

EDMOND VERNEY.

Walter of Broxbourne.

ARMS.—*Quarterly*—1, *Argent, guttée Gules, two swords in saltire, blades proper, hilts of the second, over all a lion rampant Sable,* WALTER; 2, *Argent, a bugle-horn between three trefoils slipped Sable,* PINCHPOLE; 3, *Argent, on a fess within a bordure engrailed Azure three escallops of the field,* FENNE; 4, *Azure, three battle-axes erect Or.*
CREST.—*A stork proper dipping his beak into a whelk-shell erect Or.*
    On each *a crescent for difference.*

John Walter of Crawden [Croydon],=Agnes, da. of .... Barley of Albery
co. Cambr. | Hall in co. Hertf.

24 THE VISITATION OF HERTFORDSHIRE, 1572.

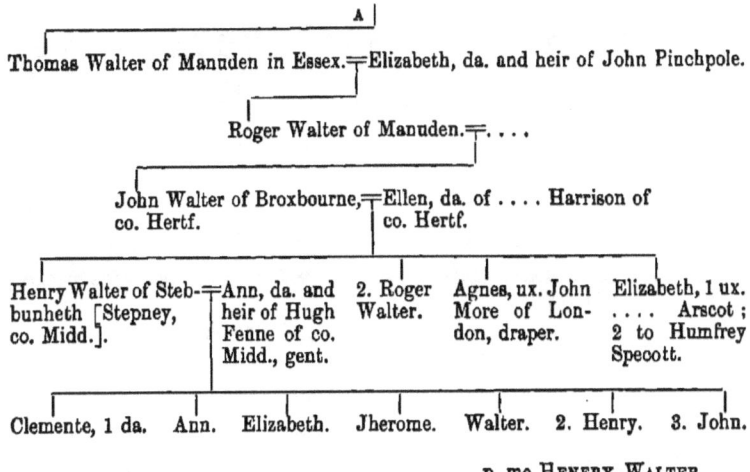

p. me HENERY WALTER.

The Visitation of Hertfordshire, 1634.

Alden of Rickmansworth.

ARMS.—*Gules, three crescents within a bordure engrailed Ermine, in the fess point an annulet Or.*

Thomas Alden of Rickmansworth, co. Hertf.=....

Edmund Alden of Rickmansworth.=....

Charles Alden of Rickmansworth.=Mary, da. of Thomas Fortherby of Rickmansworth.

1. Charles Alden of Rickmansworth, son and heir, living aº 1634.=Alice, da. of John Harmon of co. Bucks. | 2. Thomas, Chaplain to the Lord Keeper. | 3. Augustine.

Endymion, son and heir. | 2. Philip. | 3. Charles. | 4. John. | Anne, only da.

Barber of Hertford.

ARMS.—*Or, two chevrons between three fleurs-de-lis Gules, in the fess point a cinquefoil Azure;* impaling, *Argent, three greyhounds courant in bend cotised Sable between two eagles displayed of the last,* CRAY.

CREST.—*Out of a coronet a bull's head Argent, eared Gules, charged with a cinquefoil Azure.*

William Barber of London.=....

Gabriell Barber of Hertford, now living, 1634.=Elizabeth, da. of John Cray of Wichford in the Isle of Ely.

1. Gabriell Barber. | 2. John Barber. | 3. Joseph. | Elizabeth. | Anne.

Bardolf of St. Michael's.

ARMS.—*Quarterly of six*—1 and 6, BARDOLPH; 2, CRESSY; 3, MORTIMER; 4, HUSSEY, as at p. 2; 5, *Or, a cross palonce Sable*, BROCKETT.

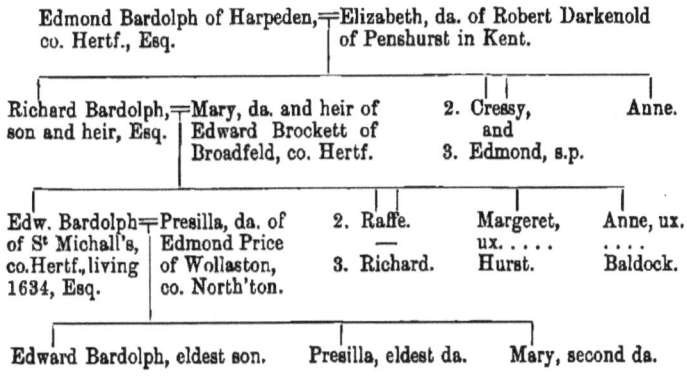

Barkley of East Barnet.

ARMS.—*Gules, a chevron between ten crosses patée Argent, a crescent on a crescent for difference.*

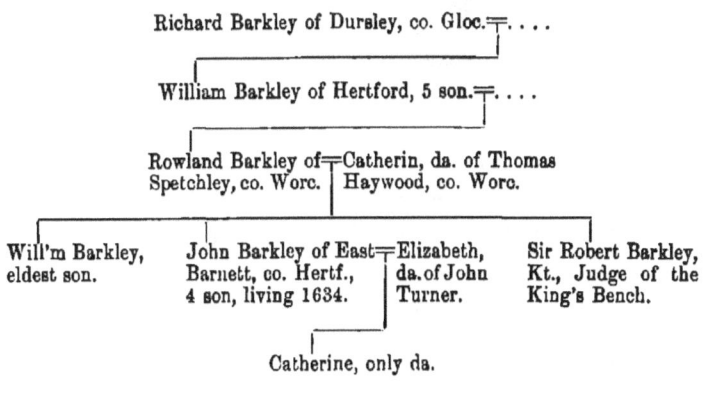

Barley of Bibsworth Hall.

ARMS.—*Barry wavy of six Ermine and Sable, a crescent for difference.*

Francis Barley of Bibsworth Hall, co. Hertf.=....

John Barley of Bibsworth Hall, 2 son.=Anne, da. of .... Inglesby.

Richard Barley, eldest son, s.p.

Robert Barley of Kimpton, co. Hertf., 2 son, now living, 1634.

Bayly of Standon.

Richard Bayly of Thorgenby, co. Linc.=....

Thomas Bayly of Thorgenby, eldest son.=Jane, da. of .... Pinarake of Burgh in the Marsh, co. Linc.

George Bayly of Standon, co. Hertf., 1634.=Scissely, da. of Richard Lumley of Wintershell, co. Sussex.

2. Thomas. — 3. Richard.

Dorathy, ux. John Munne.

Ursula, ux. Wm. Shipley.

Jane, ux. Thomas Emery of Danbury, co. Essex.

Mary, ux. John Shelley, son of Sir John.

Bayly of Hoddesdon.

ARMS.—*Argent, three torteaux, a chief Gules.*
CREST.—*Out of a coronet flory Or, a nag's head Argent maned of the first.*

John Bayly of Hodsdon, co. Hertf.=Susan, da. of William Shambrooke.

John Bayly of Hodsdon, eldest son.=Lettice, da. of Sir William Skevington of Fisherwick, co. Staff.

1. John Bayly.   2. Richard Bayly.   Elizabeth.   Lettice.

Belfeld of Studham.

ARMS and CREST as at p. 3.

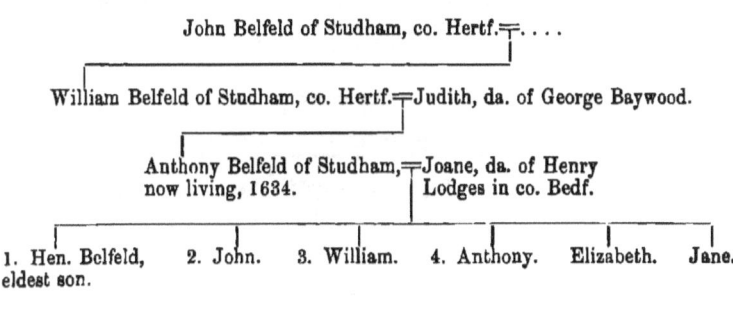

Berners of Tharfield.

ARMS.—*Quarterly—1 and 4, Quarterly Or and Vert; 2 and 3, Or, on a bend Azure three ostrich-feathers Argent.*
CREST.—*An ape proper environed about the loins and lined Or.*
MOTTO.—DEL FUGO ELLA SAVOLA.

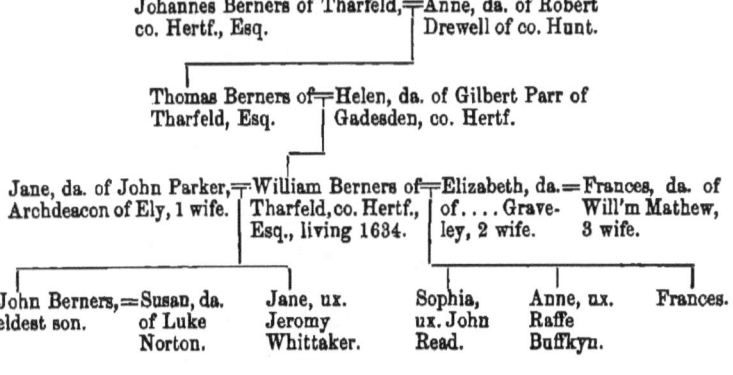

Blount of Tittinghanger.

ARMS.—*Quarterly*—1 and 4, *Barry nebulée of six Or and Gules, within a bordure gobony Azure and of the first;* 2, *Or, a lion rampant Vert, a mullet for difference,* SUTTON; 3, *Azure, a chevron Argent between three plovers Or,* WYCHARD: impaling, *Sable, three picks Argent,* PIGOTT.

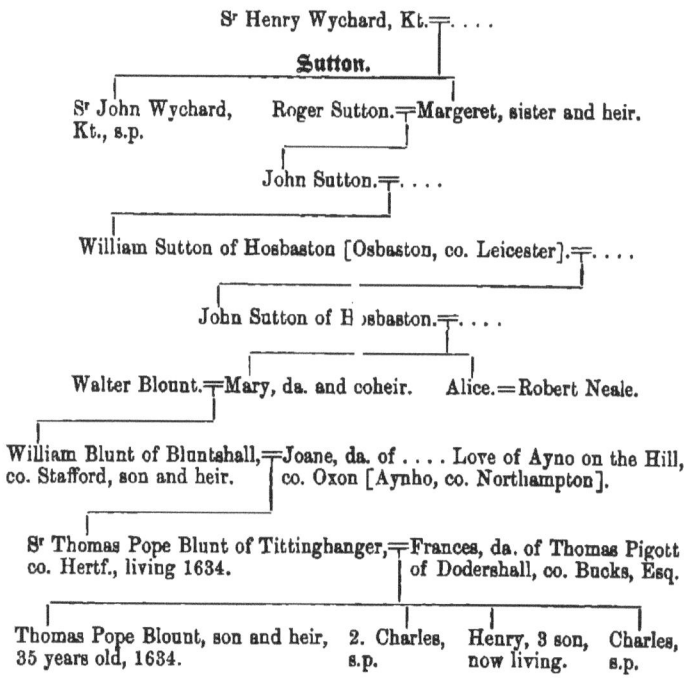

Boteler of Queen Hoo Hall.

Sir John Boteler of Watton Woodhall, co. Hertf.=. . . .

Sir Philip Boteler, eldest son.

. . . . da. of . . . .Waller, 1 wife.

=Sir Henry Boteler of Branfeld, co. Hertf., and of Woodhall.

=Alice, da. of . . . . Poulter of Wimondley, 2 wife.

30   THE VISITATION OF HERTFORDSHIRE, 1634.

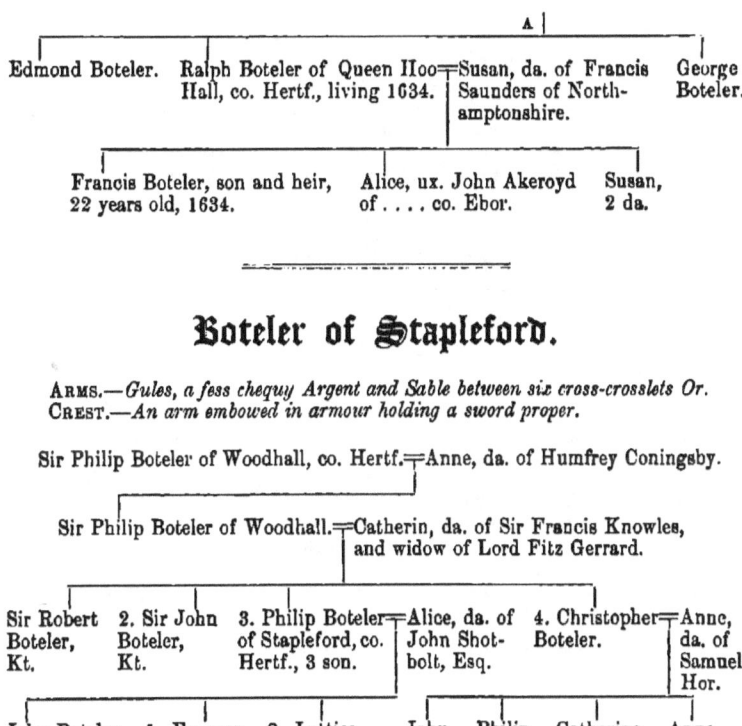

Boteler of Stapleford.

ARMS.—*Gules, a fess chequy Argent and Sable between six cross-crosslets Or.*
CREST.—*An arm embowed in armour holding a sword proper.*

Sir Philip Boteler of Woodhall, co. Hertf.=Anne, da. of Humfrey Coningsby.

Sir Philip Boteler of Woodhall.=Catherin, da. of Sir Francis Knowles, and widow of Lord Fitz Gerrard.

Sir Robert Boteler, Kt. | 2. Sir John Boteler, Kt. | 3. Philip Boteler of Stapleford, co. Hertf., 3 son.=Alice, da. of John Shotbolt, Esq. | 4. Christopher Boteler=Anne, da. of Samuel Hor.

John Boteler, eldest son. | 1. Frances. | 2. Lettice. | John. | Philip. | Catherine. | Anne.

Briggs of Rickmansworth.

The Armes are entered in the booke of Certificates in the Office.

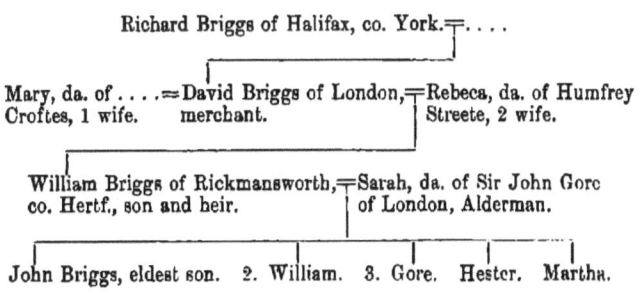

Brisco of Aldenham.

ARMS.—*Quarterly*—1 and 4, *Argent, three greyhounds courant in pale Sable;* 2, *Gules, a saltire engrailed Argent,* CROSTON ; 3, *Per pale Argent and Sable, a fleur-de-lis counterchanged,* WHINNE ; *a mullet on a crescent for difference.*
CREST.—*A greyhound courant Sable, holding in the mouth a hare proper.*

Proofe hath bene made.

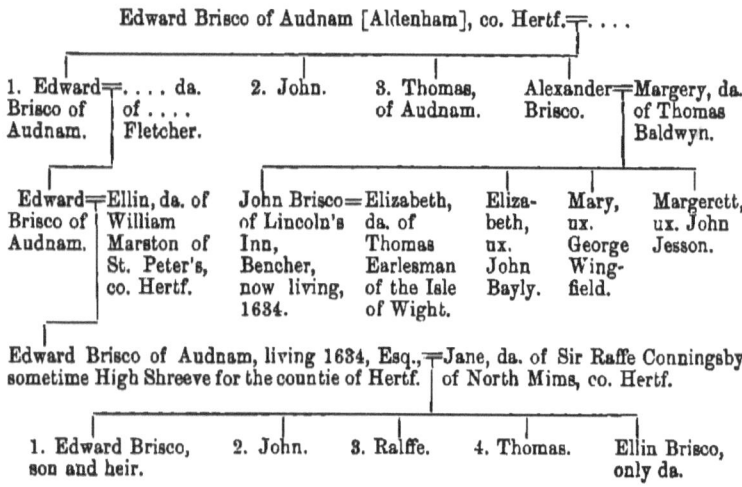

Edward Brisco of Audnam [Aldenham], co. Hertf.=. . . .

1. Edward=. . . . da.   2. John.   3. Thomas,   Alexander=Margery, da.
Brisco of | of . . . .   of Audnam.   Brisco. | of Thomas
Audnam. | Fletcher.   Baldwyn.

Edward=Ellin, da. of   John Brisco=Elizabeth,   Eliza-   Mary,   Margerett,
Brisco of | William   of Lincoln's | da. of   beth,   ux.   ux. John
Audnam. | Marston of   Inn, | Thomas   ux.   George   Jesson.
         St. Peter's,   Bencher,   Earlesman   John   Wing-
         co. Hertf.   now living,   of the Isle   Bayly.   field.
                        1634.   of Wight.

Edward Brisco of Audnam, living 1634, Esq.,=Jane, da. of Sir Raffe Conningsby
sometime High Shreeve for the countie of Hertf. | of North Mims, co. Hertf.

1. Edward Brisco,   2. John.   3. Ralffe.   4. Thomas.   Ellin Brisco,
son and heir.   only da.

Brisco of St. Michael's.

The armes not proved, nor this descent allowed to be entred, Mr. Brisco doth promise to make good prooffe with the rest of his kinred in Michellmas Tearme, which he hath since done.

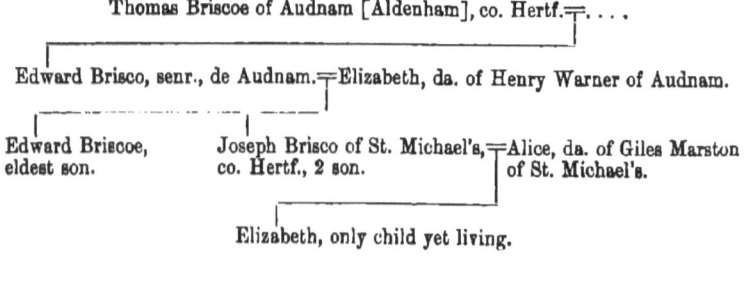

Thomas Briscoe of Audnam [Aldenham], co. Hertf.=. . . .

Edward Brisco, senr., de Audnam.=Elizabeth, da. of Henry Warner of Audnam.

Edward Briscoe,   Joseph Brisco of St. Michael's,=Alice, da. of Giles Marston
eldest son.   co. Hertf., 2 son. | of St. Michael's.

Elizabeth, only child yet living.

Brockett of Whethamstead.

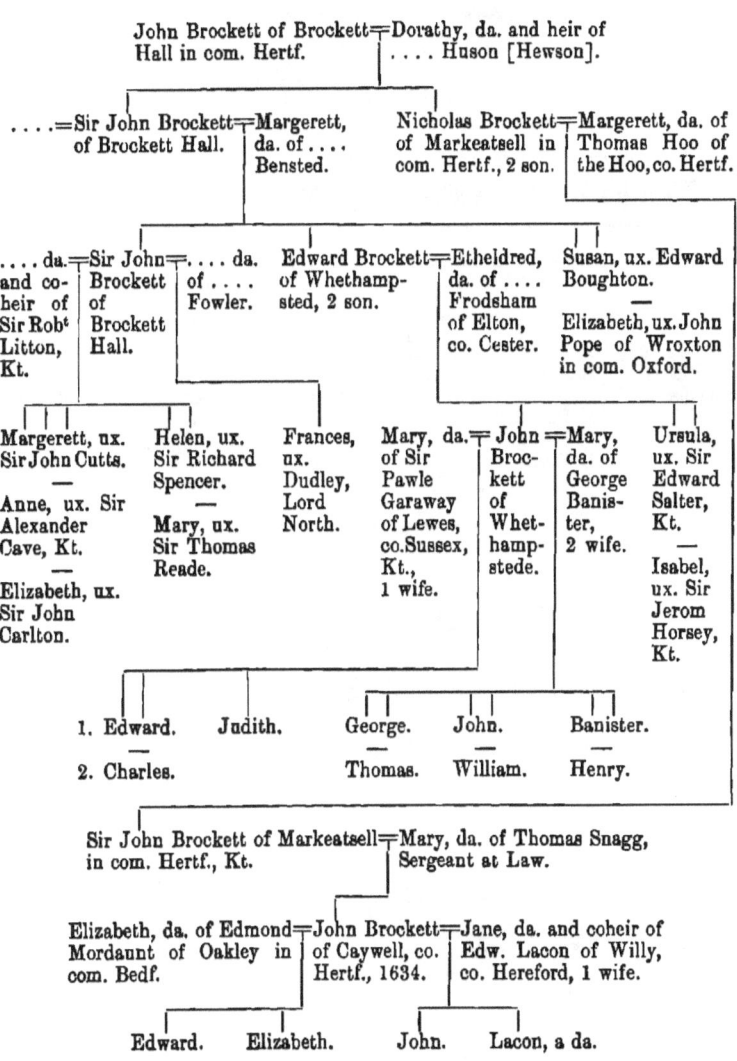

John Brockett of Brockett = Dorathy, da. and heir of
Hall in com. Hertf. .... Huson [Hewson].

.... = Sir John Brockett = Margerett,   Nicholas Brockett = Margerett, da. of
of Brockett Hall. da. of ....   of Markeatsell in   Thomas Hoo of
Bensted.   com. Hertf., 2 son.   the Hoo, co. Hertf.

.... da. = Sir John = ... da.   Edward Brockett = Etheldred,   Susan, ux. Edward
and co-   Brockett   of ....   of Whethamp-   da. of ....   Boughton.
heir of   of   Fowler.   sted, 2 son.   Frodsham
Sir Robt   Brockett   of Elton,   Elizabeth, ux. John
Litton,   Hall.   co. Cester.   Pope of Wroxton
Kt.   in com. Oxford.

Margerett, ux.   Helen, ux.   Frances,   Mary, da. = John = Mary,   Ursula,
Sir John Cutts.   Sir Richard   ux.   of Sir   Broc-   da. of   ux. Sir
—   Spencer.   Dudley,   Pawle   kett   George   Edward
Anne, ux. Sir   —   Lord   Garaway   of   Banis-   Salter,
Alexander   Mary, ux.   North.   of Lewes,   Whet-   ter,   Kt.
Cave, Kt.   Sir Thomas   co. Sussex,   hamp-   2 wife.   —
—   Reade.   Kt.,   stede.   Isabel,
Elizabeth, ux.   1 wife.   ux. Sir
Sir John   Jerom
Carlton.   Horsey,
                                                                                                       Kt.

1. Edward.   Judith.   George.   John.   Banister.
2. Charles.   Thomas.   William.   Henry.

Sir John Brockett of Markeatsell = Mary, da. of Thomas Snagg,
in com. Hertf., Kt.   Sergeant at Law.

Elizabeth, da. of Edmond = John Brockett = Jane, da. and coheir of
Mordaunt of Oakley in   of Caywell, co.   Edw. Lacon of Willy,
com. Bedf.   Hertf., 1634.   co. Hereford, 1 wife.

Edward.   Elizabeth.   John.   Lacon, a da.

Brockett of Codicot.

ARMS.—*Or, a cross flory Sable.*
Gratis. The difference to be inserted.

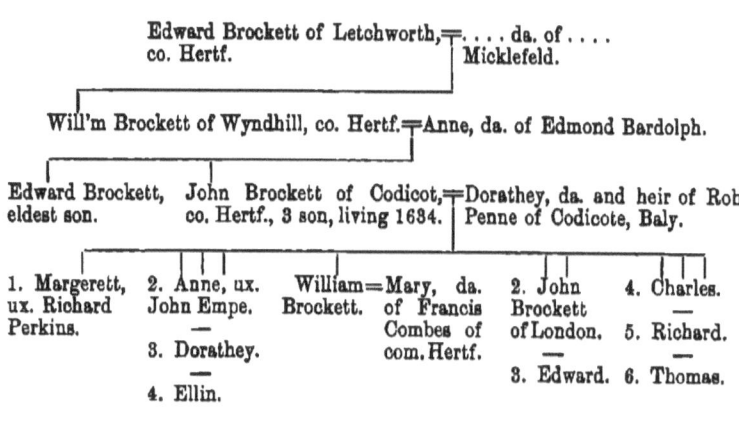

Brograve of Hammels.

ARMS.—*Argent, three lions passant Gules.*
CREST.—*An eagle with two heads displayed Ermine, each ducally crowned Or.*

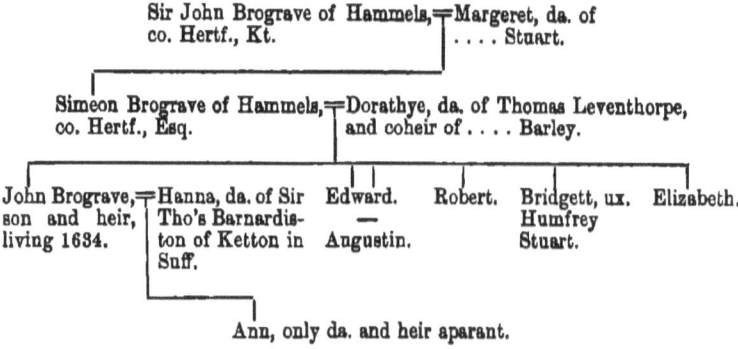

Bromley of Ware Westmill.

ARMS.—*Quarterly per fess indented Gules and Or, an inescutcheon Argent, charged with a griffin segreant Vert.*
CREST.—*A demi-lion rampant Sable issuing out of a ducal coronet Or, holding a standard Gules, charged with a lion passant of the second, the staff proper.*

The Armes and Crest respyt to London at Mich. Tearme for further prooffe.

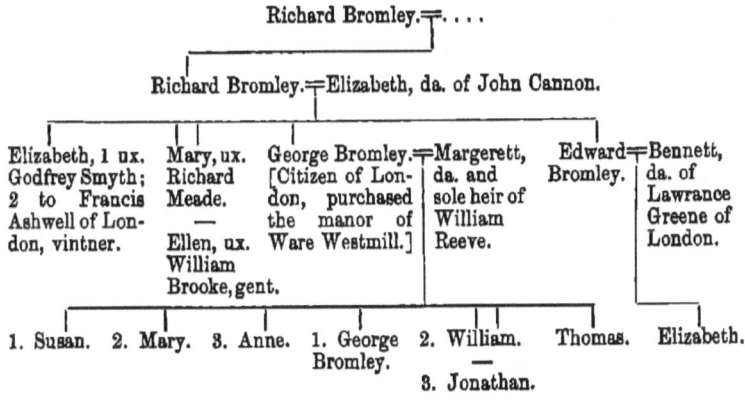

Bull of Hertford.

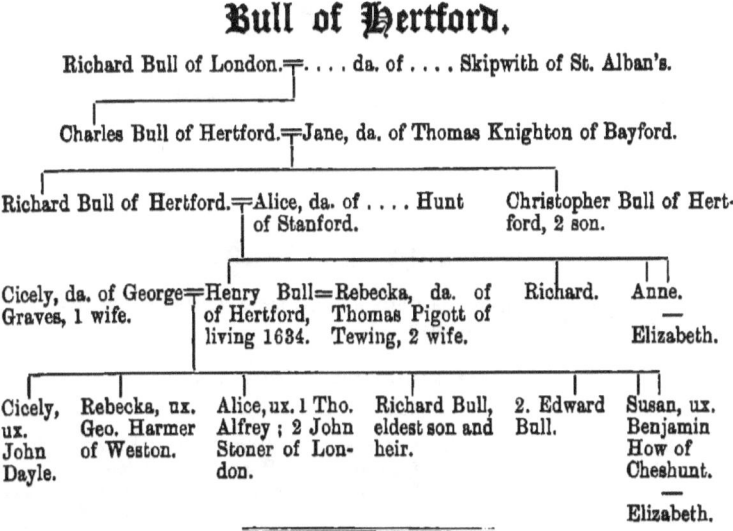

Buller of St. Alban's.

ARMS.—*Gules, on a chevron engrailed Argent between three falcons regardant Or three pellets.*
CREST.—*An antelope's head erased Ermine.*

Quere the cote of Norfolk; the arms doubtfull.

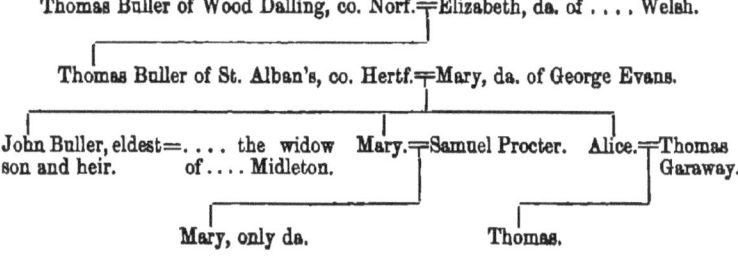

Thomas Buller of Wood Dalling, co. Norf.=Elizabeth, da. of .... Welsh.

Thomas Buller of St. Alban's, co. Hertf.=Mary, da. of George Evans.

John Buller, eldest son and heir.=.... the widow of .... Midleton. Mary.=Samuel Procter. Alice.=Thomas Garaway.

Mary, only da. Thomas.

Caesar of Sandon.

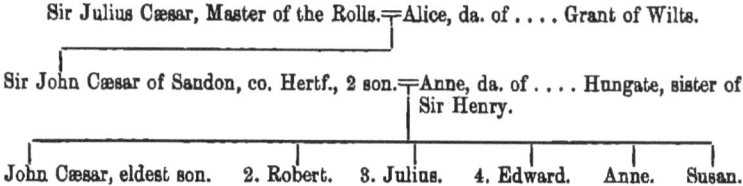

Sir Julius Cæsar, Master of the Rolls.=Alice, da. of .... Grant of Wilts.

Sir John Cæsar of Sandon, co. Hertf., 2 son.=Anne, da. of .... Hungate, sister of Sir Henry.

John Cæsar, eldest son. 2. Robert. 3. Julius. 4. Edward. Anne. Susan.

Cage of Hormead.

ARMS.—*Per pale Azure and Gules, a saltire Or, a martlet for difference.*
CREST.—*A buck statant proper.*

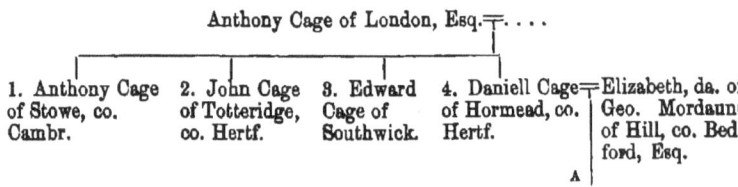

Anthony Cage of London, Esq.=....

1. Anthony Cage of Stowe, co. Cambr. 2. John Cage of Totteridge, co. Hertf. 3. Edward Cage of Southwick. 4. Daniell Cage of Hormead, co. Hertf.=Elizabeth, da. of Geo. Mordaunt of Hill, co. Bedford, Esq.

A

36   THE VISITATION OF HERTFORDSHIRE, 1634.

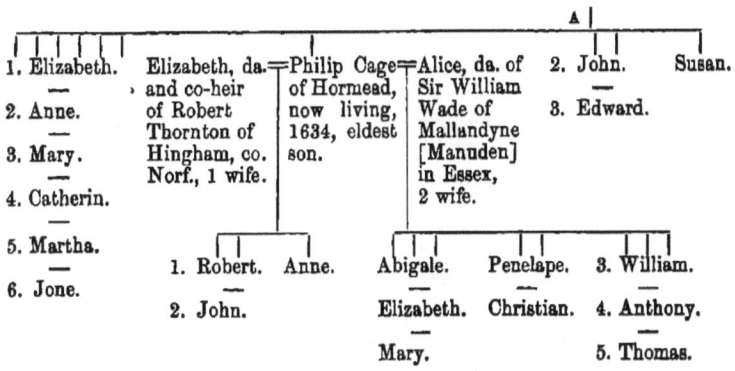

Capell of Little Hadham.

Elizabeth, da. of .... Lawrance, widow of John Hutton of Drayton and of Sir William Hinde of Madingley, Kt., 2 wife. = Sir Arthur Capell of Little Hadham, co. Hertf., Kt. = Margerett, da. of John, Lord Gray, of Pirgoe, 1 wife.

Mary, ob. s.p. — Catherine, s.p.

2. Penelapy, ux. Litton Poulter of Cottered in com. Hertf.

4. Winifred, ux. Sir Thomas Bedle of Hamerton, co. Hunts.

5. Elizabeth, 1 ux. Sir Justinian Lewen; 2 to Sir Raffe Hopton, Kt.

Margerett, ux. Anthony Stocker of Chilcompton, co. Somerset.

Dorathey, Lady Hoskins, 2 wife. = Sir John Capell, Kt., son and heir. = Theodosia, sister to Edward, Lo. Mountague, and Henry, E. of Manchester.

Anne, ux. John Corbett of Sproston, co. Norf. — Mary, ux. Hen., 2nd Earle of Marlborough.

Sir Edward Capell. — Sir Arthur Capell.

4. Humfrey.
5. William.
6. Roger.
7. Gamaliel.

Anne.

Arthur Capell of Litle Hadham, co. Hertf., Esq. = Elizabeth, da. and heir of Sir Charles Morrison, Kt. and Bart.

Henry, s.p.

Elizabeth, ux. William Wiseman of Canfield in Essex, Bart.

Theodosia, ux. Edw. Kemys of Wales. — Margerett.

Arthur Capell, son and heir, 2 years old, 1634.   Mary.   Elizabeth.

THE VISITATION OF HERTFORDSHIRE, 1634.   37

Carter of Garston.

ARMS.—*Argent, a chevron Sable between two roundles in chief and in base a Catherine-wheel Vert.*
CREST.—*On a mound Vert a greyhound sejant Argent, sustaining with the dexter paw a shield of the last charged with a Catherine-wheel of the first.*

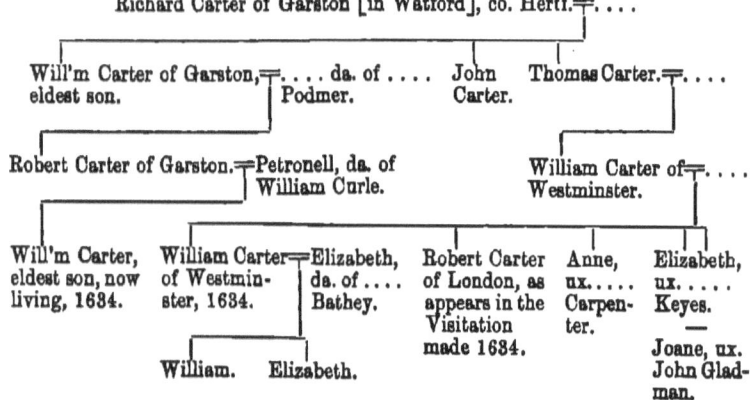

Cason of Aston Bury.

ARMS.—*Argent, a chevron Sable between three horses' heads erased Gules.*
CREST.—*A cubit dexter arm, vested Gules, charged with two bends wavy Sable, cuffed Argent, the hand proper clenched and holding a round buckle Or.*

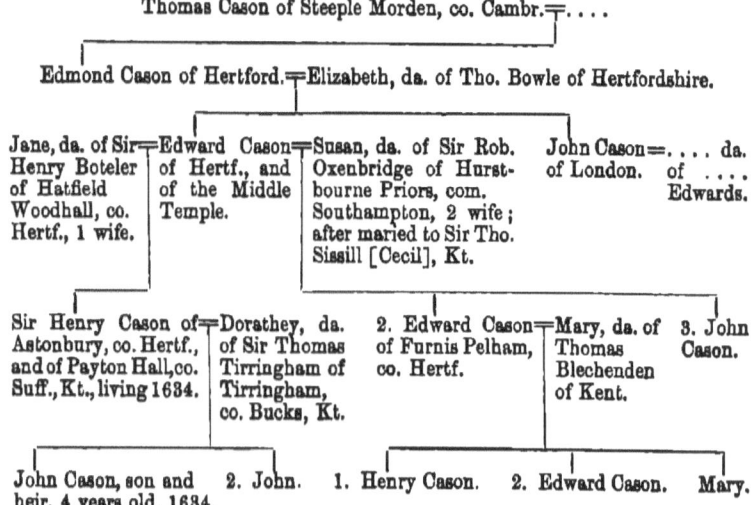

Chambers of Barkway.

ARMS.—*Argent, a chevron Azure between three trefoils slipped Gules.*
CREST.—*A bear passant Sable, muzzled, collared, and chained Or.*
On each *a crescent for difference.*

Thomas Chambers of Barkway, co. Hertf.=....

Peter Chambers of Barkway, co. Hertf.,=Ellen, da. of Thomas
one of the younger sons of Thomas. | Gregory of London.

Felix Chambers of Barkway,=Anne, da. of Steven
co. Hertf., living 1634. | Martin of co. Essex.

Thomas Chambers, eldest son and heir.　　2. Edmond.　　3. Peter.

Chauncey of Sawbridgworth.

ARMS and CREST as at p. 4, without *the crescent for difference.*

Henry Chancey of Sabridgworth, co. Hertf.=Joan, da. of .... Tendring.

William Chancey of Sabridgworth.=Bridgett, da. of John Raymond.

George Chancey=Lucy, da. and heir of Geo.　　Thomas,　　Elizabeth,　　Jone,
of Sabridgworth, | Reinolds of Great Chester-　　s.p.　　ux. ....　　ux. ....
eldest son. | ford, co. Essex.　　　　　　　　　　　　　　　Fludd.　　Parker.

George Chancey=Catherin,　　Mary, ux. Geo.　　Lucy, ux.　　2. James Chancey.
of Sabridgworth, | da. of　　Waller.　　Nathaniell　　—
eldest son, now | William　　—　　Downes.　　3. John Chancey.
living, 1634. | Clarke of　　Elizabeth, ux.　　—　　—
　　　　　　　 Wrotham,　　John Monck.　　Grace, ux.　　4. Thomas Chancey.
　　　　　　　 co. Kent.　　　　　　　　　　Ric. Smyth.

Chauncey of Yardley.

ARMS and CREST as in the previous pedigree.

D'n's Thomas Chancy, miles, Baro de Skirpenbeck in com. Ebor., a° 1375.=....
|
D'n's Gulielmus Chancy, miles, Baro de Skirpenbeck, *temp.* R. 2.

Joh'es Chancy, miles, vixit *apud* Stebenheath *juxta* London, *temp.* H. 4.

Joh'es Chauncy de Gedeleston [Geldsden] in com. Hertford, *temp.* H. 5.=....
|
Joh'es Chauncy de Gedeleston, co. Hertf., *temp.* H. 6.=....
|
John Chauncy of Crafford [Crayford] in Kent.=....
|
Henry Chancy of Gedleston, 10 H. 7.=....
|
Jane, da. and coheir of John Cornwall=George Chauncy of Gedleston,=Anne Welch, of Yardley, co. Hertf., 1 wife. | co. Hertf. | 2 wife.

Hen. Chancy=Anne, da. of	Jane, ux. Edw.	Frances,	2. George.	Judith.
of Yardley,	Giles Allen	Coe of Walter	ux.	—	
co. Hertf.,	of Haseley,	Beauchamp, co.	Ambrose	3. Charles.	
eldest son.	co. Essex.	Essex.	Porter.		

Henery Chauncy of Yardley,=Anne, da. of Peter Parkes of Totten- | 2. John
now living, 1634. | ham High Cross, co. Midd. | Chauncy.

Henery Chauncy, son and heir, 2 years old, 1634.   2. John Chauncy.

===

Chester of Cocken Hatch.

ARMS.—*Quarterly*—1 and 4, *Ermine, on a chief Sable a griffin passant Argent;
2 and 3, Quarterly, one and four, Sable, three birds' legs erased Or, a crescent
for difference; two and three, Or, a Moor's head Sable, couped Gules, wreathed
Argent; over all an inescutcheon.*

CRESTS.—1. *A demi-griffin segreant proper.*
2. *A thistle proper.*

Sir Robert Chester of Royston, Kt.,=Catherin, da. of John Throgmorton
Gent. Usher to King H. 8. | of Corse, co. Gloc.

THE VISITATION OF HERTFORDSHIRE, 1634.

Edward Chester=Catherin, da. and sole heir of   2. Oliver.   Frances, ux. Robert
of Royston, a | James Granado, Kt., an Equery   —   Filmere of Kent.
Colonel in the | to H. 8. He was knighted at   3. Robert. —
Low Countries. | Mussleborough field.   Catherin, ux. John
                                                            Forte.

Sir Robert Chester of Cocken-=Anne, da. of Henry   Mary, ux. Edward Thorn-
Hatch, near Royston in com. | Capell of Litle Had- borough of Shoddesden,
Hertford, Kt., living 1634. | ham, co. Hertf., Esq. co. Southampton.

1. Catherin, ux. Sir   2. Alice, ux. Edward   3. Theodosia, ux.   4. Elizabeth, ux.
Thomas Nightingale   Radcliff of Hitchin,   Rob't Nightin-   Samuell Hinton
of Debden, co. Essex, co. Hertf.   gale of Newport,   of Coventry.
Bart.   co. Essex, Esq.

Edward Chester=Catherin, Frances, ux.   2. Granado Chester, 4. Henry=Anne,
of Royston, son| da. of   John Pigott   Doctor in Divinity, Chester | da. of
and heir, living| John   of Alington   Rector of Broad-   of Roy- | Theo-
1634. | Stone of in Canter-   water, co. Sussex.   ston. | dore
               | London, bury [sic],   — | Reade.
               | Esq.   Esq.   3. Robert Chester,
                                         Rector of Stevenage.

Anne.   Elizabeth.   Robert Chester, son and   2. John Chester.   Cicilly.   Frances.
                    heir, 16 years old, 1634.

𝕮𝖍𝖎𝖑𝖉𝖊 𝖔𝖋 𝕷𝖆𝖓𝖌𝖑𝖊𝖞 𝕭𝖚𝖗𝖞.

ARMS.—*Azure, a fess embattled between three eagles close Or.*
CREST.—*An eagle with wings expanded Ermine, holding in the beak a trefoil slipped Vert.*

Thomas Childe of Langley Bury, co. Hertf., living 1634.

𝕮𝖍𝖚𝖓𝖊 𝖔𝖋 𝕾𝖍𝖊𝖓𝖑𝖊𝖞.

Vide the descent in the Visitation of Kent, the arms respyt.

Gregory Chune of . . . . co. Kent.=. . . .

William Chune of Rootum=Elizabeth, da. of Thomas=John Midleton of
[Wrotham], co. Kent. | Phillips of Brayntford. Sussex, 2 husband.

THE VISITATION OF HERTFORDSHIRE, 1634.

| A

John Midleton Chune of Shenley, co. Hertf., now living, 1634. = Frances, da. of William Tucke of Essenden, co. Hertf., Esq.

John Midleton Chune, eldest son. 2. Alban. 3. William. Frances. Judith.

Clarke of Tharfield and Ashwell.

ARMS.—*Argent, on a fess between three crosses patée Sable three plates.*
CREST.—*A cross patée Or between two wings Azure.*

John Clarke of Stevenedg, co. Hertf. = ...

Sir Edward Clarke of .... nere Reding in Berkshire. 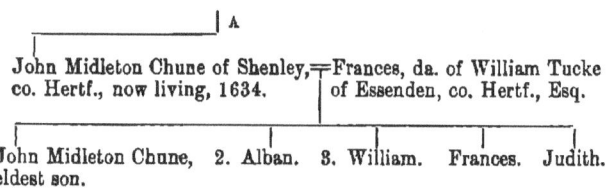   Thomas Clarke of Houghton, co. Bedf. = ...

John Clarke of Henlowbury, co. Bedford, eldest son. = Jane, da. of John Kent of Aston Bury, co. Hertf.   Sir Francis Clarke of Houghton, 2 son.

Wm. Clarke of Tharfeld, co. Hertf., son and heir, living 1634. = Susan, da. of William Aylett of Mayland, co. Essex.   2. Edward Clarke.   3. John Clarke.

Mary, ux. .... Jackson.   Susan, ux. Thomas Joscelin.   Catherin, ux. Joseph Graves.   1. Thomas = Hester, da. of Clarke of .... Anslow. London.

2. Richard Clarke. = Bridgett, da. of .... Gates.   Anne, as yet unmar.   3. John.   4. William. — 6. Robert.   7 [sic]. Aylett.

3. George Clarke of Walkern, co. Hertf. = ... da. of .... Kimpton.

George Clarke. = ...

John Clarke of Ashwell, co. Hertf. = Marian, da. and sole heir of Thomas Kimpton of Myms, co. Midd.

John Clarke of Ashwell, co. Hertf., 1634. = Judith, da. of Thomas Hawes of Bedf.

1. Judith. — 2. Elizabeth.   John Clarke, eldest son, 14 yeres old, 1634.   2. Thomas.   3. William.   3. Mary. — 4. Lettice.

Clarke of Chesfield.

The Armes are respyt till Michellmas terme.

William Clarke of Walkarne, co. Hertf.=....

George Clarke of Walkarne, co. Hertf.=Elizabeth, da. of Nicholas Bristow of Ayott St. Lawrance, co. Hertf.

Frances, da. of Nicholas Bristow of Ayott St. Lawrance.=William Clarke of Chesfeld, co. Hertford, son and heir.=Rebecka, da. of Thomas Taylor of .... Dr. of Phisick.

William Clarke.   Nicholas.   Francis.

Coghill of Bushy.

ARMS.—*Gules, on a chevron Argent three pellets, a chief Sable.*
CREST.—*A cock Erminois, wings endorsed Or.*

John Coghill of London.=Susan, da. of Dennis Viel.

John Coghill of Bushy, co. Hertf., living aº 1634.=Fayth, da. of John Sutton.

Henry Coghill, son and heir.   Elizabeth.

Cole of Shenley Hall.

Respit the Armes till the 15 of October. To be disclaymed.

John Cole of Tewxbury, co. Gloc.=....

Thomas Cole, one of the gent'n that followed the Erle of Lester, and, after, the Queen's Servant.=Isabel, da. of John Bland of ... in Yorkshire, Counsellor-at-lawe.

A

THE VISITATION OF HERTFORDSHIRE, 1634. 43

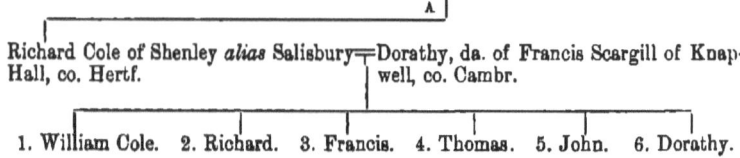

Richard Cole of Shenley *alias* Salisbury=Dorathy, da. of Francis Scargill of Knap-
Hall, co. Hertf.   well, co. Cambr.

1. William Cole. 2. Richard. 3. Francis. 4. Thomas. 5. John. 6. Dorathy.

Colles of Park Bury.

ARMS.—*Gules, a chevron Argent pellettée, charged with two bars gemelles of the field, between three lions' heads erased Or, a mullet for difference.*
CREST.—*A falcon with wings expanded, preying on a fish, all proper.*

These produced in a seale and respited to London for proofe: after proved by Mr. Cole of the Court of Wards.

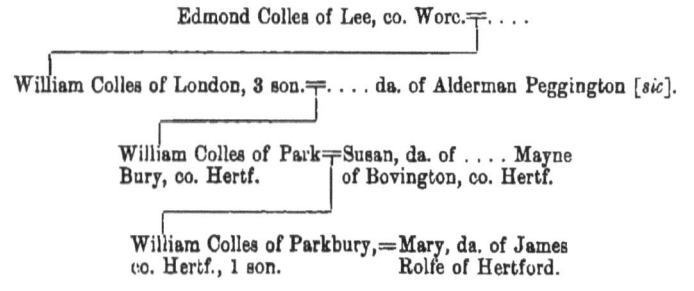

Edmond Colles of Lee, co. Worc.=....

William Colles of London, 3 son.=.... da. of Alderman Peggington [*sic*].

William Colles of Park=Susan, da. of .... Mayne
Bury, co. Hertf.   of Bovington, co. Hertf.

William Colles of Parkbury,=Mary, da. of James
co. Hertf., 1 son.   Rolfe of Hertford.

Colte of Rickmansworth.

ARMS.—*Quarterly—1 and 4, Ermine, a fess between three colts in full speed Sable; 2 and 3, Sable, a chevron Vair between three congers' heads erased Argent,* PISS.
CREST.—*A colt in full speed Sable, holding in his mouth a broken tilting-spear Or, headed Azure, the other part of the spear held between his fore-legs.*

The armes and creast with the quartered coate is testified under the hand and seale of Rob't Cooke, Clarenceux.

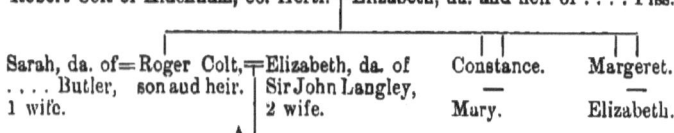

Robert Colt of Aldenham, co. Hertf.=Elizabeth, da. and heir of .... Piss.

Sarah, da. of=Roger Colt,=Elizabeth, da. of   Constance.   Margeret.
.... Butler, son and heir. | Sir John Langley,   —   —
1 wife. | 2 wife.   Mary.   Elizabeth.

A |

John Colte* of .... =Frances, da. of [Ralph] Woodcock, Alderman of London.

Sir John Colte of=Ann, da. of Albericus   Rowland Colte   Mary, wife of Richard
Rickmansworth, | Gentilis, Doctor of the   of London,   Hyem of Eastham, co.
co. Hertford. | Civill law.   2 son.   Essex.

John Colte,   2. Rowland.   3. Charles.   4. Henry.   Hester.   Anna.   Marye.
son and heir. Colte.

Combe of Hemel Hempsted.

ARMS and CREST as at p. 6.

Richard Combe of [Hemel]=Elizabeth, da. of William Marshall
Hempsted, co. Hertf. | of Edlesborough, co. Bucks.

Francis Combe,=Jane, da. of John Pope of   Elizabeth, ux. John   Susan.
son and heir. | Wroxton, co. Oxford.   Shukborough.

Francis Combe of Hemel Hempsted,=Barbara, da. of Henry Ewer
co. Hertf., eldest son, living 1634.   of the Midle Temple, Esq.

Coney of St. Alban's.

ARMS.—*Argent, a saltire Gules between four conies sejant Sable.*
CREST.—*On a mount Vert a coney sejant Or.*

Henry Cunnye of the libertie of St. Alban's.=.... da. of Sir Raph Cunnesbye.

Ralph Cunny,   2. John.   3. Henry.   Frances, wife to Mr. John   Elizabeth.
eldest son.   Harmer of St. Alban's.

---

* Clutterbuck's 'Hist. of Herts,' vol. i., 205, gives the following inscription in Rickmansworth Church : " Here under lyeth the body of *John Colte*, late of Rickmersworth in the County of Hertford, Esquier, son and heire of Roger Colte, Esquier, which John married *Frances*, one of the daughters of *Ralph Woodcocke*, late of London, Alderman, by whom he had issue, three sons, viz., *John*, *Rowland*, and *Thomas*, and four daughters, viz., *Mary*, *Ursula*, *Mary*, and *Elizabeth ;* and hee departed this life the 29th of April, A.D. 1610, being about 32 years of age. To whose memorie the said Frances, his most lovcinge wife, hath caused this monument to be erected."

THE VISITATION OF HERTFORDSHIRE, 1634.   45

Coningsby of North Mims.

ARMS.—*Quarterly of ten*—1, *Gules, three conies sejant Argent, a bordure engrailed Sable;* 2, *Vert, a pelican in piety Argent, vulned Or, nest of the last;* 3, *Azure, two chevrons Argent;* 4, ... *two lions rampant, a bordure engrailed Sable;* 5, *Per fess Azure and Or, a pale counterchanged, three lions rampant of the second;* 6, *Sable, a fess Ermine between three goats' heads erased Argent;* 7, *Sable, a cross engrailed Or;* 8, *Gules, on a fess Argent between six martlets of the second three cinquefoils of the field;* 9, *Gules, a lion rampant Argent, crowned Or;* 10, *Or, a cross engrailed Gules.*
CREST.—*A coney sejant Argent.*

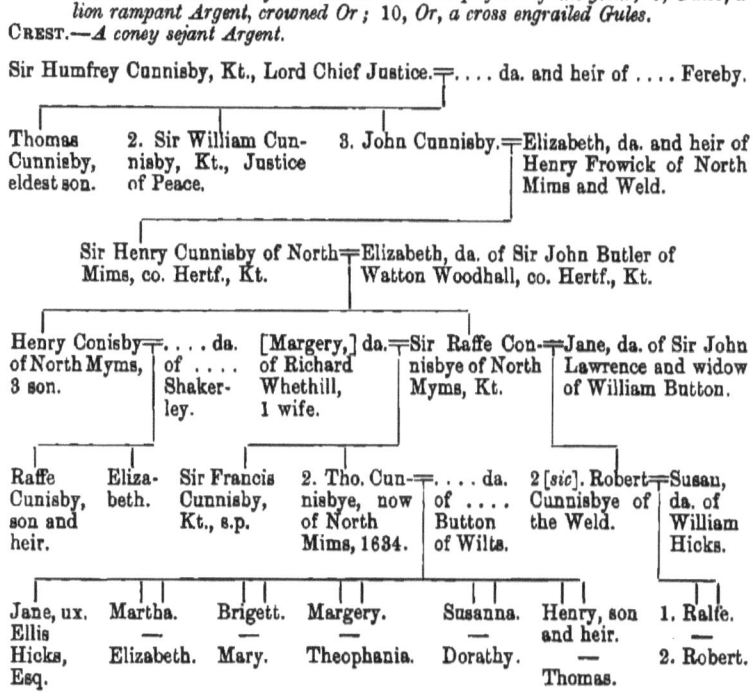

Sir Humfrey Cunnisby, Kt., Lord Chief Justice.=. . . . da. and heir of . . . . Fereby.

Thomas Cunnisby, eldest son.

2. Sir William Cunnisby, Kt., Justice of Peace.

3. John Cunnisby.=Elizabeth, da. and heir of Henry Frowick of North Mims and Weld.

Sir Henry Cunnisby of North=Elizabeth, da. of Sir John Butler of
Mims, co. Hertf., Kt.   Watton Woodhall, co. Hertf., Kt.

Henry Conisby=. . . . da. of North Myms, of . . . . 3 son. Shakerley.

[Margery,] da.=Sir Raffe Conof Richard nisbye of North Whethill, Myms, Kt. 1 wife.

=Jane, da. of Sir John Lawrence and widow of William Button.

Raffe Cunisby, son and heir.

Elizabeth.
—

Sir Francis Cunnisby, Kt., s.p.

2. Tho. Cunnisbye, now of North Mims, 1634.

=. . . . da. of . . . . Button of Wilts.

2 [sic]. Robert Cunnisbye of the Weld.

=Susan, da. of William Hicks.

Jane, ux. Ellis Hicks, Esq.

Martha.
—
Elizabeth.

Brigett.
—
Mary.

Margery.
—
Theophania.

Susanna.
—
Dorathy.

Henry, son and heir.
—
Thomas.

1. Ralfe.
—
2. Robert.

Coppin of Markeatsel.

ARMS.—*Or, a chief of one row of Vair.*
CREST.—*On a coronet a cock Or.*

Under the hand and seal of William Camden, Claren., to Sir George Coppin, 1608.

Robert Coppin, primo E. 6.=. . . .

George Coppin, who built the Crosse in Dunwich [co. Suff.].=. . . .
A

THE VISITATION OF HERTFORDSHIRE, 1634.

A

Sir George Coppin, Kt., = Anne, da. of Thomas Norton
Clarke of the Crowne. | of Bedf.

William. Robert. George.   Thomas Coppin of Markeatsel, co. = Martha, da. of
All died without issue.   Hertf., Esq., living 1634.   Luke Norton.

Thomas Coppin, eldest son.   John Coppin.   Anne.   Elizabeth.

Cotton of Flamsted.

Noate that Sir Rich. Cotton, Controller of the howse to King Edward the 6, is buried in Pitleston Church in com. Buck.

William Cotton. = ...

Daniel Cotton of Pitleston [Pightlesthorne], co. Bucks, = Alice, da. of Mr. Hill, a
Yeoman of the Mouth to Queene Elizabeth.   servant to Q. Elizabeth.

Daniel Cotton   Nathaniel Cotton   Jonas Cotton of Flamsted, = Anne, da. of Mr.
of Pitleston,   of Bovington in   co. Hertf., Marshall of the | John Hall of
eldest son.   com. Hertf., 2 son.   King's Hall.   Bovington.

1. Jonas Cotton.   2. William.   3. Thomas.   4. Nathan.   Mary.   Anne.

Cox of Beamond.

ARMS and CREST as at p. 7.

The arms and crest are confirmed to Tho. Cox of Beamonds in com. Hertf. by Rob't Cooke, Clarenceux, 1571, p. pattent and a pedegree.

Thomas Cox of Beamonds, co. Hertf. = Bridget, da. of . . . . Lanceford [Lunsford].

Alban Cox of Shenley, = Mary, da. and heir of William Lawson
co. Hertf.   of Pritlewell in Essex.

Alban Cox of Beamonds, = Mary, da. of William   William Cox of = Mary, da. of
co. Hertf., now living, Smyth of Freehowson,   Porters in Shen- | Abell Ewer of
a° 1634.   co. Hertf.   ley, co. Hertf. Greene Street,
                                                                  co. Hertf.

Crosby of Wyndridge.

Respyt the Armes till Michelmas terme.

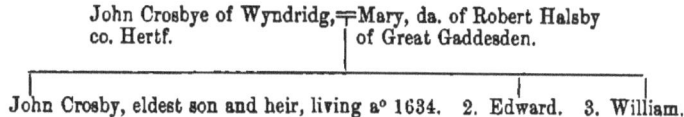

John Crosbye of Wyndridg, co. Hertf. =Mary, da. of Robert Halsby of Great Gaddesden.

John Crosby, eldest son and heir, living aº 1634.   2. Edward.   3. William.

Dacres of Chesthunt.

ARMS.—*Argent, a chevron Sable between three hurts each charged with an escallop of the field.*

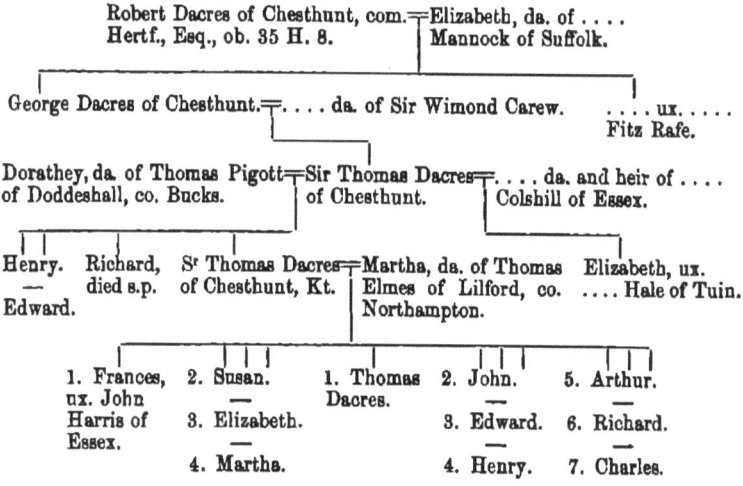

Robert Dacres of Chesthunt, com. Hertf., Esq., ob. 35 H. 8. =Elizabeth, da. of .... Mannock of Suffolk.

George Dacres of Chesthunt.=.... da. of Sir Wimond Carew.   .... ux. .... Fitz Rafe.

Dorathey, da. of Thomas Pigott of Doddeshall, co. Bucks. =Sir Thomas Dacres of Chesthunt. =.... da. and heir of .... Colshill of Essex.

Henry. — Edward.   Richard, died s.p.   Sʳ Thomas Dacres of Chesthunt, Kt. =Martha, da. of Thomas Elmes of Lilford, co. Northampton.   Elizabeth, ux. .... Hale of Tuin.

1. Frances, ux. John Harris of Essex.
2. Susan. —
3. Elizabeth. —
4. Martha.

1. Thomas Dacres.
2. John. —
3. Edward. —
4. Henry.

5. Arthur. —
6. Richard. —
7. Charles.

Dewhurst of Chesthunt.

ARMS.—*Sable, two bends within a bordure Argent.*

Barnard Duhurst of Chesthunt, co. Hertf.=Anne, da. of .... Warde.

1. Thomas.
2. Henry.
5. John.
6. Walter, s.p.

Sir Bernard Dewhurst, s.p.

Prudence,=Thomas Dacres of Chesthunt, Kt., 1 wife.

Robert Dewhurst of Chesthunt Nunnery, co. Hertf., living 1634.

=Anne, da. of Roger Dye, Citizen of London, 2 wife.

Catherin, ux. William Drywood of Warley, co. Essex, Esq.

Anne, ux. William Dormer of London.

Dixon of Braughing.

ARMS.—*Sable, a cross between four hinds' heads erased Or.*
CREST.—*On a mount Vert, a tiger sejant Ermine, ducally gorged Or.*

A Patent granted to James Dickson of London, son of William Dickson of Standrip [Staindrop] in the Bishoprick of Durham, by Robert Cooke, Clarenceux King of Arms, the 12 of September 1579.

Will'm Dixon of Standrip in the Bishoprick of Durham.=....

James Dixon of London.=Ann, da. of Thomas Jennings of London.

Thomas Dixon of Braughing, co. Hertf., living 1634.=Frances, da. of Robert Carter of Hatfeld, co. Hertf.

Mary, ux. John Dynes.

Susan, ux. Robert Hill.

Docwra of Putteridge.

He paid no fee.

Thomas Docwra, the elder, of Puttridge in the p'sh of Offley in Hertfordsh., Esq., Justice of Peace and High Shreeve, ob. æt. 84, 1602.=Mildred Hales of Canterbury, sister of John Hales of Coventry, Esq., Clarke of the Hanaper.

A

THE VISITATION OF HERTFORDSHIRE, 1634.   49

A

Helen, da. of George Horsey,=Thomas Dockwra, Esq.,=Jane, da. and coheir of
Esq., and of his wife, da. of | Justice of Peace and | Sir William Periam, Kt.,
Sir Rafe Sadler, Kt. | High Shreeve in Hert- | Lo. Cheeffe Baron of the
                                  | fordsh., ob. 1612. | Exchequer [1593–1603].

Jane, ux. Sir Henry Pakenham, Kt.

Anne, ux. Hum- | Elizabeth, | Jane,=John | Periam=Martha, | Henry
fry Walcott of | ux. James | died at | Powell, | Dockwra | sister of | Dockwra
Walcott, co. | Beverley, | Ham- | merchant | of Putt- | Oliver | of North
Salop, Esq., | Esq., | burgh. | adven- | ridge, | St. John, | Myms.
Justice of the | Justice of | | turer. | Esq., now | Earl of |
Peace and High | Peace in | | | living, | Boling- |
Shyreve. | co. Bed- | | | 1634. | brook. |
               | ford. |

Samuel Powell, | 1. Thomas | 2. Henry. | 1. Margeret. | 3. Martha.
born at Ham- | Dockwra, | —— | —— | ——
burgh. | son and heir.| 3. Lancelott.| 2. Elizabeth. | 4. Dorathe.

Raffe Dockwra=Susan | John, ob. | Frances, ux. | Helen, ux. Jasper Horsey,
of Fulborne, | . . . . | s.p. | Peter Taverner | brother of Sir Raffe Hor-
co. Cambr. | | | of Hexton. | sey, Kt.

James Dockwra of=. . . . the da. of Mr. Evelin | Thomas Dockwra=. . . . da. of
Fulborne, Captain | of Kingston upon Thames, | of Hinton, co. | Mr. Wise of
of a trained band.| Esq. | Cambr. | Hinton.

        James.   Edward.   Edward.

Edward Dockwra of Hitchin.=Elizabeth, da. of . . . . Carpenter.

Helen, ux. George | Frances, ux. Thomas East | Mildred, ux. John Conny, son
Nodes of Shephall, | of Swavesey, co. Cambr., | and heir of Sir Richard Conny
co. Hertf., Esq. | gent. | of Wissondine, co. Rutland, Kt.

Dod of Bennington.

ARMS.—*Argent, on a fess Gules between two cotises wavy Sable three crescents Or, a mullet on a crescent for difference.*
CREST.—*A serpent proper, issuing from and piercing a garb Argent.*

Resp't for difference.

Edward Dod of Great Boughton, co. Chester.=Cicelly, da. of Thomas Ball of Chester.

Thomas Dod of Great Boughton, co. Chester.=Ellin, da. of . . . .

Edward Dod, son and heir.

Hugh Dod of Bennington, co. Hertf., 3 son, living 1634.

Jane, ux. . . . . Robinson.

Drew of Broxbourne.

ARMS.—*Quarterly*—1, *Ermine, a lion passant Gules*; 2, *Argent, a chevron Sable, in chief a label of three points Gules, a mullet for difference*; 3, *Sable, a bend between two dolphins Argent*; 4, *Argent, on a bend Azure three mullets of the field.*
CREST.—*A bull's head erased Sable, holding in the mouth three wheat-ears Or.*

Vide the Visitation of Devon, 1620 [Harl. Soc.].

Emanuell Drew of St. Leonard's, co. Devon.=Anne, da. of . . . . Dillon of Chemwell, co. Devon.

John Drew of St. Leonard's in Devon, living 1620.

Robert Drew of Bratton Fleming, co. Devon.=Margeret, da. of . . . . Green.

Nathaniell Drew of Broxborne, co. Hertf., living 1634.=Alice, da. of Thomas Webb.

2. John.
—
3. Timothy.

Grace, ux. Richard Hill of Banbury.

Mary, ux. John Ward of Banbury.

1. Robert Drew, 12 years old, 1634.   2. Nathaniel.   1. Susan.   2. Elizabeth.

Eakins of Northaw.

The Armes resp't till Michelmas Termc.

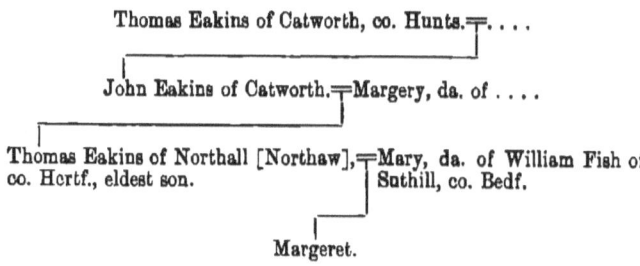

Thomas Eakins of Catworth, co. Hunts.=....

John Eakins of Catworth.=Margery, da. of ....

Thomas Eakins of Northall [Northaw],=Mary, da. of William Fish of
co. Hertf., eldest son. | Sothill, co. Bedf.

Margeret.

Ewer of The Lea and Cheshunt.

ARMS.—*Azure, a tiger passant Or, on a chief of the last three crosses pattée of the first.*
CREST.—*A pheon Or, mounted on a broken dart Gules, entwined with a serpent proper.*

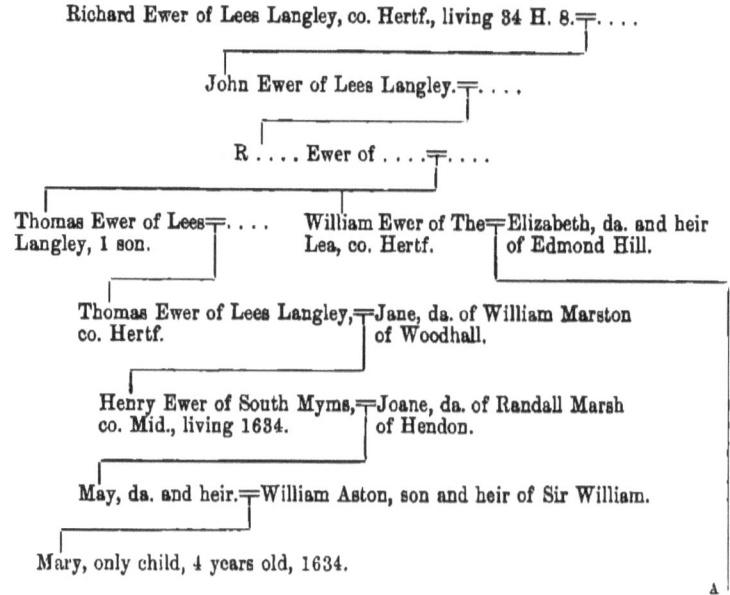

Richard Ewer of Lees Langley, co. Hertf., living 34 H. 8.=....

John Ewer of Lees Langley.=....

R .... Ewer of ....=....

Thomas Ewer of Lees=....   William Ewer of The=Elizabeth, da. and heir
Langley, 1 son.   Lea, co. Hertf.   of Edmond Hill.

Thomas Ewer of Lees Langley,=Jane, da. of William Marston
co. Hertf.   of Woodhall.

Henry Ewer of South Myms,=Joane, da. of Randall Marsh
co. Mid., living 1634.   of Hendon.

May, da. and heir.=William Aston, son and heir of Sir William.

Mary, only child, 4 years old, 1634.

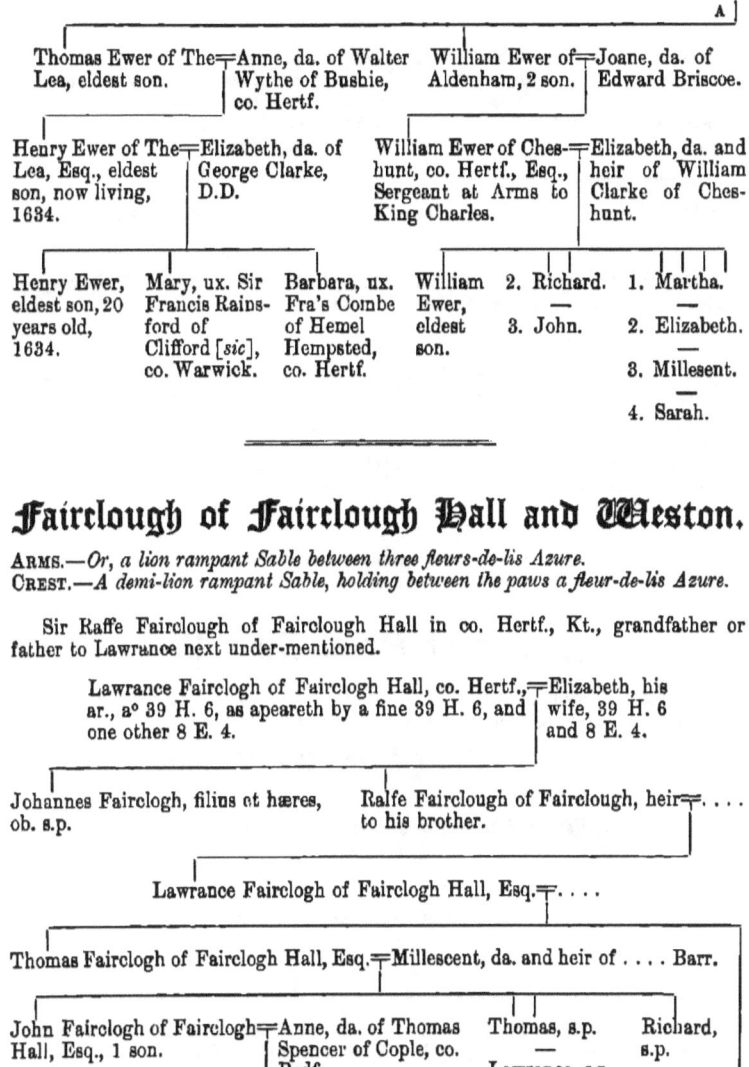

Fairclough of Fairclough Hall and Weston.

ARMS.—*Or, a lion rampant Sable between three fleurs-de-lis Azure.*
CREST.—*A demi-lion rampant Sable, holding between the paws a fleur-de-lis Azure.*

Sir Raffe Fairclough of Fairclough Hall in co. Hertf., Kt., grandfather or father to Lawrance next under-mentioned.

Lawrance Fairclogh of Fairclogh Hall, co. Hertf., =Elizabeth, his ar., a° 39 H. 6, as apeareth by a fine 39 H. 6, and | wife, 39 H. 6 one other 8 E. 4. | and 8 E. 4.

Johannes Fairclogh, filius et hæres, ob. s.p. | Ralfe Fairclough of Fairclough, heir=.... to his brother.

Lawrance Fairclogh of Fairclogh Hall, Esq.=....

Thomas Fairclogh of Fairclogh Hall, Esq.=Millescent, da. and heir of .... Barr.

John Fairclogh of Fairclogh=Anne, da. of Thomas | Thomas, s.p. | Richard, Hall, Esq., 1 son. | Spencer of Cople, co. | — | s.p. | Bedf. | Lawrance, s.p.

4. Elizabeth, ux. .... Clarke, a Deane in Ireland.

5. Frances, ux. .... Risley.

6. Rose, ux. Edward Underwood.

7. Dorathey, ux. Robert Underwood.

8. Constance, ux. Owen Hobert.

THE VISITATION OF HERTFORDSHIRE, 1634.

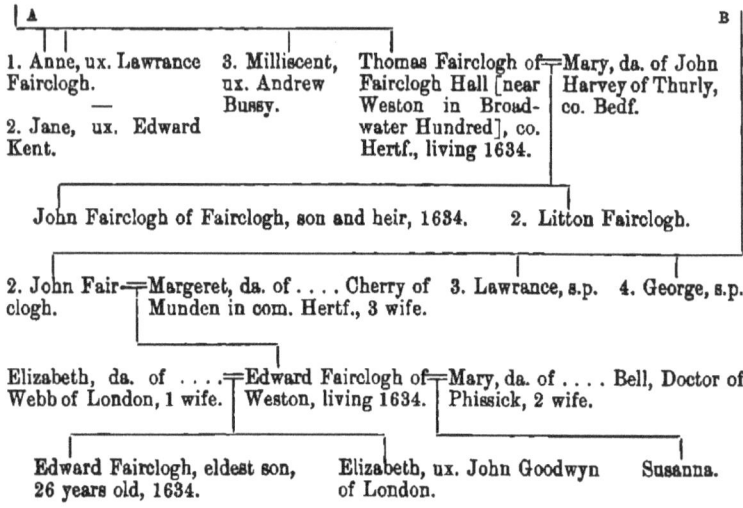

Farrar of Great Amwell.

ARMS.—*Argent, on a bend engrailed Gules three horse-shoes of the field.*
CREST.—*A horse-shoe Argent between two wings Or.*

This Arms and Crest exemplified under the hand of William Camden, Clarenceux, to John Farrer of Croxton.

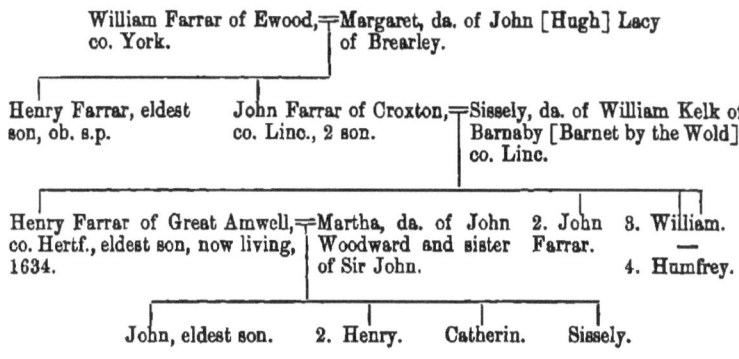

Fishe of Hatfield.

The Arms respyt for prooffe.

Thomas Fish of Litle Ate [Ayott], co. Hertf.=....da. of ....Hyde.
 |
Leonard Fishe of Litle Ate, co. Hertf.=Emme, da. of ....Graves.
 |
Thomas Fishe of Hatfeld, co. Hertf., 1634.=Alice, da. of John Eakins of co. Hertf.
 |
1. Mary. 2. Alice. Leonard Fishe, eldest son. 2. Thomas Fishe. 3. Angella. 4. Sarah.

Fish of Stevenage.

ARMS.—*Azure, a fess Argent, over all a bend Gules charged with five mullets or, a crescent for difference.*

Refer the Armes to Sir Ed. Fish of Bedfordshire.

Thomas Fishe of Litle Ate [Ayott], co. Hertf.=....da. of ....Hyde.
 |
Elizabeth, da. of ....Thompson, Auditor, 1 wife.=George Fishe of Litle Ate, co. Hertf.=Judith, da. of ....Hanby, Auditor, 2 wife.
 |
Edward Fishe of Stevenage, co. Hertf., 1 son, living 1634.=Mary, da. of Edmond Noades of Stevenage.

Fowke of St. Alban's and Flamsted.

ARMS.—*Azure, a fleur-de-lis Argent, on a chief indented of the second a lion passant Gules.*

CREST.—*A demi-eagle wings expanded Azure, double-headed, the necks crossed in saltire, beaked Or.*

A patent of this arms and crest granted unto Barthelmew Fowke, Clerk of the Spicery, after, Master of the Household to Q. Elizabeth, and made Kt. by King [James], the patent granted by William Flower, Norroy, the 1 of Feb. 1580 ; 23 of Queen Eliz.

Leonard Fowk of Flampsted, co. Hertford.=....

THE VISITATION OF HERTFORDSHIRE, 1634. 55

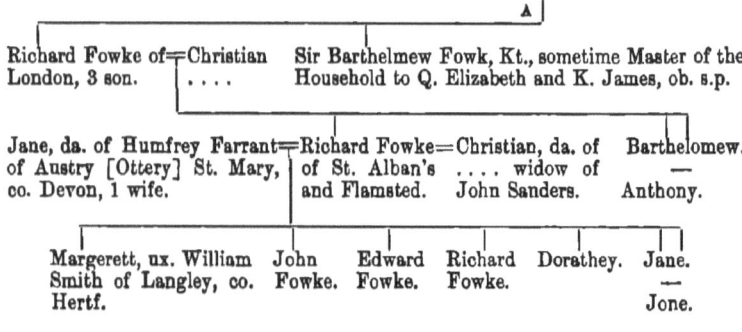

Richard Fowke of=Christian   Sir Barthelmew Fowk, Kt., sometime Master of the
London, 3 son.   ....   Household to Q. Elizabeth and K. James, ob. s.p.

Jane, da. of Humfrey Farrant=Richard Fowke=Christian, da. of   Barthelomew.
of Austry [Ottery] St. Mary, of St. Alban's   .... widow of   —
co. Devon, 1 wife.   and Flamsted.   John Sanders.   Anthony.

Margerett, ux. William   John   Edward   Richard   Dorathey.   Jane.
Smith of Langley, co.   Fowke. Fowke.   Fowke.   —
Hertf.   Jone.

Frances of Cookmaines and Salmons.*

ARMS.—*Argent, on a chevron wavy between three eagles displayed Gules as many estoiles of the first.*
CREST.—*On the trunk of a vine-tree vert, fructed "lake," an eagle wings endorsed Argent.*

[C. 28, Ind. 1, fo. 7a.]

William Frances of Cookmaines, co.=Alice, da. of .... Hill.
Hertf.; descended out of Derbigh.

William Frances=Constance, da.   3. Richard Frances=Mary, da. of   1. John
of Cookmaines, of Jo. Mathew   of Salmons in com. John Darell   Frances of
2 son, Sergeant of Soame [co.   Hertf. [youngest   of Wickham   Noake, co.
to Q. Eliz. [ser- Cantab.].   son].   [co. Bucks]. Hertf.
vant, obiit aº
1598].

1. John, s.p.   Mary, da. of=2. Mathew Frances,=Elizabeth, da. of   Elizabeth,
[eldest son].   Jo. Clark of Sergeant at Armes, Jeromy Horton,   ux. [John]
—   Crossoake,   1634 [he was Ser-   widow of James   Pennyall
3. William,   co. Hertf.,   geant at Arms to K. Rich [aº 1629].   [or Penny-
s.p. [youngest   1 wife, s.p. Ja. 1 and Ch. 1].   ale].
son].

[1.] Henry Frances, only child [aº 1634].   [2. Thomas, 2ᵈ son.]

* The additions in brackets, and the rest of the pedigree on the next page, excepting only the Christian names of Alban and William, are additions to Harl. MS. 1547 in the handwriting of Mr. Robert Dale, Suffolk Herald.

56   THE VISITATION OF HERTFORDSHIRE, 1634.

```
Alban=Elizabeth, da.    2. William,    5. John=Mary,     3. Mathew=Elizabeth,
Francis of  and heir of    and        Francis.  da. of    Francis.   da. of ...
Salmons,    Christopher  4. Thomas,             Dr.                  Ebbet.
co. Hertf., Wad, widow   ob. s.p.                Beris-
eldest son. of ....                              ford.
            Westcot.
```

```
John Francis,=Mary, da.   Jane, wife   Catherin,      1. Mathew.    3. Edward.
only son, living of William of Richard wife of        —             —
aº 1692.      Cook.       Hoper,      Heath         2. Richard.   4. James.
                          Esq.       Edwards,
John Francis, only child.             Esq.
```

```
3. Charles,  2. Alban.   Mary.   Christopher=Josepha, da. of William
ob. s.p.                         Francis,    Clark of Northamptonsh.,
                                 eldest son. and his heir.
```

[Subscribed
   The armes and descent of Mathew Frances, Esq., one of his Maties Serjeants
at Armes ratified by me
                    RI. St GEORGE, Clarenceux Kinge of Armes, 1634.]

Gardener of Watford.

ARMS.—*Or, on a chevron Gules between three griffins' heads erased Sable two lions' faces of the field.*
CREST.—*A griffin's head erased Sable.*

The armes and culler respt. to Lond.; he hath a kinsman a mercht.
at Bassinghall.

```
Gilbert Gardener of Wigan, co. Lanc.=....

   Gilbert Gardener of Wigan.=Margery, da. of .... Finning.

William Gardener of Watford,=Catherin, da. of Thomas Mauditt
co. Hertf.                    of London.
```

Gardiner of Jeningsbury.

ARMS.—*Quarterly—1 and 4, Per pale Or and Gules, a fess between three hinds passant, all counterchanged; 2 and 3, Sable, two bars Argent, in chief a talbot passant of the second*, HAWARD.

CREST.—*A Saracen's head in profile proper, erased at the shoulders Gules, wreathed round the temples Azure and of the second, and on the head a cap Or.*

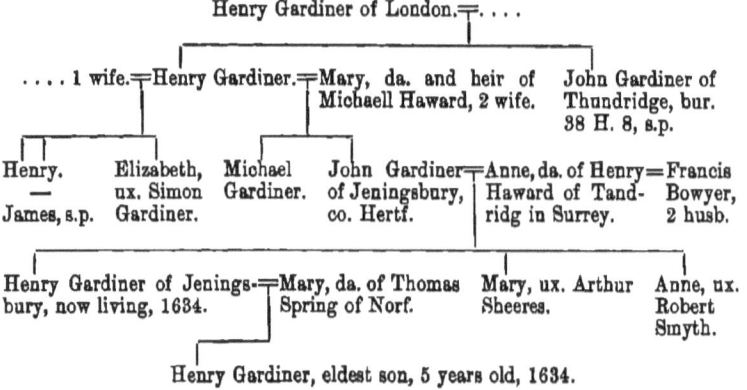

Gardiner of Thundridgebury.

ARMS.—*Per pale Or and Gules, on a fess between three hinds passant two mascles, all counterchanged.*

CREST.—*Two halberts in pale Or entwined by a snake Azure.*

These Arms and Crest granted to John Gardiner of Thundrigebury in com. Hertf., 38 of H. 8, by Christopher Barker, Garter, and do not belong to this man.

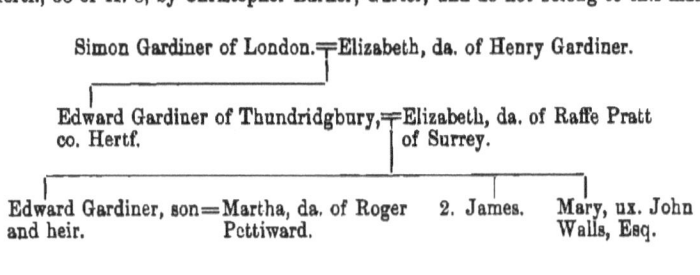

I

Gill of Anstey.

ARMS.—*Lozengy Or and Vert, a lion rampant-gardant Gules, a mullet for difference.*

George Gill of Wigill [Widdial], co. Hertf.=.... heir of .... Cannon.

Edward Gill of Anstey,=Margarett, da. of .... Brograve of Beckenham
co. Hertf., 3 son. in Kent.

Thomas Gill, eldest son, ob. s.p.

Edward Gill of Anstey,=Mary, da. of Edward Michell, and
co. Hertf., eldest son living 1634. relict of Rich. Smartfoote of Puckeridge, co. Hertf.

Edward Gill, eldest son. 2. John. 3. George. Barbara, ux. Thomas Cutler of Anstey. Susan.

[Pencilled additions in Harl. MS. 1547 make George Gill son of John Gill by Margaret, da. and heir of *George* Cannon, and make George's wife Gertruda, da. and coheir of Sir *John Perient*, Kt., and make Edward's wife Margaret the *widow* of *Henry* Brograve.]

Goodere of Hatfield.

Sir Henry Goodier of Newgate Street in the p'sh of Hatfield.=....

Francis Goodier of Hatfield, Esq.,=Catherin, da. of George Onslow of co. Stafford.
son and heir, living 1634.

2. Thomas Goodier.

Henry Goodier, son and heir, 5 yeres old, 1634. Jane.

Gourney of Hitchin.

ARMS.—*Quarterly*—1 *and* 4, *Argent, a cross engrailed Gules, depressed by another plain of the first, between four mullets of six points pierced of the second;* 2 *and* 3, *Argent, a chevron Ermines between three quatrefoils slipped Sable.*

William Gourney of Yardley,=Frances, da. of .... Hughes
co. Hertf. of Midlesex.

THE VISITATION OF HERTFORDSHIRE, 1634.   59

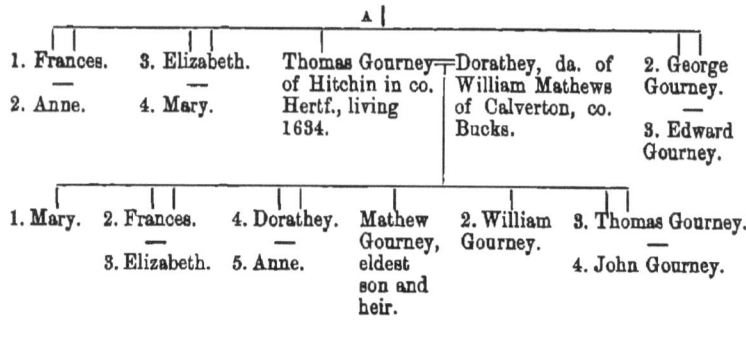

1. Frances. 3. Elizabeth.   Thomas Gourney=Dorathey, da. of   2. George
2. Anne.   4. Mary.   of Hitchin in co. | William Mathews   Gourney.
                           Hertf., living   of Calverton, co.   —
                           1634.   Bucks.   3. Edward
                                                                  Gourney.

1. Mary. 2. Frances. 4. Dorathey. Mathew   2. William   3. Thomas Gourney.
          —   Gourney,   Gourney.
          3. Elizabeth. 5. Anne.   eldest   4. John Gourney.
                                     son and
                                     heir.

Greene of East Barnett.

ARMS.—*Azure, three bucks trippant Or, attired proper, a crescent for difference.*

William Greene of Burstall, co. York.=Alice, da. of . . . . Haileharte.

Robert Greene,   Edward Greene of Bristow, Prebend=Mary, da. of . . . . Cassy
eldest son.   of the Cathedrall Church of Bristow, | of Cassys Compton, co.
                 2 son.   Gloster.

William Greene of East Barnett,=Grace, da. of Rafe Gill of the Tower, Keeper of
co. Hertf., eldest son, living | the lyons.
1634.

1. Grace.   2. Mary.   3. Martha.

Grubbe of North Mims.

ARMS.—*Quarterly—1 and 4, Ermine, on a chief embattled Gules three roses Argent; 2 and 3, Argent, two bends engrailed Sable, a label of three points Gules,* RADCLIFFE.
CREST.—*A griffin's head erased per pale Argent and Gules, charged with a rose counterchanged.*

Henry Grubb, purchased=Joane, da. of Sir Richard Radcliffe, Kt., slaine
the p'sonage of North | at the battaile of Bosworth, and heir to her
Myms a° 36 H. 8. | brother John Radcliffe who died s.p.

THE VISITATION OF HERTFORDSHIRE, 1634.

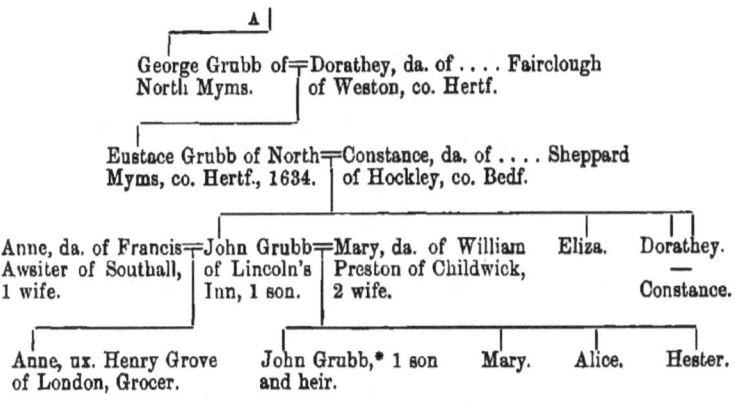

Gulston of Wydiall.

ARMS.—*Argent, three bars nebulée Gules, over all a bend Sable charged with three plates.*
CREST.—*An ostrich's wing the feathers alternately Argent and Gules, charged with a bend as in the Arms.*

Granted by William Camden, *Clarenceux.*

Thomas Gulston of Wymondham in com. Leic.=....
    |
William Gulston.=....

| John Gulston of Wydiall, co. Hertf., Esq., living 1634, one of the Justices of the Peace. | =Jane, da. of Richard Ketridg of South Mims, co. Midd. | Theodore Gulston, Doctor in Phisick, ob. s.p. |

| 1. Prudence, ux. William Manning of Woodhurst, co. Hunts. | 2. Ellin. — 3. Anne. — 4. Catherin. | 1. Richard Gulston. — 2. Theodore. | 3. Thomas. — 4. George. | 5. John. — 6. Edward. — 7. William. |

---

* [This John Grubbe, in 1663, sold to Thomas Cowlcy of St. Alban's the Rectory and lands at North Mimms, Herts, which he had inherited from his ancestor Henry Grubbe; having in the previous year, 1662, purchased the manor and estate of Horsenden in Buckinghamshire from Sir John Denham. The conveyance of North Mimms Rectory was enrolled (Close Rolls, 15 Car. II., part 25), and the vendor is therein described as "John Grubb of Horsenden in the county of Buckingham, gent." The descendants of John Grubbe were settled at Horsenden till the year 1841, when the estate was sold. See Lipscomb's 'History of Bucks,' vol. ii., 333.]

Hale of Tewin.

ARMS.—*Azure, a chevron bretessed Or, a crescent for difference.*
CREST.—*A serpent proper, entwined round five arrow-shafts Or, feathered Argent, one in pale, four saltirewise.*

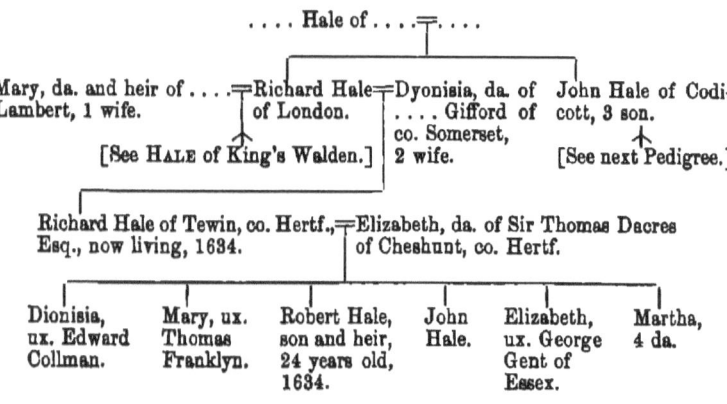

Hale of Harmer Green.

ARMS (with *a mullet for difference*) and CREST as in the preceding Pedigree.

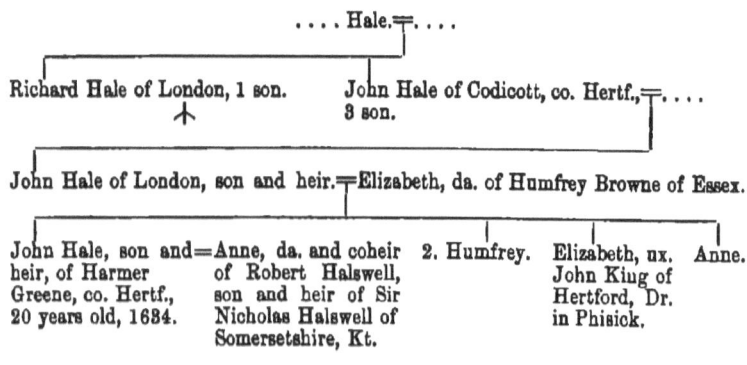

Hale of King's Walden.

ARMS.—*Quarterly*—1 *and* 4, HALE as under HALE of Tewin, *without any difference;* 2 *and* 3, *Gules, a chevron between three lambs passant Argent,* LAMBERT.

Richard Hale of London.=Mary, da. of .... Lambert.

William Hale of King's Walden,=Rose, da. of Sir George Bond of
co. Hertf., Esq. London, Kt.

| Alice, ux. John Min, son of Sir John Min of Surrey. | Anne, ux. Charles Hoskins, son of Sir Thomas. | William Hale, son and heir. | 2. Rowland=Elizabeth, Hale. da. of Alderman Garaway of London. | Bernard. — John. | Dionisia. |

Halsey of Great Gaddesden.

ARMS.—*Argent, on a pile Sable three griffins' heads erased of the first.*

Robert Halsey of Greate Gadesden,=Dorathey, da. of William
co. Hertf. Downes, co. Salop.

William Halsey of Great=Lettice, da. of Henry Stringer of Ruborow in co. Glocester
Gadesden, now living, [? Rowborrow, co. Somerset].
1634.

John Halsey, eldest son and heir.　　　Dorathey, ux. George Francklyn.

Halton of Sawbridgworth.

ARMS.—*Quarterly*—1 *and* 4, *Per pale Azure and Gules, a lion rampant Argent;* 2 *and* 3, *Sable, a fess Argent between three esquires' helmets of the second, vizors Or.* A mullet for difference.

Robert Halton of London, Sergeant-at-Law.=Jone, da. of .... Draper.

A

THE VISITATION OF HERTFORDSHIRE, 1634.   63

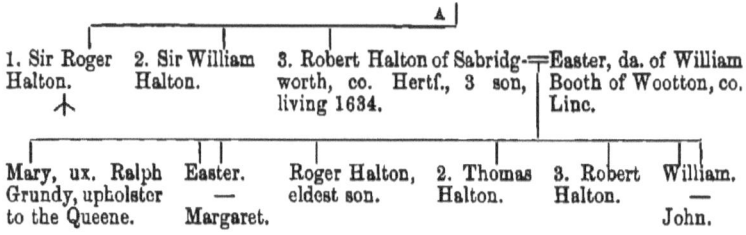

Hanchett of Braughin.

ARMS.—*Sable, three dexter hands couped at the wrist Argent.*

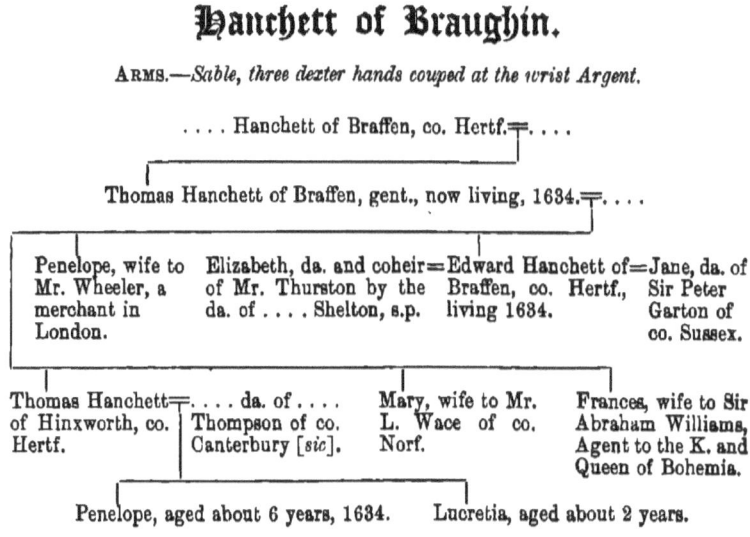

Harris of Rickmansworth.

ARMS.—*Sable, three crescents within a bordure Argent.*

Henry Harris of Rickmansworth, co. Hertf.=Thomazin, da. of Charles Spencer.
 |
 ————————————————————————————————
 | | |
John Harris of Rickmansworth, co. Hertf.,   2. Henry.   3. Frances.
eldest son, living 1634.

Hayes of Hertford.

ARMS.—*Quarterly*—1 *and* 4, *Ermine, three lions' heads erased Sable;* 2 *and* 3, *A fess embattled, in chief three martlets.*
CREST.—*A leopard's face.*

Vide the Armes of Sir Thomas Hayes of London, Alderman.

Sir Thomas Hayes, Kt., Alderman of London.=Margeret, da. of Alderman Howse of London.

Robert Hayes of Hertf., 1634.=Catherin, da. of .... Sherwood, Doctor of Phisick. | 2. Thomas. | 3. Benjamin.

Hewett of Rickmansworth.

ARMS.—*Gules, a chevron engrailed between three owls Argent.*

Here must be a Baronett's marke.

William Hewett.=....

John Hewett.=....

Sir John Hewett of Rickmansworth in co. Hertf., Bart., now living, 1634.=Catherin, da. of Sir Robert Bevill of Chesterton, co. Hunt., Kt. of the Bath.

1. Elizabeth. | 2. Catherin. | John Hewett, son and heir. | 2. Robert Hewett. | 3. Frances. | 4. Anne.

Hide of Great Hadham.

ARMS.—*Azure, a chevron between three lozenges Or, a mullet for difference.*
CREST.—*An eagle with wings endorsed Sable.*

A confirmation of this Coate and Crest to John Hide of London and Edward his brother by Robert Cook, *Clarenceux*, 1571.

Robert Hide of Norbury, co. Chester.=....

Jenkin Hide, 2 son.=....

THE VISITATION OF HERTFORDSHIRE, 1684.   65

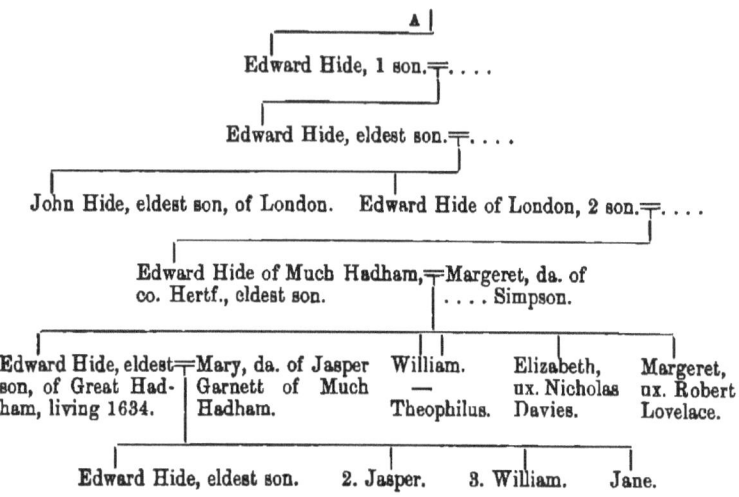

Hoo of Paul's Walden.

ARMS (quarterly of six) and CREST as at p. 12.

Thomas Hoo of Paul's Walden, co. Hertf.=Lucy, da. of .... Brockett.

Thomas Hoo of=Helen, da. of William   2. Nicholas Hoo=. ...
Paul's Walden. | Perient of Digswell.   of Flamsted.

William Hoo of=Susan, da. of George   Elizabeth, ux. John   Thomas Hoo of
Paul's Walden, | Stermont of Paul's   Harleston of Essex.   St. Stephen's,
Esq., living 1634. | Walden.   living 1634.

Thomas Hoo, son and heir, 21 years old, 1634.   Elizabeth.

Howland of St. Alban's.

Respit till Michellmas tearme to London to prove his armes.

John Howland at Stone of Wicken, co. Essex, 12 H. 7, and died .. H. 8.=. ...

John Howland at Stone of Wicken, co. Essex.=. ...
                                         A |

K

THE VISITATION OF HERTFORDSHIRE, 1634.

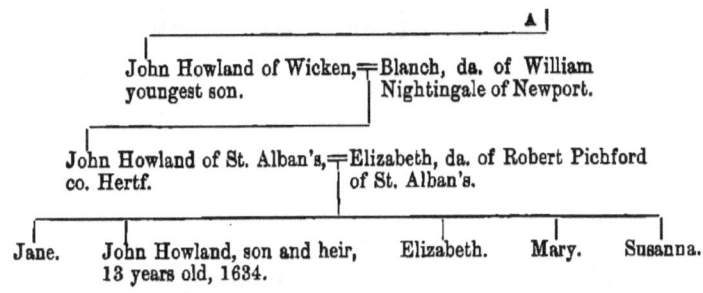

John Howland of Wicken,=Blanch, da. of William
youngest son. | Nightingale of Newport.

John Howland of St. Alban's,=Elizabeth, da. of Robert Pichford
co. Hertf. | of St. Alban's.

Jane. | John Howland, son and heir, | Elizabeth. | Mary. | Susanna.
13 years old, 1634.

Humberston of Walkarne.

ARMS.—*Quarterly—1 and 4, Argent, three bars Sable, in chief as many annulets of the second; 2 and 3, Argent, a chevron Ermines between three eagles displayed Sable; a crescent for difference.*
CREST.—*A griffin's head erased Argent, beaked Sable, charged with three annulets in pale of the second.*

John Humberston of Walkarne, co. Hertf.=. . . .

Edward Humberston of Walkarne, co. Hertf.=Annis, da. of William Winch.

Will'm Humberston of Walkarne, co. Hertf., eldest son. | 2. George Humberston=Dionis, da. and heir of Walkarne, co. Hertf., | of James Garnon of living a° 1634. | Hertford.

James Humberston, eldest son and heir. | 2. Henry. | 3. Garnon.

Hurst of Sawbridgworth.

ARMS.—*Argent, an estoile of sixteen points Gules, in dexter chief a crescent for difference.*
CREST.—*A wood proper, a crescent for difference.*

The armes respt. to the Visit. of Essex made by Mr. Raven.

Thomas Hurst of Shering, co. Essex.=Elizabeth, da. of . . . . Michell.

Roger, eldest son. | Daniell Hurst of Sabridgworth, co. Hertf.,=Martha, da. of John How of
2 sonn, living a° 1634. | Gelyon, co. Hertf.

Daniel Hurst. | Martha.

THE VISITATION OF HERTFORDSHIRE, 1634.   67

Hurst of Bishop Stortford.

ARMS and CREST as in the preceding Pedigree, *without the difference.*

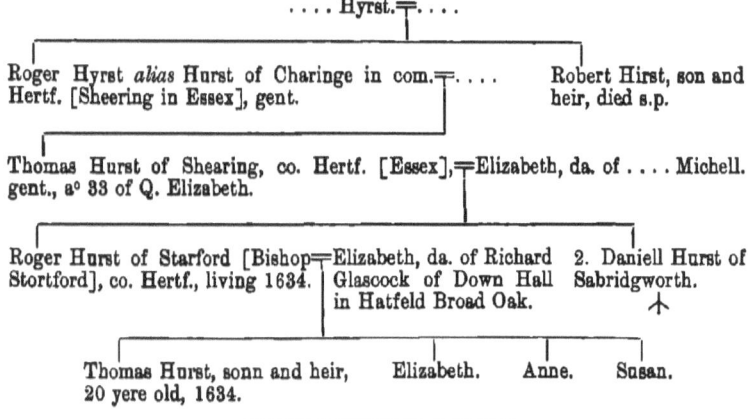

.... Hyrst.=....

Roger Hyrst *alias* Hurst of Charinge in com.=.... Hertf. [Sheering in Essex], gent.

Robert Hirst, son and heir, died s.p.

Thomas Hurst of Shearing, co. Hertf. [Essex],=Elizabeth, da. of .... Michell. gent., aº 33 of Q. Elizabeth.

Roger Hurst of Starford [Bishop=Elizabeth, da. of Richard   2. Daniell Hurst of Stortford], co. Hertf., living 1634. | Glascock of Down Hall   Sabridgworth. in Hatfeld Broad Oak.

Thomas Hurst, sonn and heir, 20 yere old, 1634.   Elizabeth.   Anne.   Susan.

Hyde of Albury.

ARMS.—*Or, a chevron between three lozenges Azure, on a chief Gules an eagle displayed of the field, on a canton Argent the badge of Ulster.*

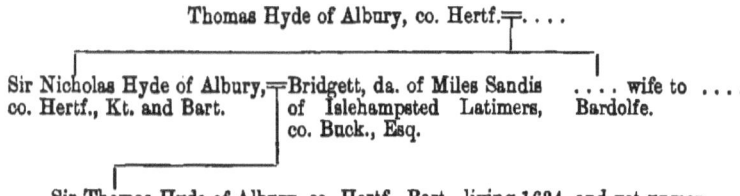

Thomas Hyde of Albury, co. Hertf.=....

Sir Nicholas Hyde of Albury,=Bridgett, da. of Miles Sandis   .... wife to .... co. Hertf., Kt. and Bart. | of Islehampsted Latimers,   Bardolfe. co. Buck., Esq.

Sir Thomas Hyde of Albury, co. Hertf., Bart., living 1634, and yet unmar.

Hyde of Throcking.

ARMS.—*Gules, a saltire engrailed Or, a chief Ermine.*

George Hyde of Throcking, co. Hertf., living 20 H. 8.=....

Lennard Hyde of Throcking, son and heir.=....   William, s.p.   William, s.p.

William Hyde of Throcking.=....
A

68   THE VISITATION OF HERTFORDSHIRE, 1634.

A

Anne, ux..... Lucy, ux. Sir   Lennard Hyde=.... George   Dudley, ux.
Bowles.   Robert Osborne.   of Throcking.   Hyde.   ....Everley.

Elizabeth, ux. Robert Hyde   2. William Hyde=....da. of Sir Martin 3. George
....Lane.   of Throcking,   of Sandon, co.   Stutevile, and widow of Hyde.
—   eldest son.   Hertf., 2 son.   Sir Robert Newdigate.
Anne, unmar.

Inkersall of Weston.

ARMS.—*Gules, a fess dancetté Ermine between six trefoils slipped Or.*
CREST.—*A griffin's head Gules, gorged with a fess dancetté Ermine, between two wings displayed Or feathered Sable.*

The Armes and Creast are testified under the hand of Sir Will'm Segar, *Garter*, as is affirmed by John Phillipot, *Somersett*.

Geffrey Inkersall of Southwell,=Dorathey, da. of Richard Moreigh of Moreigh Hall,
co. Nott.   co. Nott., and one of his heirs.

Robert Inkersall of Weston, co. Hertf., now living,=Elizabeth, da. of Richard
1634, one of the removeing Wardrobe.   Blower of Weston in co. Hertf.

Robert.   John.   Grace.   Elizabeth.   Dorathey.

Ironside of Rickmansworth.

ARMS.—*Per pale Azure and Gules, a cross patonce Or.*
CREST.—*A cubit arm vested per pale Azure and Gules, cuffed Argent, the hand proper holding a cross patonce Or.*

Richard Ironside of Rickmansworth,=Margeret, da. of Edward Brooke
co. Hertf.   of London.

1. Sarah, ux. Nicholas   3. Rachell, ux. John   1. Edward   2. John.
Heron of London.   Ivory of London.   Ironside of   —
—   —   Rickmansworth,   3. Samuel.
2. Roberta, ux. John   4. Hester.   eldest son, now   —
Hilden of London.   —   living, 1634.   4. Nathaniel.
                         5. Martha.

James of Braughin.

Vide the Visitation of Surrey.

Arnold James of London.=Mary, da. of Hans Van Hulst.

Susan, ux. .... Driver.	Mary, ux. John Jackson.	Elizabeth, ux. Henry Brereton.	John James of Braffin [Braughin], co. Hertf., living 1634.
Sarah, ux. John Aldersey.	Jane, ux. .... Garrett.	Judith, unmar.	

Joscelin of Hyde Hall.

ARMS.—*Azure, a circular wreath Argent and Sable with four hawks' bells conjoined thereto in quadrangle Or.*
CREST.—*A falcon's leg erased à la cuisse proper, belled Or.*

Alice, da. of Sir John Shelton,=Richard Josselin of=Anne, da. of ....
1 wife.   Sabridgworth.   Lucas of Bury.

.... da. of .... Barnes,=Richard Josselin,=Joice, da.   Jone.   Keyte.
Bishop of Durham [1575-   son and heir.   of Robert
1587].   Atkinson.   Mary.   Winifrid.

Sir Robert Josselin of Hyde Hall, co. Hertf., Kt.,=Bridgett, da. of Sir William
living 1634.   Smyth.

William Josselin.   2. Robert.   3. Francis.   4. Thomas.   Bridgett.   Dorathye.

Kimpton of Weston.

The Armes respyt for proofe.

The Armes are allowed w'ch is, *B., a pellican between 3 flower de luces Or.* Crest, *A demy Goate Ermyn, horned Or, collar and cheyne Sa.*

Edmond Kympton of Weston, co. Hertf.=Lucy, da. of .... Hyde of Throcking.

George Kympton of Weston, eldest son.=Catherin, da. of .... Brooke of High Cross, co. Hertf.

George Kympton of Weston.=Dorathy, da. of Henry Beecher, and sister of Sir William Beecher.

Kingsley of Sarret.

ARMS.—*Vert, a cross engrailed Argent.*
CREST.—*A goat's head Argent.*

Respyt the Armes for proofe till Michelmas terme.

Francis Kingsley of Sarret, co. Hertf.=Abigall, da. of . . . . Staynes.

William Kingsley of Sarret, co. Hertf.,=Dorathey, da. of Sir Edward Boteler of
living 1634. | Danbury, co. Essex.

William Kingsley, eldest son and heir. Dorathey.

Kitchin of Totteridge.

ARMS.—*Argent, on a pile Azure between two cross-crosslets Gules, an eagle displayed of the field charged on the breast with a torteaux.*
CREST.—*On a cap of maintenance, a pelican's head erased Azure, beaked Or, vulned Gules.*

Robert Kitchin of Leeds, co. York.=. . . .

Robert Kitchin of London.=Elizabeth, da. of John Mascall of London.

Richard Kitchin of Totteridge, co. Hertf.=Elizabeth, da. of William Nicoll of Hendon, co. Midd.

Elizabeth.=John Woodford of the Middle Temple.   Judith.=Arther Manwaring of London, son of Thomas Manwaring of Nantwich.

Elizabeth. Judith. Robert. Mary. Rose.   Thomas Manwaring.

Knighton of Bayford.

ARMS.—*Quarterly*—1 *and* 4, *Barry of eight Argent and Azure;* 2 *and* 3, *Gules, six annulets,* 3, 2, 1, *Or,* UNDERHILL.
CREST.—*Out of a ducal coronet Gules, two dragons' heads in saltire Argent, couped at the shoulders, the dexter surmounting the sinister.*

John Knighton of Bayford, co. Hertf., Esq.=. . . .

. . . . da. of . . . .=George Knighton of Bayford.=Susan, da. of . . . . White
Coventree. | of Essex.

John Knighton of Bayford, Esq.=Elizabeth, da. of Stephen Vaughan of London.

THE VISITATION OF HERTFORDSHIRE, 1634.   71

Lake of Wilstern.

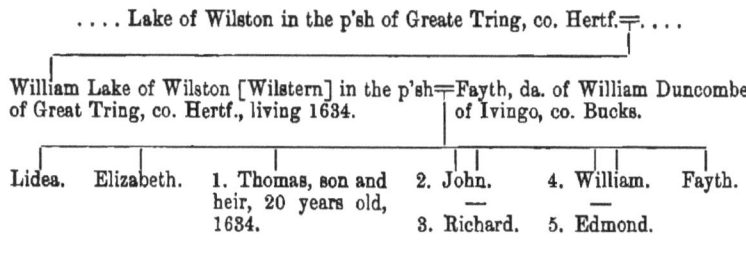

Langhorne of Bedford.

ARMS.—*Sable, a cross Argent, on a chief of the second three bugle-horns of the field, stringed Gules.*
CREST.—*A bugle-horn Sable, stringed Gules, between two wings expanded Argent.*

Under the hand of *Clarenceux* Camden.

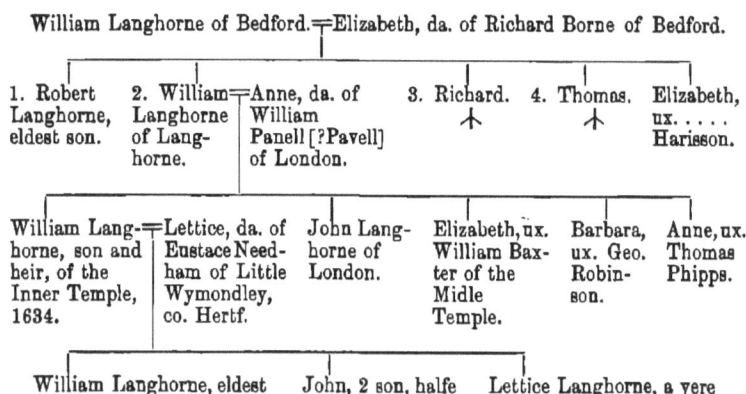

𝔏𝔞𝔳𝔢𝔫𝔡𝔢𝔯 of 𝔆𝔥𝔢𝔰𝔥𝔲𝔫𝔱.

These armes and creast, vid'z., *p'tie p. fesse Gules and Argent, a pale counter-changed, and charged with three plates*, is testified by Sir Will'm Segar, Kt., Garter, to be the aunciect coate armor of NATHANIEL LAVENDER of London, the sonn of William Lavender of Standon in the Countie of Hertford, with the grant of the creast, vid'z., *On a wreath of his cullers, a demy horse ramp. Argent, collerd with a garland of lavender proper*, under his hand and seale, dated 7 of May 1628.

Mr Lavender, being a citizen of London, desires that his descent may be transcribed and entered in that Visitation.

William Lavender of Standon, co. Hertf.=. . . .

Elias Lavender of London, citizen and marchant taylor.=Ellen, da. of Henry Bennett of London, citizen and marchant taylor.

Judith, ux. John Jenks of London.

Nathaniel Lavender of Cheshunt, co. Hertf., living 1634.=Judith, da. of Tho's Tyler of London, haberdasher, who fined for Shreeve.

Hester, ux. Humfrey Browne of London, mercer, 3 son of Jo. Browne of Essex, Kt.

Sarah, ux. Henry Westerne of London, draper.

Nathaniel Lavender, son and heir, 2 years old, 1634.   2. Elias.

𝔏𝔞𝔴𝔯𝔞𝔫𝔠𝔢 of 𝔥𝔢𝔯𝔱𝔦𝔫𝔤𝔣𝔬𝔯𝔡𝔟𝔲𝔯𝔶.

John Lawrance of Hartingfordbury, co. Hertf.=Anne, da. and heir of Thomas Frankes.

William Lawrance of Hartingfordbury.=Dorathey, da. of Walter Wrottesley of Wrottesley, co. Stafford.

William Lawrance of Hartingfordbury.=Elizabeth, da. of George Myn of Hartingfordbury.

John Darnell, one of the Secondaries in the Pipe Office.=Susan, da. and coheir.

Christopher Vernon of Hartingfordbury, Esq., living 1634.=Elizabeth, da. of John Darnell.

Anne, ux. Francis Bristow of Ayott St. Lawrance, co. Hertf.

Susan, ux. Henry Chitting, Esq., Chester Herald.

Mary Darnell.

THE VISITATION OF HERTFORDSHIRE, 1634.

Litton of Knebworth.

ARMS.—*Quarterly*—1, *Ermine, on a chief indented Azure three ducal coronets Or; 2, Argent, three boars' heads erased and erect Gules,* BOWTH *; 3, Sable, on a fess Argent between six acorns Or three leaves Vert; 4, Ermine, on a cross Or five escallops Gules.*
CREST.—*A bittern proper in flags Vert.*

This Sir Robert was knighted at the creation of H. 8., when hee was made Duke of York.

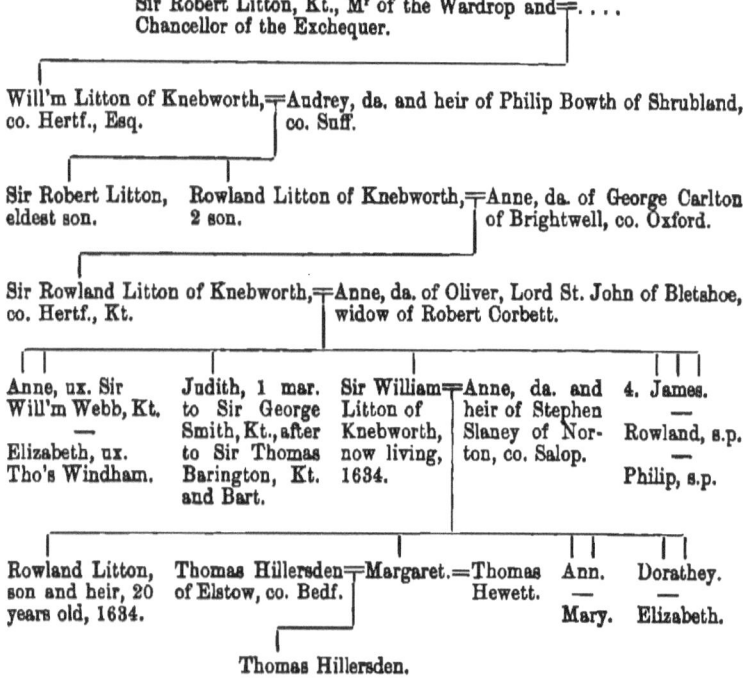

Sir Robert Litton, Kt., Mr of the Wardrop and=. . . .
Chancellor of the Exchequer.

Will'm Litton of Knebworth,=Audrey, da. and heir of Philip Bowth of Shrubland,
co. Hertf., Esq.   co. Suff.

Sir Robert Litton,   Rowland Litton of Knebworth,=Anne, da. of George Carlton
eldest son.   2 son.   of Brightwell, co. Oxford.

Sir Rowland Litton of Knebworth,=Anne, da. of Oliver, Lord St. John of Bletahoe,
co. Hertf., Kt.   widow of Robert Corbett.

Anne, ux. Sir   Judith, 1 mar.   Sir William=Anne, da. and   4. James.
Will'm Webb, Kt.   to Sir George   Litton of   heir of Stephen   —
—   Smith, Kt., after   Knebworth,   Slaney of Nor-   Rowland, s.p.
Elizabeth, ux.   to Sir Thomas   now living,   ton, co. Salop.   —
Tho's Windham.   Barington, Kt.   1634.   Philip, s.p.
   and Bart.

Rowland Litton,   Thomas Hillersden=Margaret.=Thomas   Ann.   Dorathey.
son and heir, 20   of Elstow, co. Bedf.   Hewett.   —   —
years old, 1634.   Mary.   Elizabeth.

Thomas Hillersden.

𝔏𝔬𝔴𝔢 of 𝔖t. 𝔄lban's.

ARMS.—*Argent, on a bend Azure three wolves' heads erased of the field.*
CREST.—*Out of a mural coronet Gules, a wolf's head pierced through the neck with a broken spear Or, armed of the second.*

A confirmation of this coat and grant of this crest to Humfrey Lowe of South Mills in the parish of Blunham in com. Bedford, Esqʳ, by Sir Will'm Segar, Kt., *Garter*, the 28 July 1628.

William Lowe of .... co. Lancaster.=....

John Lowe of St. Alban's, co. Hertf.=Ellin, da. of William Pointer of .... co. Salop.

Humfrey Lowe of St. Alban's, co. Hertf., =Sarah, da. of Christopher Borough of and of Blunham, co. Bedf. | Wix Abbey, co. Suff.

1. Francis Lowe, son and heir. 2. John Low. 3. Humfrey. 4. Thomas. 5. Christopher. Sarah. Dorathye.

𝔐arston of 𝔥emel 𝔥empstead.

ARMS.—*Azure, a chevron embattled Argent between three tigers' heads erased ducally crowned Or.*
CREST.—*A tiger's head erased per chevron Azure and Or ducally crowned of the second.*

William Marston of Hemel Hempsted, =Alice, da. of .... co. Hertf. | Pudifoote.

William Marston of Hemel Hempsted, =Sibbell, da. of John Ewer of the Lea in eldest son. | Watford, co. Hertf.

Joseph Marston of Hemel Hempsted, eldest son, now living, 1634. =Mary, da. of Thomas Porter of Aiat [Ayott] St. Lawrance, co. Hertf.   Mary, ux. John Emes of Little Gaddesden, co. Hertf.

1. William Marston, eldest son.   2. Joseph Marston.   3. Henry.

Mayne of Bovington.

ARMS.—*Argent, on a bend Sable three dexter hands couped at the wrist of the first.*
CRESTS.—1. *Out of a ducal coronet Or, a dragon's head Vert.*
       2. [An addition.] *A buck's head erased Argent.*

This Arms and Crest is entered in the Visitation of Warr. made by Mr. Leonard, and the descent of John Mayne of Elinton, but he must make further prooffe.

Richard Mayne of Bovington, co. Hertf.=.... da. of.... Bradshawe.

Henry Mayne of Bovington.=Alice, da. and co-heir of .... William. Richard.
                            Randolfe of co. Berks.

James Mayne of Bovington.=Mary, da. and heir of John Andrew   Simon. John.
                         of Hitchin, co. Hertf.

James Mayne = Dorathy, da. and   Alice, ux. Daniell   Mary, ux. Reynes   Elizabeth.
of Boving-   heir of John   Caldwell of Horn- Lowe of Clifton,   —
don, living   Hawes of Lon-   don, co. Essex.   co. Bucks.   Anne.
1634.   don, merchant.   —
                                                                                                                        Sarah.

Meautis of Hertford.

ARMS.—*Azure, a unicorn salient Erminois armed Or.*

Henry Mewtis of Westham,=.... da. of .... Jermy, sister of
co. Essex.   Sir Thomas Jermy.

Thomas Mewtis of Westham,=Elizabeth, da. of Sir Henry Connisby of North
co. Essex.   Myms, co. Hertf.

Elizabeth, ux.   Anne, ux.   1. Henry Mewtis=Elizabeth,   2. Edmond.   4. Philip.
John Clopton   William   of Hertford,   da. of Sir   —   —
of Suff.   Glover of   eldest son, now   William   3. Thomas, 5. John.
   —   Midd.   living, 1634.   Glover of   one of the
Frances, ux.   London.   Clarks of
Sir John   the Privie
Thorowgood   Counsell.
of Norf.

1. Henry Mewtis.   2. Thomas.   3. William.   4. John.   5. Peter.   6. Philip.

Monox of Charleywood.

ARMS.—*Argent, on a chevron Sable between three leaves Vert as many bezants, on a chief Gules a dove between two anchors of the first.*
CREST.—*A dove "Blewish," membered Gules, holding in the beak a branch of three acorns Vert, fructed Or.*

Confirmed by William Harvy, *Clarenceux*, 1561.

Richard Monox of Barkhamsted, co. Hertf.=....

Thomas Monox of Sissiter [Cirencester], co. Gloster.=Jone, d. of .... Swindlehurst.

George Monox of Charleywood, co. Hertf., Esq., fined for Sheriff of London.=Mary, da. of Mathew Perrey of London.

Anne, ux. Robert Newman of London.

Mary, ux. Abraham Chambers.

Morgan of Bushey Hall.

ARMS.—*Or, a griffin segreant Sable, on the breast a rose.*

Vide the Armes in the Visitation of Glamorgan.

John Morgan of Pencoyt in Wales.=Joanne, da. of .... Kemis.

John Morgan of Pencoyt in Wales.=Jane, da. of .... Reynolds.

William Morgan of Bushey Hall, co. Hertf., now living, a° 1634.=Jone, da. of John Bolar, the widow of Henry Hickman.

Morrison of Sandon.

ARMS.—*Or, on a cross Sable five fleurs-de-lis of the field, in dexter chief a crescent for difference.*

Thomas Morrison of Cadeby, co. Linc.=.... da. of .... Moyne.

THE VISITATION OF HERTFORDSHIRE, 1634.   77

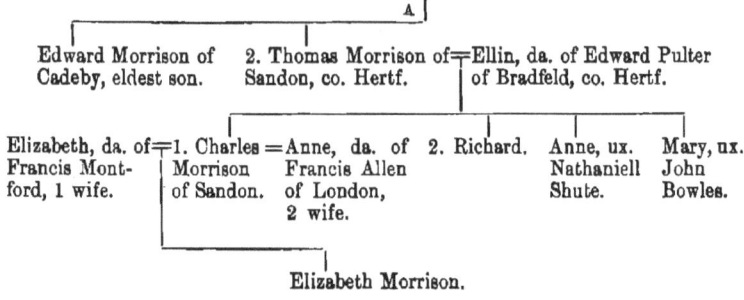

Needham of Little Wymondley and Welwyn.

ARMS.—*Argent, on a bend engrailed Azure between two bucks' heads, cabossed Sable, an escallop Or.*
CREST.—*Out of a pallisado coronet Or, a buck's head Sable, attired of the first.*

This descent and arms testified under the hand and Seale of Robert Cooke, *Clarenceux*, 1586.

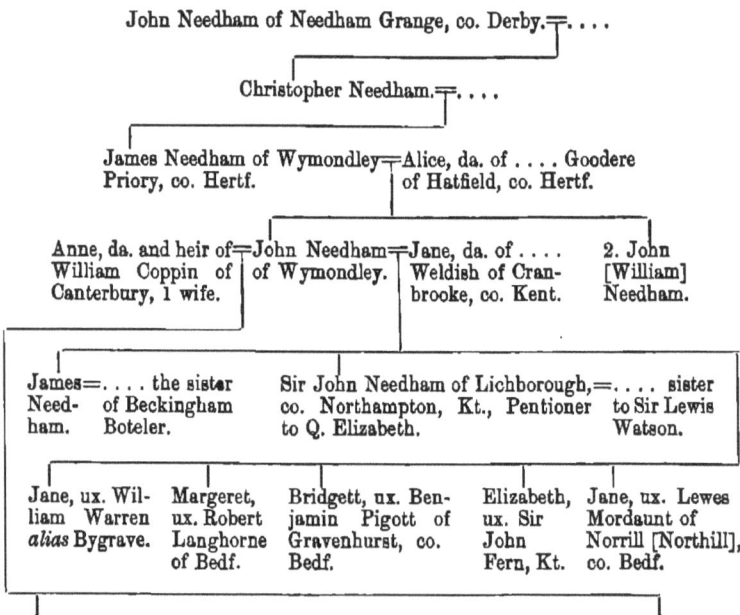

78   THE VISITATION OF HERTFORDSHIRE, 1634.

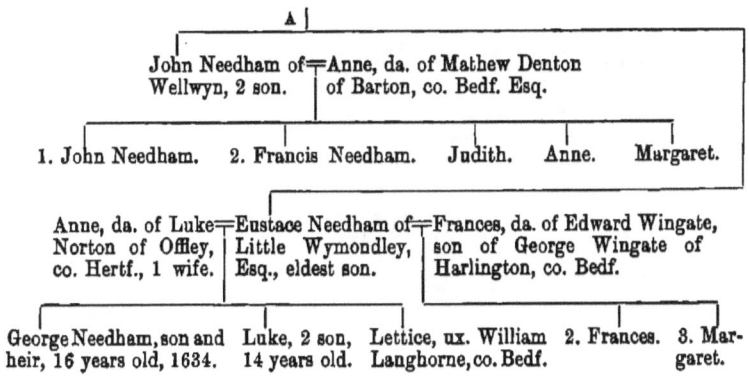

Newce of Much Hadham.

ARMS.—*Sable, two pales Argent, a canton Ermine.*
CREST.—*On a mound Vert, a garb Or.*

This Coat and Crest as is here depicted is confirmed unto Clement Newce of Much Haddam in the countie of Hertford, gent., by Robert Cooke, *Clarenceux*, 1575, the 17 of Queene Elizabeth.

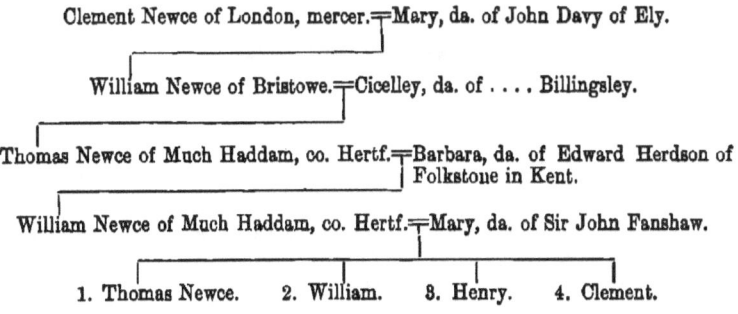

Newcomen of Bishop Stortford.

ARMS.—*Argent, a lion's head erased Sable between three crescents Gules.*
CREST.—*A lion's gamb erased Sable.*
  On each *a crescent for difference.*

John Newcomen of Saltfleetby, = Alice, da. of John Gascoigne of
co. Linc. Lasingcrofte, co. York.

John Newcomen, eldest son.

2. Thomas Newcomen of Haydon, co. Essex. = Prudence, da. of Robert Luckin of Takely, co. Essex.

Mary, da. of John Cooke of London. = Thomas Newcomen of Stortford, co. Hertf., eldest son. = Catherin, da. of .... Montjoy.

1. Mary.
2. Prudence.
3. Elizabeth.
4. Jane.
Ellin. Dynamithe.

Thomas Newcomen, only son yet living.

Newport of Furneux Pelham.

John Newport of Sandonbury, = ... da. of .... Greene of Sandonbury.
co. Hertf.

John Newport of Sandon and Ruston [Rushden], and of the manor of Garmuck, ob. 7 E. 6. = Grace, da. of Robert Newport of Furnix Pelham, co. Hertf.

Robert Newport of Sandon, son and heir. = Jane, da. of .... Barrington, Kt.

Jane, ux. .... Scroggs.

Anne, da. and one of the heirs of James Riley, 1 wife. = Edward Newport, sometime High Shreeve of co. Hertf. = Anne, da. of Thomas Everard of Linsted, co. Suff., 2 wife.

John Newport of Furnix Pelham, co. Hertf., now living, 1634. = Mary, da. and sole heir of Thomas Suliard of Suffolk.

Robert Newport of Great Chesterford, co. Essex. = Jane, da. and heir of Edward Baker of Great Chesterford.

80   THE VISITATION OF HERTFORDSHIRE, 1634.

```
        ┌───────┬───────┬───────┐ ┌───────┬───────┬───────┐
        A│      │       │       │ │       │       │       │
1. John  2. Edward. 5. Thomas. 1. Anne.   4. Bridgett. 7. Dorathey.
Newport.
         3. William.  6. Charles.  2. Mary.    5. Elizabeth.
         4. Robert.                3. Frances. 6. Martha.
```

Nodes of Shephall.

ARMS.—[Apparently an addition.] *Sable, on a pile Argent three trefoils slipped of the first.*

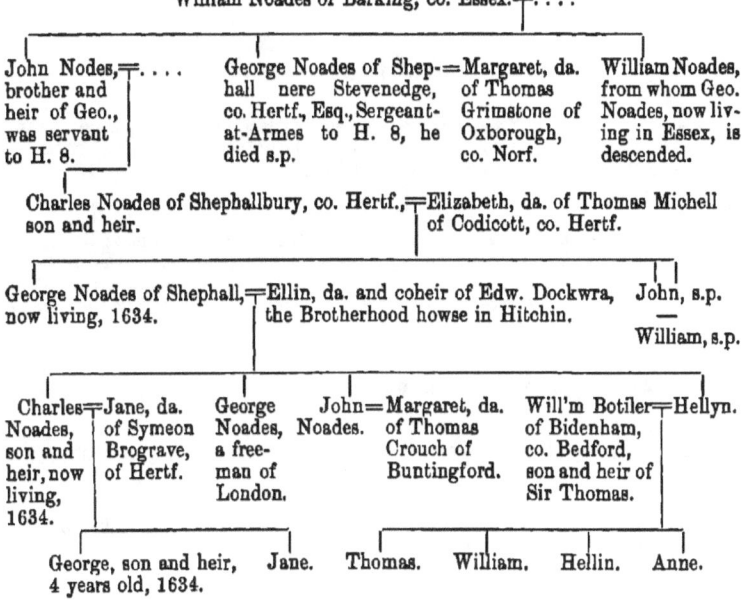

William Noades of Barking, co. Essex.=. . . .

John Nodes,=. . . .
brother and
heir of Geo.,
was servant
to H. 8.

George Noades of Shep-=Margaret, da.
hall nere Stevenedge, of Thomas
co. Hertf., Esq., Sergeant- Grimstone of
at-Armes to H. 8, he   Oxborough,
died s.p.   co. Norf.

William Noades,
from whom Geo.
Noades, now liv-
ing in Essex, is
descended.

Charles Noades of Shephallbury, co. Hertf.,=Elizabeth, da. of Thomas Michell
son and heir.   of Codicott, co. Hertf.

George Noades of Shephall,=Ellin, da. and coheir of Edw. Dockwra,   John, s.p.
now living, 1634.   the Brotherhood howse in Hitchin.
                                                                    William, s.p.

Charles=Jane, da.   George   John=Margaret, da.   Will'm Botiler=Hellyn.
Noades, of Symeon   Noades,   Noades. of Thomas   of Bidenham,
son and Brograve,   a free-   Crouch of   co. Bedford,
heir, now of Hertf. man of   Buntingford. son and heir of
living,   London.   Sir Thomas.
1634.

George, son and heir, Jane.   Thomas.   William.   Hellin.   Anne.
4 years old, 1634.

Norton of Marketcell.

ARMS.—*Gules, a fret Argent, over all a bend vairé Or and of the first.*

Quere better [proofe] of these armes, p. R. C., *Clarenceulx.*

Elizabeth, da. of Robert=Thomas Norton of Sharpen=Elizabeth, da. of Robert
Merry of Northall, 1 wife. │ howe, co. Bedf.   Marshall of Hitchin, co.
                          A   Hertf., 4 wife [*sic*].

THE VISITATION OF HERTFORDSHIRE, 1634.   81

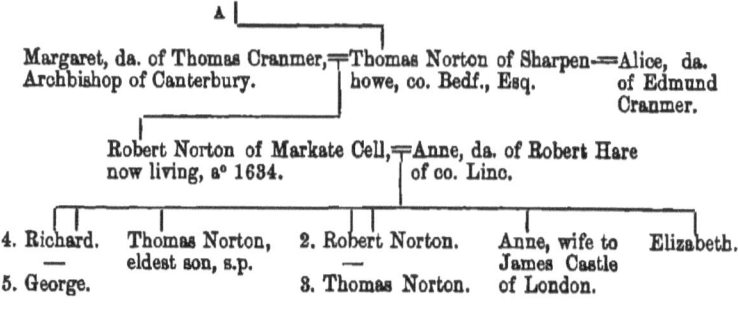

Pemberton of St. Alban's.

ARMS.—*Quarterly*—1 and 4, *Argent, a chevron between three buckets Sable hooped and handled Or* ; 2 and 3, *Argent, three dragons' heads couped erect Sable.*
CREST.—*A dragon's head couped and erect Sable.*
  On each *a crescent for difference.*

I have entered this descent with this coate and creast uppon sight of Receipt of £3 6s. 8d. rec. by Mr. Leonard for entrance of a certifficate after the death of Mr. Ralfe Pemberton who died 6 of December 1627; which coate and creast I find entered in the office of Armes, in the booke of Certifficates of Funeralls; and as he pretends his ancestors came out of Cheshier.

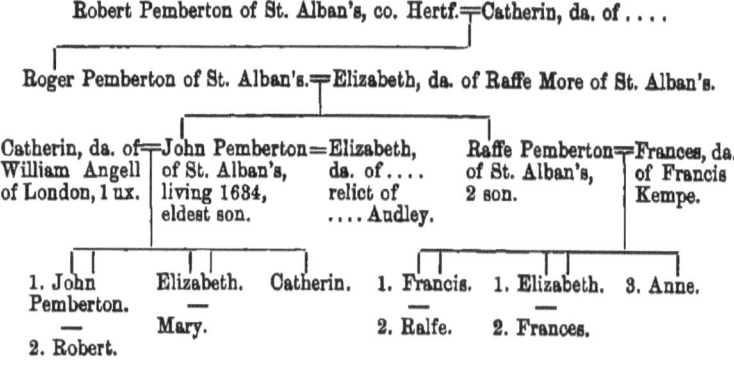

Penne of Codicote.

ARMS.—*Quarterly*—1 *and* 4, *Argent, on a fess Gules, between three peacocks Azure, a lion passant-gardant Or between two combs of the first ;* 2 *and* 3, *Or, three horses' heads couped Sable, bridled Argent,* CHEVALL.
CREST.—*A demi-lion rampant Gules, holding between the paws a comb Argent.*

Thus quartered under the hand of William Harvy, *Clarenceux.*

Thomas Penne of Coddicott,=Margery, da. of Thomas Saunders of Agmondisham
co. Hertf.   [Amersham], co. Bucks.

John Penne of Broughton,=Margaret, da. of   Susan.   Mary.   Lucy.
co. Bucks.   Henry Charge.

Thomas Penne of Codicot,=Alice, da. of Simon Lambert
co. Hertf.   of Buckingham.

1. John=Susan, da. of Henry   2. Thomas.   5. Chevall.   7. Francis.   Ellin.
Penne,   Wallis of Upper   —   —   —   —
eldest   Chissell, co. Essex.   3. William.   6. Jonathan.   8. Simon.   Alice.
son.   —
   4. Robert.

Pichford of St. Alban's.

ARMS.—*Azure, a cinquefoil between six martlets Or.*
CREST.—*An ostrich Argent, membered and ducally gorged Or.*

Vide the hand of Robert Cooke, *Clarenceux.*

John Pichford of Lee Brockhurst, co. Salop.=. . . .

John Pichford of Lee Brockhurst,=Jone, da. of . . . . Besford of
co. Salop.   co. Salop.

1. Thomas   2. William.   5. Robert Pichford of=Jane, da. of   4. Andrew.
Pichford.   —   St. Alban's, co. Hertf., ... North
   3. John.   living 1634.   of Coventree.

Plomer of Radwell.

ARMS.—*Vert, a chevron between three lions' heads erased Or.*

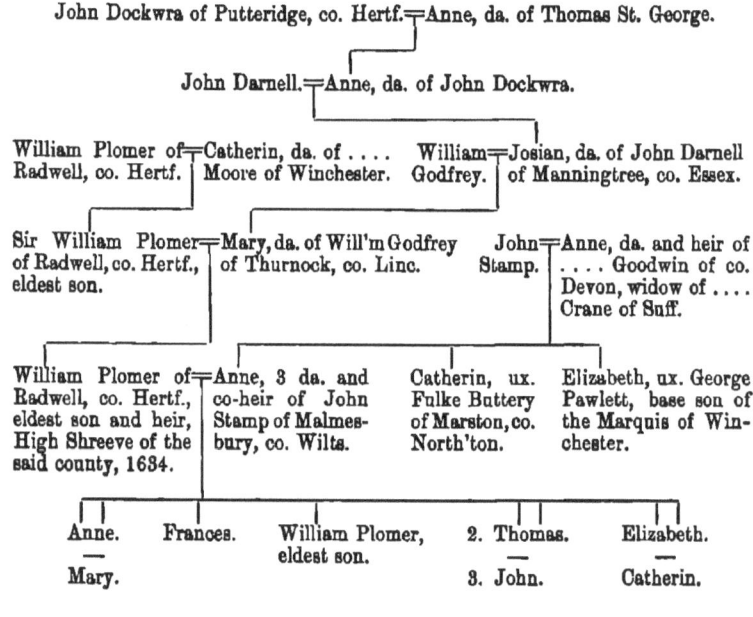

Powell of St. Alban's.

ARMS.—*Sable, three roses Argent seeded Or.*
CREST.—*Out of a ducal coronet, a Lancaster rose-tree proper between two wings erect Gules.*

Under the hand of William Segar, *Garter*.

Howell ap David ap Griffith Vychan ap Madock ap Jerwarth Vychan,=....
2 son to Jerwarth ap David ap Grono.
　　　　　　|
　　　Lewis ap Howell of St. Alban's, ob. 1560.=....
　　　　　　|
　　Thomas ap Howell of St. Alban's.=Margaret, da. of .... Johnson.

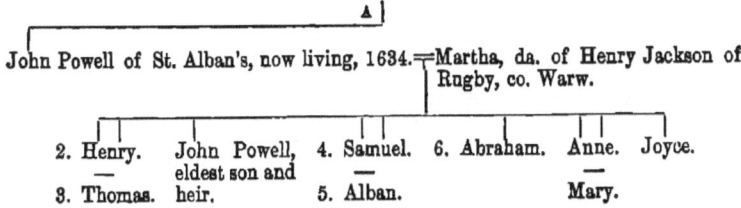

John Powell of St. Alban's, now living, 1634.=Martha, da. of Henry Jackson of Rugby, co. Warw.

| 2. Henry. | John Powell, | 4. Samuel. | 6. Abraham. | Anne. | Joyce. |
| 3. Thomas. | eldest son and heir. | 5. Alban. | | Mary. | |

Preston of Childwick.

ARMS.—*Argent, two bars Gules, a bordure Sable charged with eight cinquefoils Or.*
CREST.—*Out of a mural coronet Or, a demi-fox rampant Sable, gorged with a collar Ermine.*
ANOTHER SHIELD.—*Quarterly*—1 *and* 4, PRESTON ; 2 *and* 3, *Gules, a chevron quarterly Ermine and Ermines between three pheons Or,* ARNOLD.

The Arms and Crest granted to William Preston of Chilwick in co. Hertf. by l'res patents by Sir Richard St. George, *Clarenceux,* dated 1629.

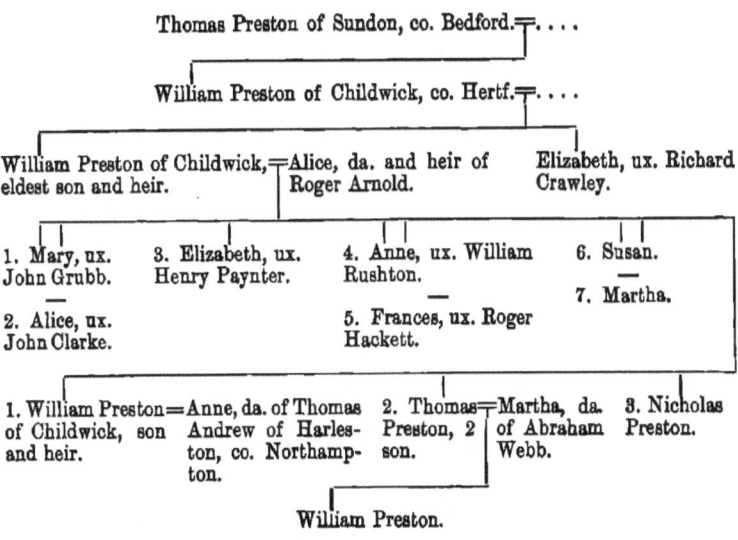

Thomas Preston of Sundon, co. Bedford.=....

William Preston of Childwick, co. Hertf.=....

William Preston of Childwick,=Alice, da. and heir of Roger Arnold.   Elizabeth, ux. Richard Crawley.
eldest son and heir.

| 1. Mary, ux. John Grubb. | 3. Elizabeth, ux. Henry Paynter. | 4. Anne, ux. William Rushton. | 6. Susan. |
| 2. Alice, ux. John Clarke. | | 5. Frances, ux. Roger Hackett. | 7. Martha. |

1. William Preston=Anne, da. of Thomas   2. Thomas=Martha, da.   3. Nicholas
of Childwick, son Andrew of Harles-   Preston, 2 | of Abraham   Preston.
and heir.   ton, co. Northamp-   son.   Webb.
   ton.

William Preston.

Pulter of Bradfield.

ARMS.—*Quarterly of eight*—1, *Argent, two bendlets Sable, in sinister chief a Cornish chough proper;* 2, *Gules, an eagle displayed Argent;* 3, *Quarterly Argent and Sable, four crosses potent saltirewise counterchanged;* 4, *Azure, fretty Argent;* 5, *Ermine, on a bend Sable three congers' heads erased Argent;* 6, *Argent, a chevron Vert between three popinjays of the second, membered Or;* 7, *Argent, on a bend Gules three martlets Or;* 8, *Ermine, on a bend Gules two chevronels Or.*

Edward Pulter of Bradfeld, co. Hertf. =Mary, da. of Rowland Litton of Knebworth, co. Hertf.

Litton Pulter of Cotterel, co. Hertf. =Penelapy, da. of Sir Arthur Capell of Litle Hadham, co. Hertf.

Arther Pulter of Bradfeld, now living, 1634.=Hester, da. of James [Ley], Erle of Marleborough.

1. Mary. 3. Margeret. James Pulter, son and heir. William Pulter. 4. Hester. 5. Penelapy.
2. Jane.

Radcliffe of Hitchin.

ARMS.—*Quarterly*—1, RADCLIFFE, as at p. 19; 2, *Azure, on a saltire Ermine a lion rampant Gules,* WILCOX; 3 and 4, *blank,* but stated to be those of EDOLPH and MAY.
CREST.—*A bull's head Sable, armed or, gorged with a ducal coronet of the last, charged on the neck with a cross-crosslet.*

Rafe Radcliffe of Hitchin, co. Hertf., a second son. =Elizabeth, da. of .... Marshall of Hitchin.   ....=.... da. and heir of Wilcox. .... Edolfe.

1. Rafe.   Elizabeth, ux. William Fryar of Stevenadge.   3. Sir Edward Radcliffe=Martha, da. and of Hitchin.   co-heir.
2. Jeromy.

Edward Radcliffe of Hitchin, Esq., son and heir.=Anne, da. of Sir Robert Chester of Royston, co. Hertf., Kt.

Rich of Anstey.

ARMS.—*Gules, a chevron between three crosses botonée Or.*

Respyt the arms for difference.

Edward Rich of Horndon on the Hill, co. Essex.=.... da. of .... Saunders.

1. Edward Rich=Judith, da. of Sir Richard Saltonstall, Kt.
of Horndon.

2. Sir Robert Rich, Kt., one of the Masters of the Chancery.

Edward Rich of Anstey,=Susan, da. of Thomas Percye of Emmesbury [Amesbury], co. Wilts.
co. Hertf.

1. Edward Rich.   2. Peter Rich.   Susan.

Robinson of Cheshunt.

ARMS.—*Or, a mitre Argent lined Gules, the framework bezantée, the pendants Sable platée.*
CREST.—*A buck's head Pean, double antlered Or.*

John Robinson of London, descended=Jone, da. of .... Skinner
from Litle Banlow in Westmoreland | of Buntingford, co. Hertf.
[? Little Banton, co. Cumberland].

Peter Robinson of London.=Anne, da. of Thomas Marston of London.

William Robinson of Chesthunt,=Elizabeth, da. of Richard Burrell
co. Hertf. | of London.

1. Peter Robinson.   2. William.   3. John.   Jane.   Elizabeth.

Robotham of St. Alban's.

ARMS.—*Per fess Argent and Sable, a fess counter-embattled between three bucks, all counterchanged.*
CREST.—*A demi-griffin Azure, gutte de l'armes, ducally gorged Or.*

The Arms and Crest granted by Laurence Dalton, *Norroy*, to Robert Robotham of Roskill [? Raisgill] in the County of York, servant to King Edward 6, Queen Mary, and Queen Elizabeth, dated 8th of December 1560, the 3 of Eliz.

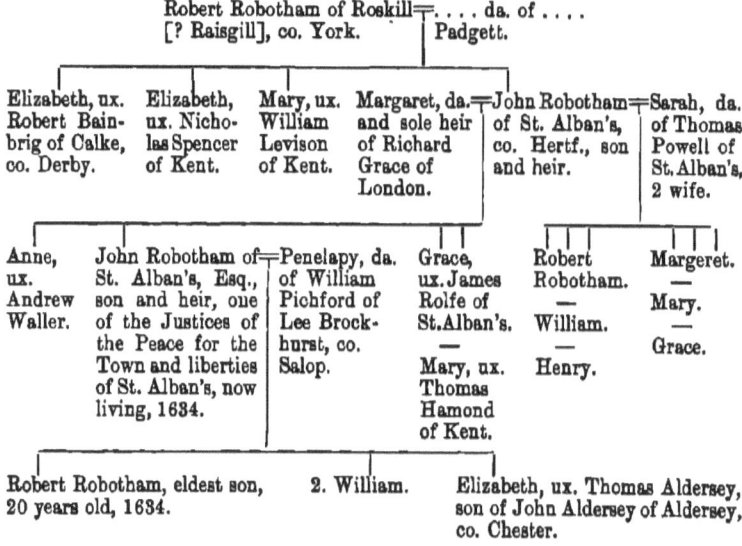

Rogers of Maydencroft.

Respyt the Armes till Michellmas tearme. Further respyt per Mr. Skinner.

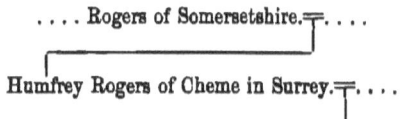

Humfrey Rogers of Maydencrofte = Anne, da. of William Cock, Esq., and relict in the p'sh of Ippollets, co. Hertf., of Sir William Fryer, Kt., gentleman living 1634. Pentioner to King James.

Rolfe of St. Alban's.

ARMS.—*Argent, three ravens Sable, ducally gorged Or.*
CREST.—*A raven wings expanded Sable, ducally crowned Or, in the beak a five-leaved branch slipped Vert.*

.... Rolfe, servant in ordinary to K. H. 7.=....

William Rolfe of Barton in the Clay,=Dorathey, da. of .... Ireland
and of St. Alban's, co. Hertf. of Hertford, gent.

James Rolfe of St. Alban's, Comissary and Official=Grace, da. of John Robotham
to the Bishops of Lincoln and London, one of the of St. Alban's.
Masters of the High Court of Chancery.

Nicholas Rolfe of St.=Margaret, da. of William Mary, ux. William
Alban's, co. Hertf., Colles of Parkbury, co. Colles of Parkbury.
living 1634. Hertf., gent.

Susan Rolfe, Mary Rolfe, 2. Nicholas 1. James, dyed. Margeret Rolfe, aged
aged 9 years, aged 8 years, Rolfe, son — 3 years, 1634.
a° 1634. 1634. and heir. 3. Richard, dyed. —
 Margeret, dyed.

Rotheram of Farle, co. Bedford.

ARMS.—*Vert, three bucks passant Or, over all a bend Argent.*

George Rotheram of Farly, co. Bedf.=....

Joane, da. of .... Helder=George Rotheram=Elizabeth, da. of
alias Spicer. of Farly. .... Wallop.

George Rotheram Thomas Rotheram of=Talbot, da. of Luke Norton
of Lewton. Farly, living 1634. of Offley, co. Hertf.

Sadler of Sopwell.

ARMS.—*Quarterly*—1, *Or, a lion rampant per fess Azure and Gules;* 2, *Per chevron Or and Gules, in chief two lions combatant Sable,* LEE; 3, *Gules, three swords in pale Argent between twelve estoiles Or, a bordure engrailed of the second;* 4, *Sable, three pales Ermine, on a canton Argent a lion rampant Azure; a crescent on a crescent for difference.*
CREST.—*A demi-lion rampant Azure, ducally crowned Or; with the same difference.*

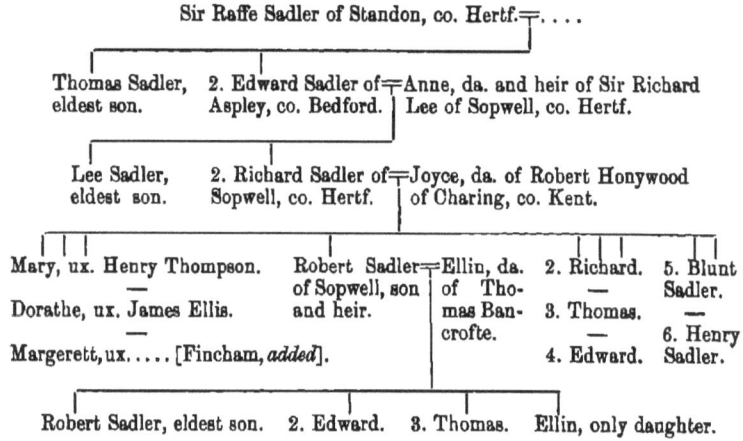

Sadler of Standon.

ARMS and CREST as in the last Pedigree.
MOTTO.—SERVIRE DEO SAPERE.

Sir Raffe Sadleir, Kt. Banerett, Lord of the Manor of=Margerett, Standon, co. Hertf., Chanceller of the Dutchie of | da. of Mr. Lankaster, and a Privie Counseller to H. 8, E. 6, and | Michell. Q. E., ob. 30 March 1587.

Anne, ux. Sir George Horsey of Digswell, co. Hertf.

Mary, ux. Thomas Bolle.

Jane, ux. Edward Rash.

Dorathy, ux. Edward Elrington.

THE VISITATION OF HERTFORDSHIRE, 1634.

.... da. of =Sir Thomas=Gertrude, Edward Sadleir Henry Sadleir of Everley,
Sir John   Sadleir of da. of Rob't of Temple, co. co. Wilts, 1 m. the da. of
Sherington, Standon,   Markham   Hertf., Esq., m. Gilberte Everley; 2 to
Kt., 1 wife. Kt.   of Cotham,   the da. and heir Ursula, da. of John Gill
                       2 wife.   of Sir Richard   of Wydiall, co. Hertf.,
                                    Lee of Sopwell. Esq.

Raffe Sadleir of=Anne, da. of Sir Edward Cooke, Gertrude, ux. Sir Walter Aston,
Standon, Esq.   Kt., Lord Cheiffe Justice of   Baron of Fayrford in Ireland.
                 England.

Saltonstall of Barkway.

ARMS.—*Or, a bend between two eagles displayed Sable, in dexter chief a mullet for difference.*
CREST.—*Out of a ducal coronet Or, a pelican Azure vulning its breast Gules, a mullet for difference.*

Sir Richard Saltonstall of London, Kt.,=Susan, da. of .... Poyntz, sister
and of South Okenden, co. Essex.   of Sir Gabriel Poyntz.

Sir Peter Saltonstall of Barkway,=Christian, da. of Sir John Pettus, Kt., of
co. Hertf., Kt.   Norfolk.

Susan.=Robert Castell Bridgett. James Salton- 2. Peter Salton- Ann.
       of East Hat-   —   stall, eldest stall.   —
       ley, co. Cambs. Christian. son.   Elizabeth.

Robert Castell.

Saunders of Beechwood.

A branch of Sanders of Harington, with the elephants' heds.

Thomas Saunders.=....

John Saunders of Agmondisham,=Elizabeth, da. and heir of Edward Puttenham,
co. Bucks.   a younger brother of Sir George.

THE VISITATION OF HERTFORDSHIRE, 1634.   91

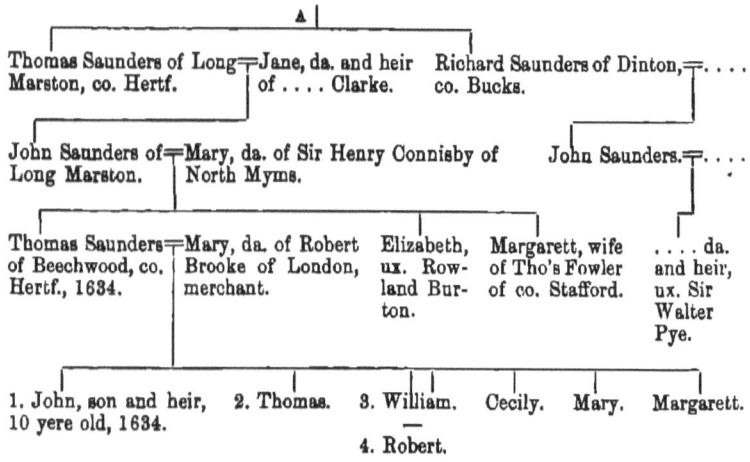

Sedley of Digswell.

Richard Sedley of Diggeswell,=Elizabeth, da. of John Darell
co. Hertf., Esq.   of Calehill, co. Kent.

William Sedley,=Anne, da. of   Anne, ux. Edward   2. John   Eliza-=George
son and heir.   . . . . Boteler Maddison of the   Sedley.   beth. Tucker.
                of London.   Midle Temple.

1. George.   2. Francis.   3. Robert.   Elizabeth.

Selioke of St. Alban's.

ARMS.—*Quarterly*—1 *and* 4, *Argent, three oak-leaves Vert;* 2 *and* 3, *Argent, on a chief Sable two mullets pierced Or, a bordure engrailed Gules.*
CREST.—*Out of a mural crown Or, a cubit arm vested proper charged with a pale of the first, holding in the hand also proper an oak-branch Vert fructed of the first.*

John Selioke of Haselborough,=Dorathey, da. of Sir George Chaworth
co. Darby.   of Wiverton, co. Notts.

92   THE VISITATION OF HERTFORDSHIRE, 1634.

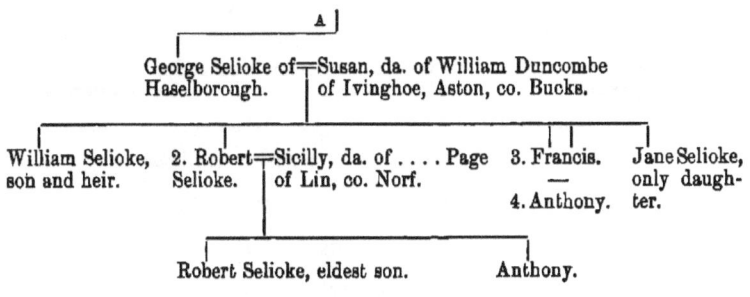

𝔖ennoke of 𝔏ayston.

ARMS.—*Argent, a chevron between three acorns Gules.*

Respyt till Michelmas tearme.

The Coate of Senoke, Lord Mayor of London, is B., 7 *acorns Or*, 2, 3, and 2.

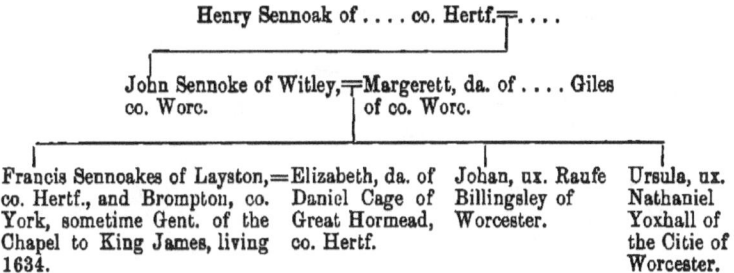

𝔖impson of 𝔖t. 𝔄lban's.

ARMS.—*Argent, on a chief Vert three crescents of the first, a mullet for difference.*
CREST.—*Out of a tower Azure, a demi-lion rampant-gardant Argent, holding in the dexter hand a sword erect Gules.*

This coate Mr. Simpson affirmeth hee hath under Clarenceux' hand but cannot find it, but he sheweth it ould upon a picture.

.... Simpson.=....
|
Giles Simpson of London,=Christian, da. of John Ferne,
Goldsmith.   and sister of Sir John Ferne.

THE VISITATION OF HERTFORDSHIRE, 1634.

▲

John Simpson of St. Alban's,=Sarah, da. of Thomas Gooderidge   2. Jeromy
co. Hertf., 1634.   of St. Alban's.   Simpson.

John Simpson, eldest son.   Sarah, eldest daughter.

Skinner of Hitchin.

ARMS.—*Gules, three cross-bows unbent Argent, furnished Or, in middle chief an annulet of the last.*
CREST.—*On a mound Vert, a buck couchant Gules, attired Or, charged on the body with an annulet of the last.*

Thomas Skynner *alias* Skener, came out of Flaunders,=. . . .
temp. H. 7, and seated himselfe in Sussex.

1. Richard   2. Thomas Skynner of Norwich,=. . . . da. of . . . .
Skynner.   youngest son, *temp.* H. 8.   Plumsted.

This Richard had   Richard Skynner of Norwich,=Ann, da. of . . . .
21 children.   Register for that Dioc.   Benjamin.

John Skynner of Hitchin, one of the=Mary, da. of . . . .
yongest sons, now living, 1634.   Wright.

John Skynner,=Grace, da. of Richard Rochdale   Ralfe Skynner,
eldest son.   of London.   second son.

Mary Skynner.   Elizabeth.

Sterne of Hoddesdon.

ARMS.—*Or, a chevron between three crosses patonce Sable.*
CREST.—*A falcon rising proper.*

Robert Sterne of Malden, co. Cambr.=Bettris, da. of . . . . Bonas.

William Sterne,   Edward Sterne of Hoddesdon,=Mary, da. of Richard Blackman,
eldest son.   co. Hertf., 4 son, living 1634. the relict of William Pedley.

Robert Sterne, eldest son and heir.   Frances Sterne.

Sterne of Barkway.

ARMS.—As in the last Pedigree.

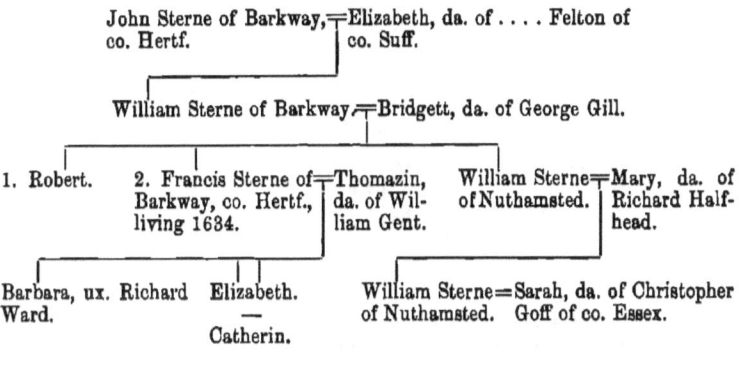

Steward of Braughin.

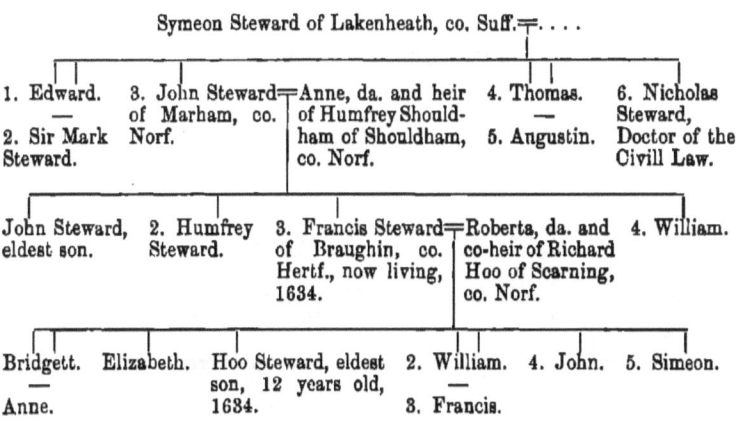

Stratford of Meesden.

ARMS.—*Barry of ten Argent and Azure, over all a lion rampant Gules, membered Or.*

This descent and Armes is testified under the hand of Robert Cooke, *Clarenceux*, downe to Henry and Richard Stratford of Hawling, w'ch maried with the da's of Cole and Churchman.

John Stratford of Farncote, co. Glouc.=Margerett, da. of Richard Howell.

- John Stratford of Farncote, co. Glouc.=Margerett, da. of Robert Tracye.
- William Stratford of Gyting, 2 son.=Joyce, da. of Richard De la Mott.
- Richard Stratford of Hawling, co. Glouc.=Margerett, da. of .... Combe.

- Henry Stratford of Hawling, eldest son, ob. s.p.=Abigale, da. of William Cole.
- Richard Stratford of London, 2 son.=Alice, da. of Robert Churchman of London.

- Henry Stratford of Hawling, co. Gloc., heir to his uncle, 1634.
- 2. Richard.
- 3. Anthony Stratford of Meeseden, co. Hertf. 1634.=Abigale, da. of Robert Dover of Child's Wickham, co. Gloc.
- George Stratford of Meeseden, 4 son, living 1634.=Sibilla, da. of Robert Dover, sister of Abigale.

Catherin, da., 4 yeres old, 1634.

Taverner of Hertonbury.

ARMS.—*Quarterly—1 and 4, Argent, a bend lozengy Sable, in sinister chief a torteaux; 2 and 3, Ermine, on a chevron Sable three crosses engrailed Argent,* SILVESTER.
CREST.—*A dove with wings expanded Argent, in the beak a branch of laurel Vert.*

Alice, da. and heir of Robert Silvester of North Elmham, co. Norf., 1 wife.=John Taverner of North Elmham, co. Norf.=Anne Crane of Norfolk, was the 2 wife of John. Her sister was the mother of Sir John Petty of Norfolk, Kt., father of Sir Augustin Petty, Kt.

A   B

THE VISITATION OF HERTFORDSHIRE, 1634.

A | B |

James Taverner = ... da. and heir of Mr. Russell   Thomas Taver- = ... da.
of Northelmham. | of Wighton, near Walsingham, | ner of Kerdis- | of Mr.
the widow of Edmond Beding- | ton, co. Norf. | Grim-
feld. | | stone.

Thomas Taverner = ... da. and heir of   Frances, ux. Sir William Denny, Kt.,
of Northelmham. | Mr. Riches of Norf. | of Gray's Inn, Recorder of the City
of Norwich.

Henry, etc.

2. Roger Taverner of Upminster, co. Essex, Esq., Surveyor of the = ... da. of
King's Wood on this side Trent. | ....

.... da. of .... Wentworth = John Taverner of Upminster, = ... sister of Sir
of Lillingstone in Northamp- | Surveyor General of the Woods | Henry Whitehead
ton, and had no issue by her. | to Q. E. and K. James on this | of co. Hants.
side Trent.

Roger Taverner of Upminster, now living.

.... da. of Sir John = 1. Richard Taverner of Wood = Margerett, da. of Walter
Harecourt of Stanton | Eaton, co. Oxford, was Clarke | Lambert, grandfather of
Harecourt, Kt., 2 | of the Signet to H. 8 and E. 6, | Sir Oliver, Lord Lam-
wife. | Justice of the Peace, and High | bert, Kt., 1 wife.
Shreeve of Oxon 12 Eliz.

Harecourt   Richard = ... da.   Peter Taverner = Frances, da. of Tho-
Taverner. | Taverner | of Francis | of Hexton, co. | mas Dockwra the
— | of Wood | Heyton of | Hertf. | elder of Putteridge
Penelape, ux. | Eaton. | Surrey, Esq. | | in Hertf., Esq.
Mr. Pettitt.

Francis = Jane, da. of George   John Taverner,   Margerett. = Edw. Wingate
Taverner | Needham of Wim- | Professor in | | of Welwyn, co.
of Hex- | ondly Priory, co. | Gresham Col- | | Hertf.
ton, Esq., | Hertf., Esq. | lege, p'son of
Justice of | | Newington.
Peace.

Richard   Jane.   Edward Win- = Mary, da. and heir   Frances, ux. Eustace
Taverner. | | gate of Wel- | of Raffe Allway of | Needham of Wim-
wyn. | Cannons, co. Hertf. | ondly. C | D

THE VISITATION OF HERTFORDSHIRE, 1634.   97

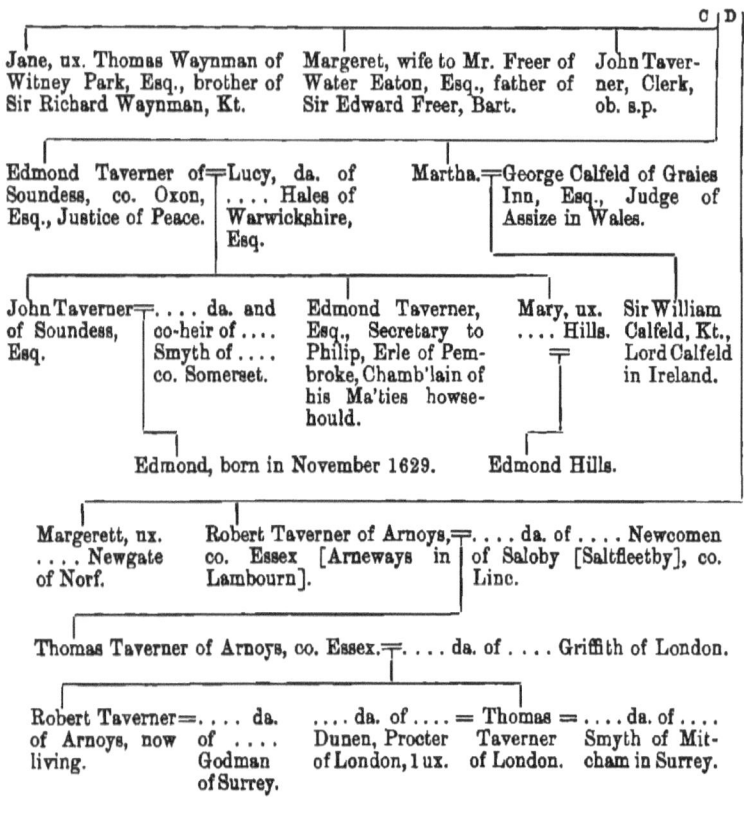

Thompson of Watton-at-Stone.

ARMS.—*Or, on a fess dancettée Azure three estoiles of the field, on a canton of the second the sun in glory of the first.*
CREST.—*An arm erect vested Gules cuffed Argent, holding in the hand proper five ears of wheat Or.*

Robert Thompson, came out of the North.=....

Morris Thompson of Cheston=Catherin, da. of ....
[Cheshunt], co. Hertf.   Harvey.
               A

98   THE VISITATION OF HERTFORDSHIRE, 1634.

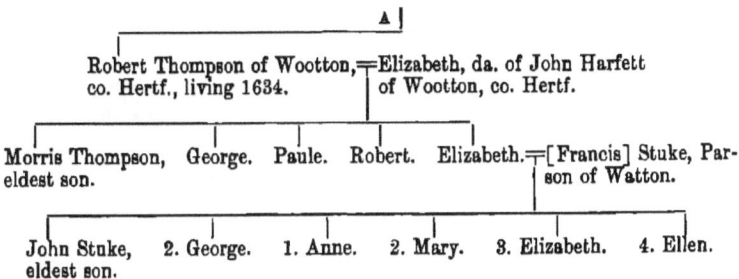

Thorogood of Tharfield.

ARMS.—*Sable, three pilgrims' staves one in pale and two in saltire Or, banded Argent,*
   GARTON.
CREST.—*A leopard's head erased and affrontée.*

To come to London for better proofe.

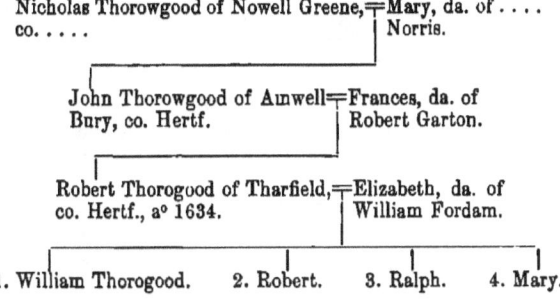

Tooke of Wormley.

ARMS.—*Per chevron Sable and Argent, three griffins' heads erased counterchanged.*
CREST.—*A griffin's head erased Sable, holding in the beak a sword erect Argent
   pomelled Or.*

A Pattent under the hand and seal of William Camden to Walter Tooke granted the 17 day of April 1600, and in the 42 year of Queen Elizabeth.

William Toque *alias* Tooke of Godengton [near Ashford],=. . . .
   co. Kent, Auditor of the Court of Wards.
|
Walter Tooke.=. . . .
   ▲

THE VISITATION OF HERTFORDSHIRE, 1634.

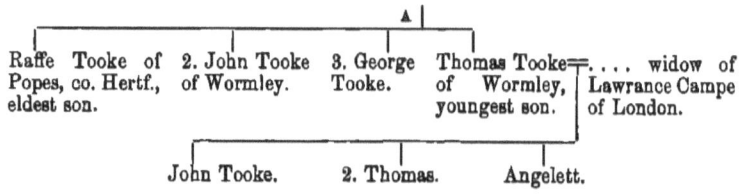

Tooke of Popes.

ARMS and CREST as in the last Pedigree.

A confirmation under the hand and seal of William Camden, *Clarenceux*, the 17 day of April 1600, and in the 42 year of Queen Elizabeth, to Walter Tooke.

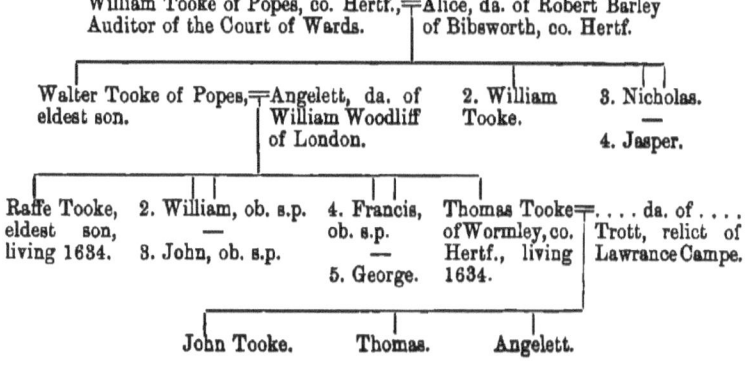

Vernon of Hertingfordbury.

ARMS.—*Quarterly*—1 and 4, *Argent, fretty Sable, on a canton Gules a mullet Or*; 2 and 3, *Quarterly, one and four, Argent, a cross raguly Sable, in chief a bezant*, LAWRENCE; *two and three, Vert, a saltire engrailed Or*, FRANKES.
CREST.—*Out of a coronet Argent, a boar's head erased Sable maned and tusked Or.*

Sir William Vernon of Haddon, co. Darby,⹋Margerett, da. and heir
made his will and died 1467. | of Sir Robert Pipe.

Sir Hen. | 2. Richard | William Vernon of⹋.... | 4. Raffe. | Elizabeth. | Bridgett.
Vernon, | Vernon. | Stewkley, co. Hunts, | — | — | —
Kt., s.p. | — | 3 son. | | Margerett. | Alice.

THE VISITATION OF HERTFORDSHIRE, 1634.

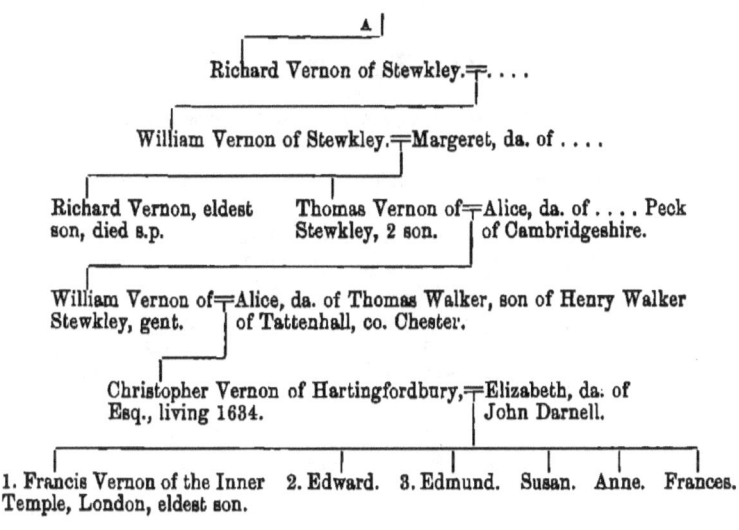

1. Francis Vernon of the Inner Temple, London, eldest son. 2. Edward. 3. Edmund. Susan. Anne. Frances.

Warren of Colney.

ARMS.—*Chequy Or and Azure, on a canton Gules a lion rampant Argent.*
CREST.—*A wyvern Argent, tail nowed, wings expanded chequy Or and Azure.*
On each *a mullet within an annulet for difference.*

Lawrance Warren of Pointon, co. Chester, a younger son of Lawrance Warren of Pointon.=....

John Warren of Harrow, co. Midd., a younger son.=.... da. of .... Edlin of Midlesex.

Gilbert Warren of Aldenham, co. Hertf.=Martha, da. of John Long, Alderman of London.

Gilbert Warren of Colnye, co. Hertf.,=Margery, da. of Thomas Hickman now living, 1634. of London, Haberdasher.

Warren alias Waller of Ashwell.

ARMS.—*Chequy Or and Azure, a fleur-de-lis Argent within a bordure engrailed Sable, on a canton Gules a lion rampant double-queued of the third.*

These Armes are entred for his kinsman amongst the Certificates.

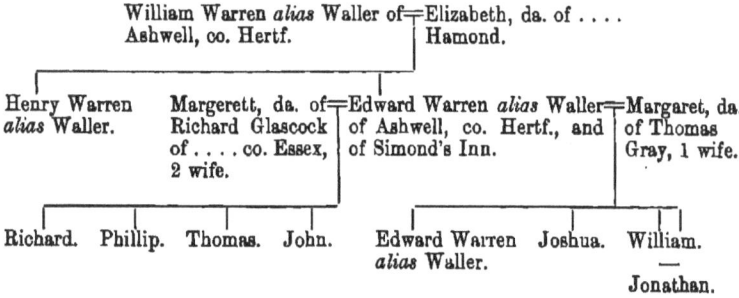

Wathe of St. Alban's.

ARMS.—*Sable, three bars wavy Argent, a chief Or.*
CREST.—*A dragon's head erased Sable.*

This descent from Sir Nicholas Wathe is respited for further proofe.

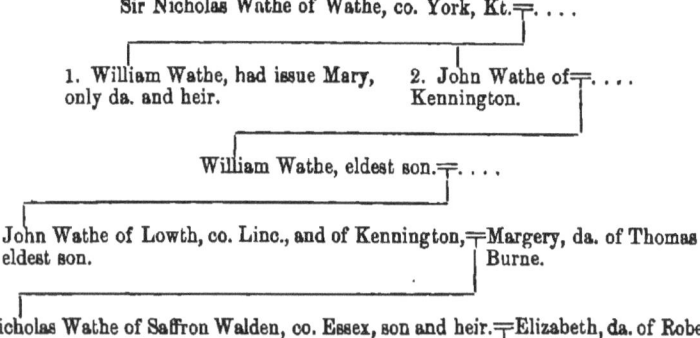

A

Twyford Wathe of Slipton, co. Northampton, living=Edith, da. and heir of William
1634, son and heir, now of St. Alban's. | Hemington of co. Northampton.

Anne Wathe, da. and coheir.   Frances Wathe, 2 da. and coheir.

This descent, with a more auntient w'ch I have, was left me by my auncestors.
                                                        TWYFORD WATHE.

And saith that he was entered by Mr. Vincent, *Rouge Rose*, in the last Visitation of Northamptonshire.

Watts of Thundridge.

Sir John Watts of London, Alderman.=Margaret, da. of Sir James Hawes.

Sir John Watts,   Thomas Watts of Thundridge, co. Hertf.,=Elizabeth, da. of
eldest son.   5 son, living 1634.   .... Vavasor.

1. Elizabeth. 2. Diana. 4. Dorathye. Thomas Watts, 2. John.   4. Francis.
                                        eldest son.
               3. Ursula. 5. Mary.   3. George.

Watts of Ware.

ARMS (added).—*Argent, two bars Azure, in chief three pellets.*
CREST.—*A sea-dog's head proper.*

Thomas Watts of Buntingford, co. Hertf.=....

Sir John Watts, Kt., sometime Lord Maior=Margarett, da. of Sir James Hawes, Kt.,
of the Citie of London [1606]. | Lord Maior of London [1574].

Thomas   Sir John Watts of Ware,=Mary, da. of Thomas Bayn-   Magdalen, ux.
Watts.   co. Hertf., Kt., at the ing of Suffolk, elder brother Sir Henry
          Expedition to Cales 1625, to Pawle and Andrew Bayn- Apleton, Kt.
          in which he was a great ing, Aldermen of London.   and Bart.
          commander.   A

THE VISITATION OF HERTFORDSHIRE, 1634.   103

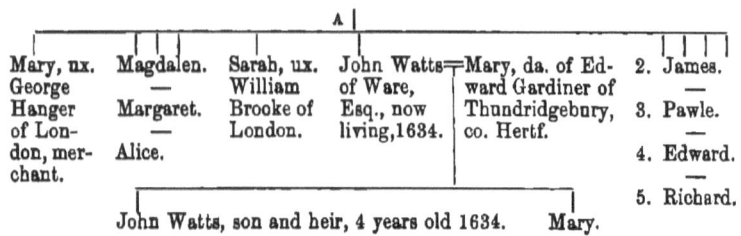

Mary, ux. George Hanger of London, merchant. | Magdalen. — Margaret. — Alice. | Sarah, ux. William Brooke of London. | John Watts of Ware, Esq., now living, 1634. = Mary, da. of Edward Gardiner of Thundridgebury, co. Hertf. | 2. James. — 3. Pawle. — 4. Edward. — 5. Richard.

John Watts, son and heir, 4 years old 1634.   Mary.

Weld of Widbury Hill.

ARMS.—*Azure, a fess nebulée between three crescents Ermine, a mullet for difference.*
CREST.—*A wyvern ducally gorged, a mullet for difference.*

This descent and Armes are resp. for further proofe at London the 3 of November 1634.

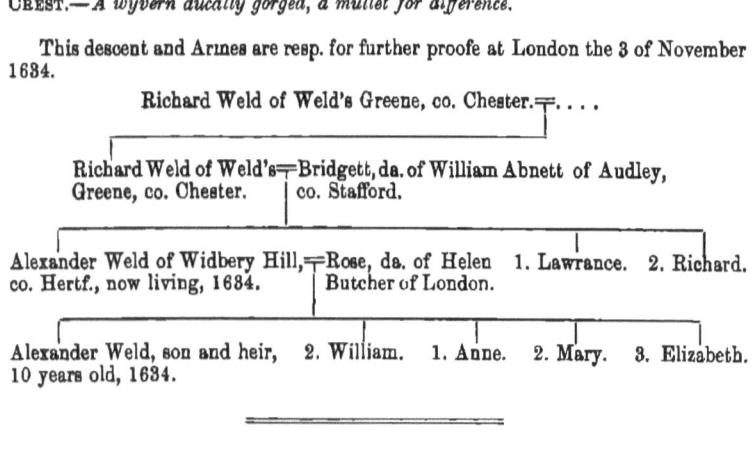

Richard Weld of Weld's Greene, co. Chester. = ...

Richard Weld of Weld's Greene, co. Chester. = Bridgett, da. of William Abnett of Audley, co. Stafford.

Alexander Weld of Widbery Hill, co. Hertf., now living, 1634. = Rose, da. of Helen Butcher of London.   1. Lawrance.   2. Richard.

Alexander Weld, son and heir, 10 years old, 1634.   2. William.   1. Anne.   2. Mary.   3. Elizabeth.

Whitaker of Ashwell.

ARMS.—*Sable, three mascles Or, a fleur-de-lis for difference.*

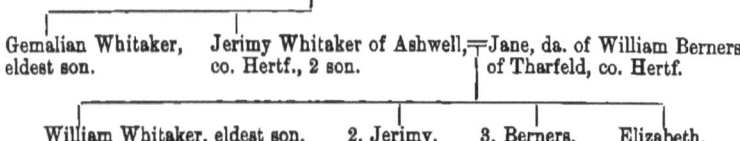

Edward Whitaker of Thornhill, co. York. = Elizabeth, da. of John Gomershall of Gomershall, co York.

Gemalian Whitaker, eldest son.   Jerimy Whitaker of Ashwell, co. Hertf., 2 son. = Jane, da. of William Berners of Tharfeld, co. Hertf.

William Whitaker, eldest son.   2. Jerimy.   3. Berners.   Elizabeth.

𝔚illimott of 𝔎elshall.

ARMS.—*On a fess between three greyhounds courant three roundles.*
CREST.—*An eagle displayed.*

These produced in an ould seale, but respyt for proofe.

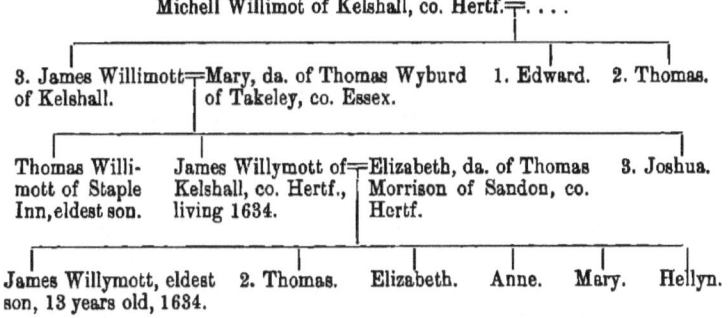

𝔚illis of 𝔅alls.

ARMS.—*Quarterly—1 and 4, Per fess Gules and Argent, three lions rampant counterchanged, a bordure Ermine; 2, Argent, a lion rampant Vert crowned Or,* HENMARSH; *3, Two bars, in chief three annulets.*
CREST.—*Two lions' gambs erased, the dexter Argent, the sinister Gules, supporting an escucheon Or.*

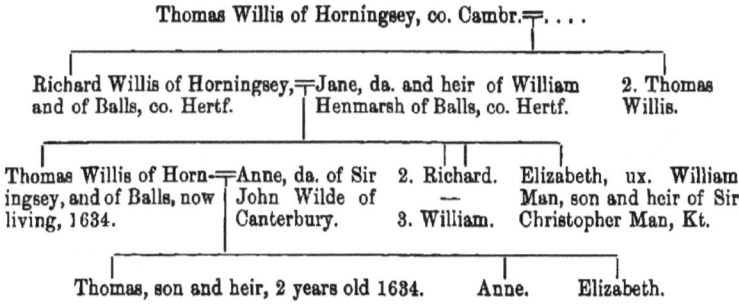

Wilson of Willion.

ARMS.—*Quarterly*—1 and 4, Sable, a wolf salient Or, in chief three estoiles Argent; 2 and 3, Azure, crusily Or and a lion rampant Argent.
CREST.—*A demi-wolf salient Or, a crescent for difference.*

Under the hand of Sir William Segar, Kt., *Garter.*

Elizabeth, da. and heir of Freeman Lambert, 1 wife. =Edward Wilson of Walkarne, co. Hertf., married to his 2 wife Elizabeth, da. of Edmond Kimpton. =Marian, da. of .... Hyde, 3 wife.

Margarett, da. of William Goldwell of Kent, 1 wife. =Edward Wilson of Wilyen. =Joane, da. of Robert Sunings of London, 2 wife.

Edward Wilson of Wyllen [Willion], co. Hertf., now living, 1634. =Jane, da. of Tho's Bolle of Wallington, Esq. | Mary Wilson, wife to Benj. Bonwick of Surrey. | Thomas Wilson of Wylyen, co. Hertf. =Lucy, da. of Anthony Jenkinson, Esq.

Mary, da. of Edward Pulter. =Raphe Wilson, son and heir. =.... da. of .... Campe of London. | Edward Wilson, eldest son and heir. | 2. John. | Judith.

Edward. | Thomas. | Susan.

Wingate of Lockleys.

ARMS.—*Quarterly*—1 and 4, Sable, a bend Ermine cotised Or between six martlets of the last; 2 and 3, Azure, a fess between three guttes d'Or. On an escucheon of pretence : *Or, a talbot passant Sable, on a chief of the second three martlets of the first*, ALLWAY.
CRESTS.—1, *A wicket-gate, a crescent for difference.*
2, *A hind's head couped proper.**

* This Creast only used by the Clarke of the Check.

William Wyngatt of Lockleys in Wellwin, 2 son of George Wyngatt of Harlington in Bedf., Esq. =Margerett, da. of Peter Taverner of Hexton, co. Hertf., Esq., and Frances Docwra his wife.

Edward Wyngate, only son and heir, living 1634. =Mary, da. and heir of Rauf Allway of Cannons in Shenley, co. Hertf., gent. | Francis, ux. Needham of Wymondley, co. Hertf., Esq. | Eustace | Jane.

Edward Wyngate, son and heir, aged 3 years. | George Wyngate, aged 1 year.

Wroth of Youngs.

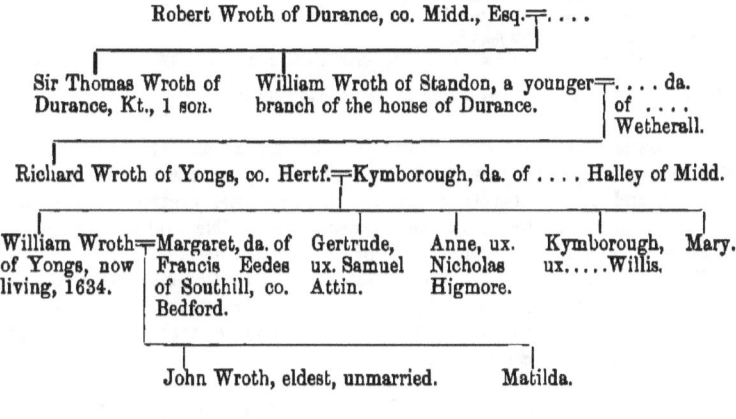

Robert Wroth of Durance, co. Midd., Esq.=....

Sir Thomas Wroth of Durance, Kt., 1 son.

William Wroth of Standon, a younger branch of the house of Durance. =....da. of .... Wetherall.

Richard Wroth of Yongs, co. Hertf.=Kymborough, da. of .... Halley of Midd.

William Wroth of Yongs, now living, 1634. =Margaret, da. of Francis Eedes of Southill, co. Bedford.

Gertrude, ux. Samuel Attin.

Anne, ux. Nicholas Higmore.

Kymborough, ux.....Willis.

Mary.

John Wroth, eldest, unmarried.

Matilda.

Wyndowt of Radwell.

ARMS.—*Per fess Gules and Or, a lion rampant per fess Argent and Azure guttée counterchanged between three escallops counterchanged of the first and second.*
CREST.—*A cubit arm vested Argent, glove Gules, between two wings Sable, holding a falcon Azure beaked and belled Or.*

This Armes and Creast graunted by Thomas Benolt, *Clarenceux*, and Thomas Wryothesley, *Garter*, to Barthelmew Wyndowt, aº 1515, 7 yere of Henry 8; and noe Armes belongeth to John de la Wood.

Barthelmew Wyndowt of Radiswell [Radwell], co. Herts.=....

Catherin, da. and heir, wife to John de la Wood.

The Town and Borough of Hertford.

SEAL.—*On the sinister side a tower triple-domed, on each dome a cross. In front, on the dexter side, and partly obscuring the tower, a stag statant, between the attires a cross patée fitchée.*
LEGEND.—✠ R. D. C. THE SEALE OF THE BOROUGHE TOWNE OF HARTFORD.
SHIELD.—*Argent, on a mount a stag couchant both proper.*

The towne of Hertford, time out of minde, has bin an antient towne endowed w'th many priveleges by prescription, incorporated by the name of Burgesses of Hertford, and by all that time had two markets weekly upon Saturday and Wednesday, and sent Burgesses to the Parliament, with divers other priveleges as appeares by the Booke of Doomsday and by diverse other Records.

[The entry then refers to Letters Patent, dated 26 November 31 Elizabeth, confirming their ancient rights and privileges, and incorporating them by the name of Bayley and Burgesses ; and also Letters Patent, dated 8 August 3 James, confirming the same ; and continues thus :]

For the presente William, Earl of Salisbery, is *High Steward*, George Hoppie is now *Mayor*, John Kelinge, Esq., *Steward*, and Henry Bull, Esq., *Justice* of the Peace ; John Roberts, Robert Dawson, X'pofer Brown, Edward Lawrence, Gabriell Barber, Esq., John Dyer, Edward Offley, gent., and Joseph Halton, *Burgesses*; and John Gaddesden, *Towne Clarke*.

The Town and Borough of St. Alban's.

ARMS, ON A SEAL.—*A saltire.*
LEGEND.—S. COMMUNE VILLE SANCTI ALBANI.

[This entry refers to Letters Patent, dated at Westminster 12 May 7 Edward 6, incorporating the Borough of St. Alban's in the County of Hertford ; and also Letters Patent, dated at Westminster 17 December 8 Charles, confirming the same ; and continues thus :] of which said Borough, at the time of this Visitation this thirteenth day of August Anno D'ni 1634, Henry Gape is *Mayor*, and Edward Eames in this yeare (being in the yeare next after his precedent mayoraltie) is a *Justice* of the Peace ; William Humfrey, Ralfe Pollard, Raphe Pemberton, gent., Richard Ruthe, William Newce, Robert Ivory, Gavin Crosfeilde, Thomas Oxton, and Thomas Cowley are principall *Burgesses* of the said Borough.

Also, by the said l'res Patent of our said soveraign Lord the King's Ma'tie that now is, the right hon'ble Thomas, Lord Coventry, Lord Keeper of the Great Seal of England, is assigned, named, constituted, and made the first and now *High Stewarde* of the said Borough ; and that after the death of the now Under Steward they shall have a *Recorder* instead of their Under Steward, and to bee a Justice of Peace as the now Steward is with others as above ; and also they have thereby a Town Clerke and a Coroner within themselves.

The Town and Borough of Berkhampstead.

ARMS.—*Or, a castle embattled, tripled-towered, and domed Azure, on each of the side domes a banner charged with a cross, all within a bordure Sable bezantée.*

A SEAL *bearing the same arms without tinctures.*

LEGEND.—SIGILLUM BALL. ET BURG. DE BARKHAMSTEAD S'TI PETRI.

APPENDIX I.

Anderson of Pendley in Aldbury.

ARMS.—*Argent, a chevron between three crosses patonce Sable, a fleur-de-lis Gules for difference.*
CREST.—*Out of a ducal coronet Argent, a hind's head Or pierced through the neck with an arrow of the first.*

John Andersonn.=Margerett, da. and heir of .... Anderton of .... co. Lanc.

Thomas Andersonn.=....

Thomas Andersonn=.... da. of .... Hopton of co. of London, Grocer. | Salop; renupt. .... Garraway.

- Sir John Andersonn,=Elizabeth, da. of Francis Bowyer of London, Alderman. Kt., Shreeve of London 1602, free of the Grocers.
- Christian, ux. John Robinson of London, ob. 24 April 1592; buried at St. Hellen's, London.
- Elizabeth, ux. Sir William Garraway of London, Kt.

- Frances, s.p.
- Frances, ux. Robert Needham of Shavington, co. Salop.
- Mary, ux. John Spencer of Offeley, co. Hertf.
- Sarah, ux. Sir Charles Wilmot, Kt.

- Catherin, ux. Thomas Derham of West Derham in Norf., Esq.
- Elizabeth, ux. Thomas Cowley of London, Merchant.
- George Andersonn, ob. s.p.
- 2. Sir Richard Andersonn of Penley, co. Hertf., Kt., ob. 3 Aug. 1632.=Margerett, da. of Robert Spencer, Baron of Wormleighton, co. Northampton.

- 1. Elizabeth, ux. Robert Peyton, son and heir of Sir John Peyton of Dunnington in the Isle of Ely.
- 2. Mary.
- 3. Frances. Margerett, s.p.
- 4. Margerett.
- 5. Catherin. Dorothy, s.p.
- 6. Penelope.
- 7. Anne.
- 8. Bridget.

- Henry Anderson=Jacomina, da. of Sir Charles Cæsar of Benington, Kt. of Penley, Esq.
- 2. Robert.
- 3. John.
- 4. William.
- 5. Richard, s.p.

Anne.

Barnwell of St. Alban's.

ARMS.—*Per pale Sable and Azure, on a fess dancettée Or three crosses patée fitchée of the first;* impaling, *Per chevron embattled Argent and Sable, three cinquefoils counterchanged,* HILL.

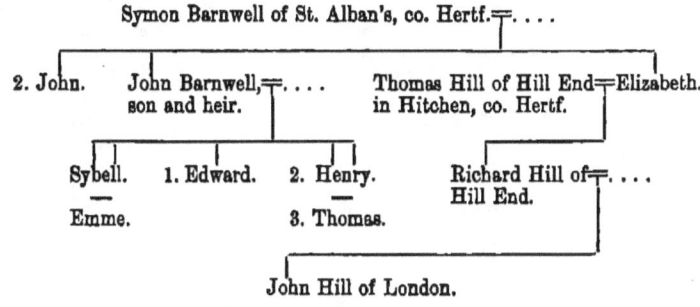

Symon Barnwell of St. Alban's, co. Hertf.=. . . .

2. John.   John Barnwell,=. . . .   Thomas Hill of Hill End=Elizabeth.
           son and heir.   in Hitchen, co. Hertf.

Sybell.   1. Edward.   2. Henry.   Richard Hill of=. . . .
                                   Hill End.
Emme.   3. Thomas.

John Hill of London.

Boraston of Aldenham.

ARMS.—*Quarterly Argent and Sable, on a bend cotised Gules three crosses patée fitchée Or.*
CREST.—*Out of a mural crown Sable, a griffin's head Or, gorged with a fess cotised Gules.*

Per Camden, *Clarenceulx.*

Thomas Boraston of The Rocke, co. Worc., gent.=. . . .

Henry Boraston of Aldenham, co. Hertf.=Alice, da. of Raphe Taylor of the North.

Phillip Boraston of Aldenham, gent.=Luce, da. to William Pulter of Hertford.

Pulter Boraston,   Edward Boraston,   Phillip, 2 son, dyed in Denmark,
ob. s.p.   son and heir.   s.p., and buried in Elsinore.

Boteler of Woodhall.

ARMS.—*Quarterly of nine*—1, *Gules, a fess counter-compony Argent and Sable between six cross-crosslets of the first;* 2, *Argent, a sword in bend Sable;* 3, *Gules, two bars Ermine,* PANTOLPH; 4, *Quarterly Or and barry of six Argent and Vert, a bordure Sable charged with lucies hauriant of the second,* GOBION; 5, *Argent, a fess Gules;* 6, *Vair, a fess Gules fretty Or;* 7, *Azure, a bend Argent, a bordure of the second bezantée;* 8, *Paly of six Or and Azure, a chief dancettée Vert;* 9, *Or, a bull passant Gules between three roaches hauriant Argent, a chief chequy Azure and of the third,* ROCHE.

CREST.—*An arm embowed in armour proper, in the hand a sword Sable, hilt Or.*

Ralfe le Boteler, Lord and Baron of Wemme in the right of his wife. =Maude, da. and heir of William Pantolph, Lord of Wemme.

William le Boteler, Baron of Wemme. =Margaret, da. of Richard, Earle of Arundell. John, s.p. Gawen, s.p.

William le Boteler, Lord of Wemme, temp. E. 3. =Ella, da. to .... Handslagh *alias* Hansacre. Sir Raphe le Boteler, Kt., Lord of Woodhall. =Hawise, da. and heir to Richard, son of Hugh Gobion.

William le Boteler. =Johanna, 1 da. and co-heir of John, Lord Sudley. Raphe le Boteler. =.... da. of .... Hanlow. Sir Raphe Boteler, Kt. =Maude, da. to Sir Philip Marmion, Kt.

Thomas le Boteler, Lord of Sudley. =Alice, da. to John Beauchamp, Lord Powick. Elizabeth, da. and heir, 1 ux. to Thomas Mollington, in her right Baron of Wemme; after to Robert Ferrers, in her right Baron of Wemme. John Boteler, 13 E. 4. =.... Raphe Boteler of Woodhall. =Katherin, da. to .... Kilpeck.

Raphe Boteler, Lord of Sudley, K.G. and Treasurer of England. =.... Ralfe, ob. s.p. Edward, s.p. Sir John Butler of Woodhall, Kt. =Grissell, da. and heir of .... Roche.

Sir Thomas Boteler, Kt., ob. s.p.

1. Sir Phillipp Boteler of Woodhall, Kt. =Anne, da. of John Conisby. .... ux. .... Conisby. .... da. of .... Waller, 1 ux. 2. Henry Butler of Hatfield Woodhall, Kt. =Alice, da. of Edw. Pulter, Esq, 2 ux. 3. Thomas. — Nicholas. — William.

APPENDIX I.

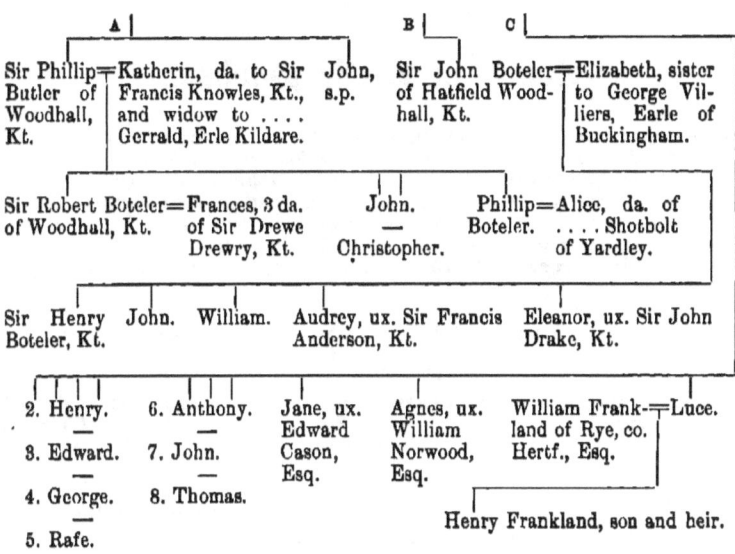

Bowles of Wallington.

ARMS.—*Argent, on a chevron between three boars' heads couped Sable as many escallops Or, within a bordure engrailed Vert bezantée.*
CREST.—*Out of a ducal coronet Or, two wings Gules billitée of the first, between them a boar's head couped Sable.*

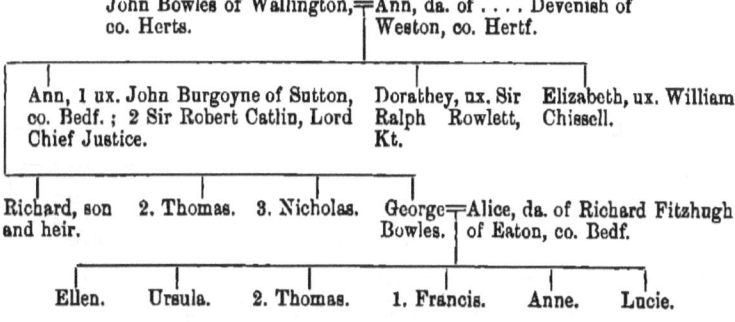

Capell of Little Hadham.

ARMS.—*Quarterly of six*—1, *Gules, a lion rampant between three cross-crosslets fitchée Or;* 2, *Argent, a chevron Gules between three torteaux, on a chief Azure a fret between two cinquefoils Or;* 3, *Argent, on a chevron Azure three garbs Or;* 4, *Sable, a chevron Ermine between three escallops Argent,* CHEDDER; 5, *Gules, a chevron between three fleurs-de-lis Or;* 6, *Argent, crusily and a lion rampant Gules, ducally crowned Or.*

CREST.—*A demi-lion rampant holding a cross-crosslet fitchée Or.*

Sir John Arundell, Kt.=Katherin, da. to Sir John Chidioke, Kt.

| John Capell of=Joane. Stoke Leyland, co. Suff. | Sir Thomas=Katherin, da. Arundell, to Sir John Kt. Dynham, Kt. | Sir John=Mabell, da. and Newton, heir of Thomas Kt. Chedder. |

| Sir William Capell, Kt., Lord Maior of=Margaret, da. London and Draper 1503, knighted to Sir Thomas by H. 7. Arundell, Kt. | Elianor, da.=Thomas to the Lord Newton. Daubenie. |

| Dorothey, ux. the Lord Zouch. | Elizabeth, ux. William Paulett, Marquis of Winchester. | Sir Giles Capell,=.... da. of Thomas, Kt. and heir of Sir John Newton, Kt. |

| Sir Henry=Anne, sister to Thomas Capell, Kt. Manners, Earle of Rutland. | 2. Sir Edward=Anne, da. to Sir William Capell, Kt. Peckham, Kt. |

| Arthur. | Edward. | John. | Gabriell. | Robert. | Mary.—Anne. | Agnes. | Frances. |

| 2. Gyles Capell. | Anne, ux. Ralfe Hyde. | Mary.=Weston Browne. | Elizabeth, ux. John Wentworth. | Grace, ux. ....Burton. |

| Katherin, da. to Thomas=Henry=Mary, da. of Anthony=John, Lord Gray, Manners, Earle of Rutland. Capell. Browne, Lord Viscount brother to the Mountague. Marquis Dorset. |

| Anne, ux. .... Chester, son to Captaine Chester. | Mary, ux. Humfrey Mildmay of Essex. | 2. Gamaliell Capell=Jane, da. and of Rookwood Hall co-heir to Weston Browne. in Essex. |

A

APPENDIX I.

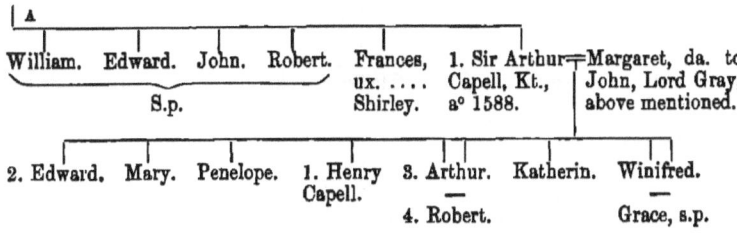

William.	Edward.	John.	Robert.	Frances, ux. .... Shirley.	1. Sir Arthur Capell, Kt., aº 1588.	=Margaret, da. to John, Lord Gray, above mentioned.
S.p.						

| 2. Edward. | Mary. | Penelope. | 1. Henry Capell. | 3. Arthur. — 4. Robert. | Katherin. | Winifred. — Grace, s.p. |

Fanshaw of Ware Park.

ARMS.—*Or, a chevron between three fleurs-de-lis Sable.*
CREST.—*A wyvern's head erased Or, breathing " fier."*

.... =Thomas Fanshaw of Ware Park, co. Hertf.,=Jane, da. of Thomas Smyth of
   Remembrancer of the Exchequer.   London, Customer, 2 ux.

| 1. Sir Henry Fanshaw of Ware Park, Kt. | =Elizabeth, da. of Thomas Smyth of London, Customer. | Thomas. — William. | Alice, ux. Sir Christopher Hatton, Kt. |

Horsey of Digswell.

ARMS.—*Quarterly—1, Azure, three horses' heads couped Argent, bridled Or; 2, Azure, a chevron between three cross-crosslets fitchée within a bordure engrailed Or; 3, Argent, three bars wavy Gules, over all a saltire Or; 4, Gules, a chevron engrailed between three lions' heads Or; over all a crescent for difference.*
CREST.—*A horse's head in armour Argent, plumed and bridled Azure and Or.*

George Horsey of Diggeswell,=Ann, eldest da. of Sir Rafe Sadler,
co. Hertf., Esq., Receiver   Kt. and Bannerett and Chancellour
Generall of the Dutchy of Lanc. of the Dutchy of Lanc.

| Mary, ux. Roger Revell, son to Roger, Surveyor to Q. Elizabeth. | 2. Jesper Horsey of Willen, co. Hertf. | =Hellen, da. of Thomas Dockwray. |

| Hellen. | Gertrud. | Jane, ux. Robert Pagenham of Nottingham. | 1. Jesper. | 2. George. |

| 1. Sir Raphe Horsey of Digswell, Kt. | =Edyth, sister of Sir Reignold Mohun. | Ann, ux. Richard Whalley of Screveton, co. Nott. | Ellen, ux. Thomas Dockwray. |

APPENDIX I.

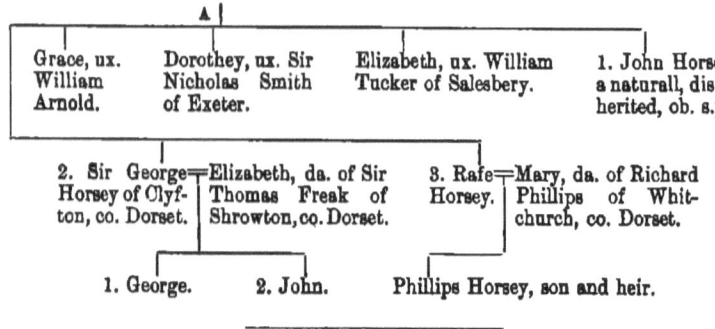

Lewen of Hertford.

ARMS.—*Per pale Gules and Azure, three bucks' heads erased Or.*

John Lewen of Coffley, had two wives.=....

1. Thomas Lewen.=....   2. John Lewen of Hertford.=Jane, da. to .... Plomer.

| Thomas, slaine in a parke. | Elizabeth, ux. Thomas Pembridge. | .... a da., ux. .... Thompson. | .... a da., ux. .... Rigby. |

| Margery, ux. John Howe of Somersett. | Elizabeth, 1 ux. Thomas Mayott, 2 to William Sherington of London, Merchant. | 1. John Lewen of Coffley. | =Sibell, da. of Sir William Allen, Kt., Alderman of London. | Ann, da. of .... Thorogood. | =2. Thomas Lewen. | =Ann, da. of .... Beamond. |

Litton of Knebworth.

ARMS (quarterly) and CREST as at p. 73.

Sir Rowland Lytton of Knebworth,=Anne, da. of Oliver, Lord St. co. Hertf., Kt.; he died the 23 of John of Bletso, the relict of June 1615. Mr. Corbet of Shropshire.

| Anne, ux. Sir Richard Webb. | Elizabeth. — Jane. | Judeth, ux. Geo. Smith. | Sir William Litton of Knebworth, Kt., son and heir. | =Anne, da. of Stephen Slaney. | Rowland. — Philip. |

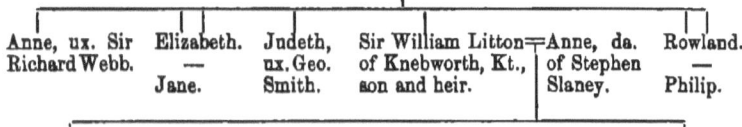

Rowland Litton, half a year old at the death of his grandfather.   Margaret.

Morrison of Cashiobury.

ARMS.—*Or, on a chief Gules three chaplets of the field.*
CREST.—*A pegasus Or.*

Sir Richard Morison, Kt. = Bridgett, da. of John, Lord Hussey; remar. to Henry, Erle of Rutland. = Francis Russell, Earl of Bedford, 3 vir.

    Sir Charles Morison of Cashowbury in the parish of Watford, co. Hertf., Kt. = ... da. of .... Clarke.

Sir Charles Morisson of Cashowbury, Kt. and Bart. = ... da. and co-heir of Sir Baptist Hicks, Kt.

Bridgett, ux. Robert, Erle of Sussex.

Penne of Codicote.

ARMS (quarterly) and CREST as at p. 82.

John Penne of Coddicott, co. Hertf., Grome of the Privy Chamber and Barber to H. 8. = Lucye, da. and heir of Edmond Chevall of Coddicott.

2. Robert.
—
3. John.

Thomas Penne of Coddicott. = Margery, da. of Thomas Saunders of Agmondisham, co. Bucks.

Ellenor, ux. .... Barre.

Elizabeth.
—
Dorothey.

John Penne.   Susan.   Mary.   Lucy.

Pulter of Wymondley.

ARMS.—*Quarterly*—1 and 4, 2 and 3, as 1, 2, and 3 at p. 85.

Edward Pulter of Greate Wymondley, co. Hertf., Esq. = Julian, da. and sole heir of Edmond Cave, Citizen and Draper of London, mar. to .... Hansbott. = Sir Thomas Cotton of Oxenheath in West Peckham in Kent.

APPENDIX I.

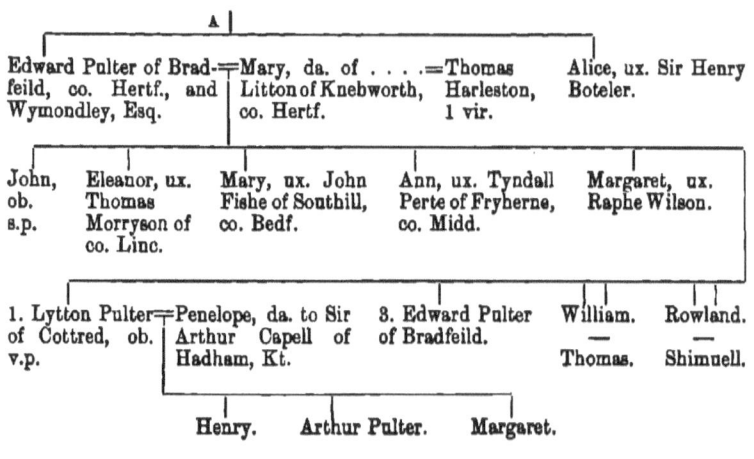

𝔗horogood of 𝔠heshunt.

ARMS.—*Azure, on a chief Argent three square buckles of the field.*
CREST.—*A wolf's head Argent, charged with a square buckle.*

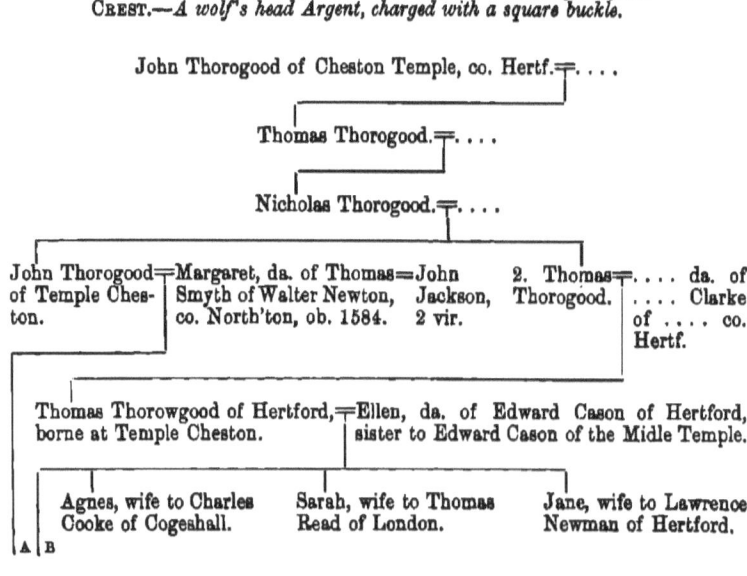

APPENDIX I.

A | B

George Thorow=Elizabeth, da.　Edward Thorow-　Elizabeth, wife to Nicholas
good of London,　of Thomas　good of London.　Richold of Cogeshall, co.
aº 1634.　Vinton of　　　　　　　　　　Essex.
　　　　　　London.

George Thorow-　2. John.　Edward.　Elizabeth, wife to　Susan.　Hannah.
good, eldest son.　　　　　—　　Stephen White of　—
　　　　　　　　　　　　　　Joseph.　London, Merchant.　Sarah.

Thomas Thoro-=Bridget, da.　Susan, mar. to　Jane, mar. first　Elizabeth, first
good of Wal-　of ....　William Man-　to John Hob-　mar. to Edward
mesford, co.　Kell of co.　esty of co.　son of London;　Henson of
North'ton.　Bucks.　Hunt., and had　2 to Thomas　London; 2 to
　　　　　　　　　Robert and　Holdich, Clark.　Sir Peter Proby
　　　　　　　　　William.　　　　　　　　of London,
　　　　　　　　　　　　　　　　　　　　　　Alderman.

　　　　　　　　John.　Elizabeth.　Bridget.

2. William　Nicholas Thoro-=Dorothey,　Anne, ux. Law-　Frances, mar. to Edward
Thoro-　good of Temple　da. of ....　rence Fisher of　Winch of Chiping Wick-
good, ob.　Cheston, eldest　Alley of　Buckden, and　ham, co. Bucks.
s.p.　son.　co. Bedf.　had Dorothy
　　　　　　　　　　　　　　East.

John Thorogood　Frances, mar.　2. Nicholas Thoro-=Jane, da. of　Joane, mar.
of Temple Ches-　to William　good of Nassing-　William　to ....
ton, eldest son,　Purdey of co.　ton, co. North'ton,　Poole of　Turner of
ob. s.p.　Leic.　aº 1618.　Screveton,　Eye, co.
　　　　　　　　　　　　　　co. Nott.　North'ton.

1. Nicholas and Frances,　2. Daniel, 3 years　Dorathey.　Jane.　Frances.
both ob. s.p.　old 1618.

Jane, mar. to　Margaret, mar.　Elizabeth, first　4. John Thoro-=Elizabeth, da.
Jacob New-　to Christopher　mar. to Francis　good of Wel-　of .... Earle
man of Wy-　Cooper of Yax-　Johnson; 2 to　borne, co. Linc.　of .. co. Linc.
tering, co.　ley, co. Hunt.　John Capet of
North'ton.　　　　　　　　Gretford, co.
　　　　　　　　　　　Linc.

Augustin=Elizabeth, da. of William Walcot　Nicholas.　Margaret.　Elizabeth.
Thorogood.　of Walcot, co. Linc.

Waterhouse of Berkhampstead.

ARMS.—*Quarterly of six*—1, *Or, a pile engrailed Sable;* 2, *Gules, three bends Vair;* 3, *Per pale indented Argent and Gules;* 4, *Argent, a chevron between three cross-crosslets fitchée Sable, a fleur-de-lis for difference;* 5, *Argent, three castles Gules;* 6, *Chequy Or and Vert, a bend Ermine,* SPARKE.

CREST.—*A demi-hound salient Ermine, eared Sable, collared Gules, a mullet for difference.*

Gilbert Waterhouse of Kirton in Low Lyncey, Esq. = Isabel, da. and heir of John de Longevale.

Sir John Castell, Kt. = Jone, da. of John Hastings. *Or, a maunch Gules.*

Richard Smyth. *Ermine, three torteaux.* = Mary, da. of Nich. Bonevyle. *Or, on a bend Sable three mullets of six points Argent.*

Roger Waterhouse, Esq. = Joane, da. and heir of Sir John Castell.

John Smyth. = Elizabeth, da. of Henry Wake. *Gules, a crosse Ermine.*

James Waterhouse, Esq. = Mary, da. of John Smyth.

Alis, da. of Edmond Tempest. *Argent, a bend between six martlets Sable.* = William Waterhouse of Litle Stirley. = Maude, da. of Roger Preston of Alderney, by Joane his wife, da. of John Fitz Andrew. *Argent, two bars Gules, on a canton of the second a cinquefoil pierced Or;* impaling, *Argent, a chevron between three escallops Gules, a chief Vair.*

Thomas Waterhouse, Esq. = Anne, da. of Thomas Umfrevile. *Gules, a cinquefoil between six cross-crosslets within a bordure Or.*

William, died in Normandy, s.p.

Anne, ux. Christopher Medcalf. *Argent, three calves passant Sable.*

John Waterhouse. = Elizabeth, da. of John Blewet. *Or, a chevron between three eaglets displayed Vert.*

Thomas, s.p.

James Waterhouse of Ludlow. = Anne, da. of Thomas Damport, sister and co-heir of John Damport.

Francis Waterhouse of Ludlow. A = Elizabeth, da. of Thomas Farington. *Argent, a chevron Gules between three leopards' faces Sable.*

Anne, ux. Thomas Fitzhugh. *Sable, three chevronels interlaced in base and a chief Or.*

Mary, ux. Henry Baynard. *Gules, three chevronels Ermine.*

APPENDIX I.

A |

- Constance, da. of Francis Waterhouse and sister of John, ux. Andrew Whaddon.
- John Waterhouse, who descended of .... Waterhouse of Ludlow, co. Salop, son of Francis Waterhouse. = Anne, da. and heir of .... Sparke of London.
- Robert Waterhouse, Chaplaine to the King.

Children:
- Thomas Waterhouse, Rector of Ashrugh, co. Hertf., ob. s.p.
- John Waterhouse of Whitchurch, co. Buck., Esq., lyeth bur. at Berkhampsted. = Margerett, da. of Henry Turner of Blunt's Hall in Essex, Esq.
- Elizabeth, ux. Rich. Langdale. *Sable, a chevron between three mullets Argent.*
- Agnes, ux. Robert Combe. *Ermine, three lions passant-gardant Sable bezantée.*

- 1. John Waterhouse of Whitchurch, buried at Berkhampsted. = Ann, da. of Henry Birkenhed of Huxley, co. Chester. *Sable, three garbs Or, a bordure engrailed Azure.*
- Elizabeth Villiers, 1 ux.
- 3. Sir Edward Waterhouse of Woodchurch in Kent, Chauncellor of the Exchequer, and one of the Privie Councell in Ireland, ob. s.p. = Margaret, da. of .... Spilman of Kent, 2 ux.; Debora, widow to .... Harlakenden of Kent, Esq., 3 ux.

- Thomas Waterhouse of Whitchurch, buried in Acton. = ... da. and heir of Vallentyn Pigott of Bechampton, co. Buck., Esq.
- 2. Charles. —
- 3. Clifford. S.p.
- 4. John Waterhouse of Whitchurch, cozen and heir male. = ... da. of .... Muschampe of .... co. Surrey.

John Waterhouse of Whitchurch, s.p. = ... da. of .... Nutting of co. Midd.   Anne.

- 5. Edward.
- 6. Henry.
- Katherin. Susan, s.p.
- Elizabeth, ux. John Bassett of Fledborough, co. Nott., Esq.
- Grace, ux. .... Tuke of Essex.
- Anne, ux. Tho's Spicer of .... co. Bedf.

- 4. Arthur Waterhouse, mar. Grace, da. of John Hanshott in co. Hertf., ob. s.p.
- 2. Thomas Waterhouse of Berkhamsted, co. Hertf. = Mary, da. of John Kirkby of Nottingham. *Argent, two bars and a canton Gules.*
- 5. Charles Waterhouse of Baltra in Ireland. = Ursula, da. of .... Andrewes, cosen to Sir Eusebius Andrewes, Kt.

- Edward Waterhouse of Berkhamsted. = Elizabeth, da. to Sir William Lane of Horton, co. North'ton, Kt.
- 2. Arthur.
- Edward of Baltra.
- Charles.

Thomas Waterhouse, son and heir, æt. 14 annor. 1618.   2. Hennage.   Mary.   Philipp.   Judith.

Wilson of Willion.

ARMS.—*Quarterly of six—1, Sable, a wolf salient and in chief three estoiles Or; 2, Barry wavy of six Argent and Azure, SONGER; 3, Argent, a chevron engrailed Gules between three Cornish choughs proper, LAMBERT; 4, Sable, a fess Ermine between three escucheons Argent, SONINGS; 5, Argent, a chevron countercompony of the first and Azure between three martlets Gules, HAMPTON; 6, Argent, two pales and a bordure engrailed Sable, CROUCH.*
CREST.—*A demi-wolf salient Or.*

Thomas Wilson of Stroby, =.... co. Linc., Esq.

James Songer of Stoking = Jane Pelham, co. Hertf. | Norris.

William Wilson of Stroby, =.... da. of .... Dighton of co. Linc.
son and heir.

John Songer =.... da. of William of Stoking | Wood of Essex. Pelham.

1. William Wilson of Stroby, ancestor to Secretary Wilson.

Thomas Wilson of Codreth, = Margaret, da. co. Hertf. | and heir.

Edmond. | Rafe and Jane, ob. s.p. | Alice, wife to .... Conniswell. | .... wife to .... Greene; after to .... Eliott of Stanford Rivers.

Lambert.

Thomas Lambert of Wheathampstead. =....

Thomas Lambert = ... of Wheathampstead, co. Hertf.

John Lambert of Hinxworth, and Shreive of London *temp.* H. 6.

Thomas Hill = ... da. of Symon of Hill End Barnwell of St. in Hitchin, Alban's. co. Hertf.

Freman Lambert = ... da. of of Bridewell Ashe | .... High- in Sandridge, co. | nowe. Hertf.

Thomas Graveley = Agnes, da. to = Edward of Graveley, co. | Thomas Hill; | Wilson Hertf., 1 vir. | mar. to .... | of Cod- Gascoigne, her | reth, 2 3 vir. | vir.

Henry Graveley, s.p. John Graveley, son and heir. = Elizabeth Randall.

Thomas Graveley.

Elizabeth, da. = Edward Wilson of = Mary, da. and heir to | Walkhorne; mar. | to .... Freman Lam- | Elizabeth, da. of | Hide, 3 ux. bert, 1 ux. | Edmond Kimp- ton of Weston, 2 A | ux. B

Robert = Margery, da. and heir to Sonn- | William Hampton of ings of | Kent by the da. and heir Lon- | of .... Crouch of Kent. don. C

R

APPENDIX I.

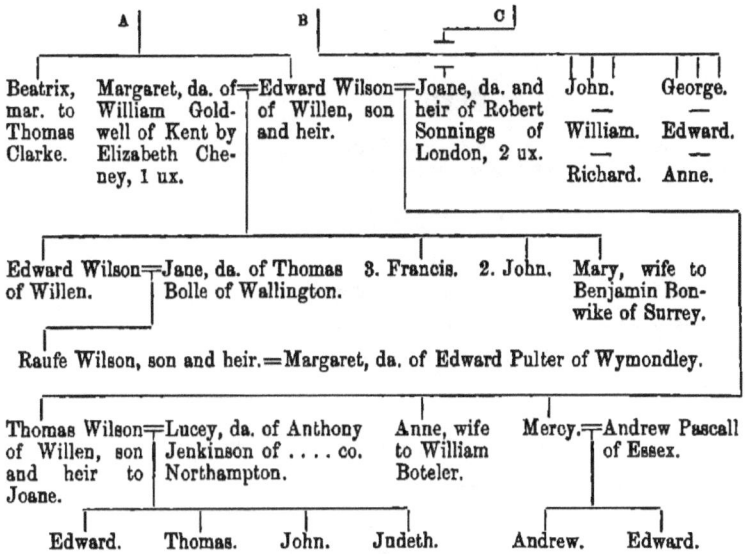

A | B | C
Beatrix, mar. to Thomas Clarke. | Margaret, da. of William Goldwell of Kent by Elizabeth Cheney, 1 ux. =Edward Wilson of Willen, son and heir. =Joane, da. and heir of Robert Sonnings of London, 2 ux. | John. William. — Richard. | George. Edward. — Anne.

Edward Wilson of Willen. =Jane, da. of Thomas Bolle of Wallington. 3. Francis. 2. John. Mary, wife to Benjamin Bonwike of Surrey.

Raufe Wilson, son and heir.=Margaret, da. of Edward Pulter of Wymondley.

Thomas Wilson of Willen, son and heir to Joane. =Lucey, da. of Anthony Jenkinson of .... co. Northampton. Anne, wife to William Boteler. Mercy.=Andrew Pascall of Essex.

Edward. Thomas. John. Judeth. Andrew. Edward.

APPENDIX II.

Andrew of Hitchin.

ARMS.—*Argent, on a bend cotised Sable three mullets pierced of the field.*
CREST.—*A stag's head erased Argent.*

William Andrew.=....
    |
James Andrew.=....

William Andrew of St. Alban's,=Joane, da. of William Skipwith of St. Alban's,
co. Hertf.   Esq., and Jone his wife.

William Andrew of St. Alban's.=.... da. of .... Babham.

John Andrew of Libery, co. Hertf.=Anne, da. of William Browne of Essex.

John Andrew=Susan, da. of Thomas	Sir William Andrew of	Catherin, ux.
of Hitchin, co.	Duncombe of Brick-	Lathbury, co. Bucks,	John Marsh
Hertf.	hill, co. Bucks.	*vide* Bucks.	of Barnett.

Mary, da. and heir, ux. James Mayne of Bovington, co. Hertf.

Antrobus of St. Alban's.

ARMS.—*Lozengy Or and Azure, on a pale Gules three estoiles of the first.*
CREST.—*Out of rays Or a unicorn's head Argent, gorged with a wreath of laurel Vert.*

William Antrobus of Antrobus,=Felix, da. of .... Constantyne of Whit-
co. Chesh.   church. *Or, six fleurs-de-lis Sable.*

Thomas Antrobus=Mary, da. of Richard Fitzwalter. *Quarterly Or and Gules, on*
of Antrobus.   *a bend Azure three fleurs-de-lis Argent.*
▲

APPENDIX II.

A

Henry Antrobus, who sould the = Elizabeth, da. of John Machelsfeld of Guysnes.
Mannor of Antrobus to .... | *Gules, a cross engrailed Ermine.*
Venables.

Rafe Antrobus of Pever, co. Chesh. = ...

1. John Antrobus of Pever. | William Antrobus of Knottesford the bigger. = ... | 2. Robert Antrobus of Chelford. | Edward Antrobus of Tabley. | Henry, ob. s.p. — Rafe, ob. s.p. | 4. Philip Antrobus of Northwiche.

John Antrobus of Knottesford. | 2. William Antrobus of St. Alban's. | Robert of St. Stephen's, near St. Alban's. | Antrobus = Rose, da. of Tudor Daye of Holywell. | Walter Antrobus of St. Alban's. = ...

Richard Antrobus of Clifford's Inn in London. = Dorathea, da. of Nicholas Selyard of Kent. *Azure, a chief Ermine.* | Thomas. — Roger, by another wife. | John Antrobus of Aldenham, co. Hertf., by another wife, I think. | William Antrobus of St. Alban's.

Robert Antrobus.

William Antrobus. = Elizabeth, da. of Thomas Hollingshead of Shead, co. Chesh. | Henry Antrobus. = ...

William Antrobus of Little Knottesford. = Jane, da. of .... Millington. *Azure, three millstones Argent.* | George Antrobus. = ...

Thomas Antrobus of London. = Elizabeth, da. of Rafe Woodcock of London, Alderman. | Henry Antrobus of Little Knottesford. = ...

1. Thomas Antrobus of Heathouse nigh Petersfeld, co. Southampton, Esq. = Elizabeth, da. of Sir Richard Norton of Rotherfeld, co. Southampton, Kt. | 2. John Antrobus. | 3. Richard Antrobus of Lincoln's Inn. | George Antrobus of London. = ...

Thomas Antrobus.

Baldwin of Red Heath.

ARMS.—*Quarterly*—1 *and* 4, *Argent, six leaves slipped in pairs, two in chief and one in base, Sable, the leaves bent downwards over the stalks, a canton of the second ;* 2 *and* 3, *Ermine, a fess chequy Or and Azure.*
CREST.—*A squirrel sejant proper holding a pair of leaves as in the arms.*
On each *a mullet for difference.*

```
                    John Baldwin of Redheth, co. Hertf.=....
    ┌──────────────────────────────────┬──────────────────────────────┐
Thomas Baldwin of Redheth, Esq.,   Richard Baldwin of=Anne, da. of Richard
Comptroller of the King's Buildings.  the Midle Temple. │ Sawell.
    │
Richard Baldwin of High=Anne, da. of William Towers=William Cheney of ....
Holborne, co. Midd.    │ of Thornock, co. Linc.   co. Northampton, 1 vir.
    ┌──────────────────────┬───────────────────┬─────────┬────────────┐
1. Thomas Baldwin, 9 yeres  2. Richard Baldwin, 5 yeres  Catherin.  Anne, ob.
old 1 March 1630, drowned   old on Barthelmew day 1631,            yong.
with his brother by the     drowned with his brother by
breach of Izer.             the breach of Izer.
```

Bash of Stansted Bury and St. Margaret's.

ARMS.—*Quarterly*—1 *and* 4, *Per chevron Argent and Gules, in chief two moor-hens Sable beaked and legged of the second, in base a saltire Or ;* 2 *and* 3, *Per chevron Argent and Sable, three towers triple-towered counterchanged.*
CREST.—*A griffin segreant per pale Argent and Sable, holding in the beak a broken spear of the first.*
ANOTHER COAT for BAKER, wife to Edward Bash: *Argent, on a chevron Gules between three hinds Sable bezantée as many lozenges Vair.*

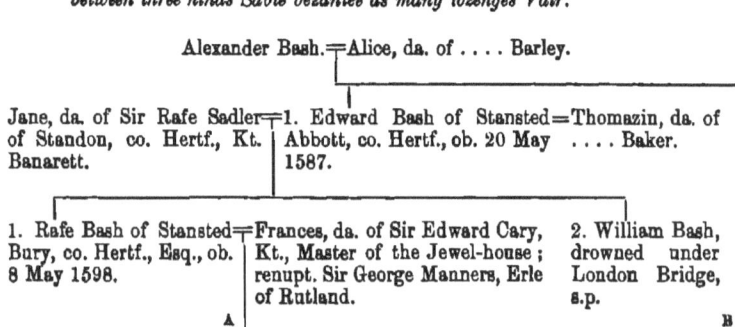

```
                    Alexander Bash.=Alice, da. of .... Barley.
                                    │
Jane, da. of Sir Rafe Sadler=1. Edward Bash of Stansted=Thomazin, da. of
of Standon, co. Hertf., Kt. │ Abbott, co. Hertf., ob. 20 May  .... Baker.
Banarett.                   │ 1587.
    ┌───────────────────────┬────────────────────────────┬──────────────────┐
1. Rafe Bash of Stansted=Frances, da. of Sir Edward Cary,  2. William Bash,
Bury, co. Hertf., Esq., ob. │ Kt., Master of the Jewel-house ;  drowned under
8 May 1598.                 │ renupt. Sir George Manners, Erle   London Bridge,
                            │ of Rutland.                        s.p.
```

APPENDIX II.

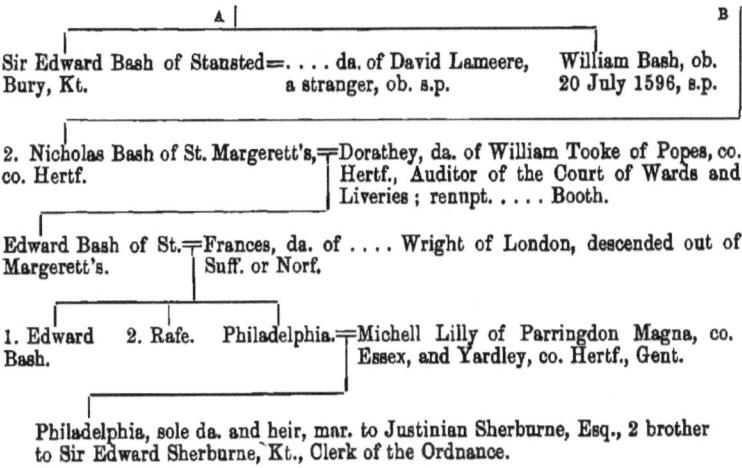

Philadelphia, sole da. and heir, mar. to Justinian Sherburne, Esq., 2 brother to Sir Edward Sherburne, Kt., Clerk of the Ordnance.

Bestney of St. Alban's.

ARMS.—*Per pale Sable and Gules, a lion rampant-gardant Argent ducally crowned Or.*
CREST.—*Out of a ducal coronet, a demi-griffin segreant Sable, clawed, beaked, and winged close Or.*

This descent is annexed to a Pattent of the single Coat and Crest of Bestney dated the 20th of March 1558, p. Lawrence Dalton, *Norroy King of Armes*, and was copied by the originall p. me Mundy.

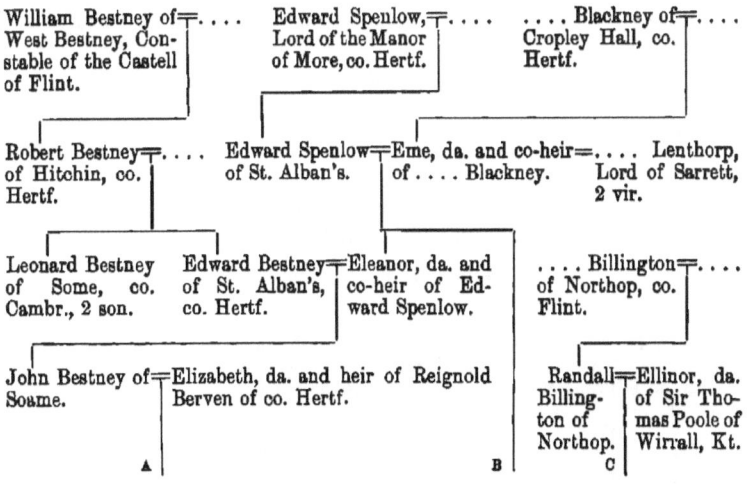

APPENDIX II.

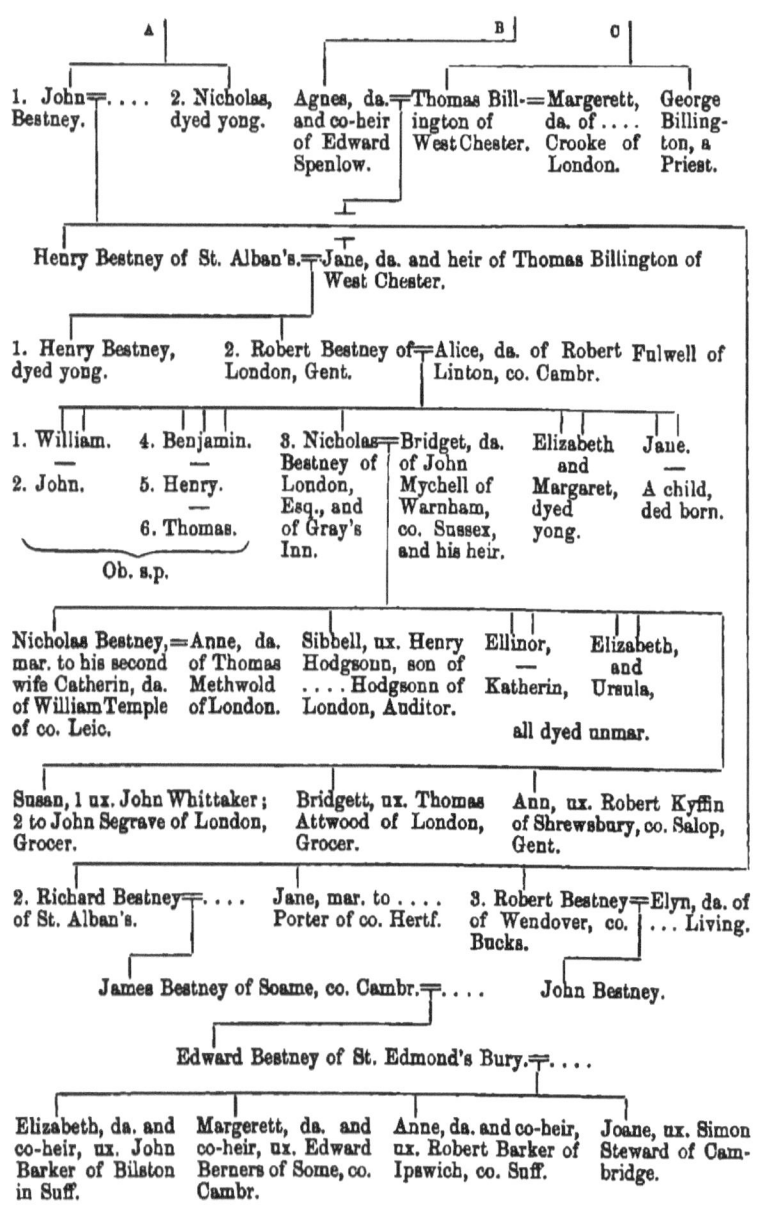

A.
1. John Bestney.=....   2. Nicholas, dyed yong.

B.
Agnes, da. and co-heir of Edward Spenlow.=Thomas Billington of West Chester.=Margerett, da. of .... Crooke of London.

C.
George Billington, a Priest.

Henry Bestney of St. Alban's.=Jane, da. and heir of Thomas Billington of West Chester.

1. Henry Bestney, dyed yong.   2. Robert Bestney of London, Gent.=Alice, da. of Robert Fulwell of Linton, co. Cambr.

1. William.   4. Benjamin.   3. Nicholas Bestney of London, Esq., and of Gray's Inn.=Bridget, da. of John Mychell of Warnham, co. Sussex, and his heir.   Elizabeth and Margaret, dyed yong.   Jane. A child, ded born.
2. John.   5. Henry.
6. Thomas.
Ob. s.p.

Nicholas Bestney,=Anne, da. of Thomas Methwold of London.   mar. to his second wife Catherin, da. of William Temple of co. Leic.   Sibbell, ux. Henry Hodgsonn, son of .... Hodgsonn of London, Auditor.   Ellinor, — Katherin,   Elizabeth, and Ursula, all dyed unmar.

Susan, 1 ux. John Whittaker; 2 to John Segrave of London, Grocer.   Bridgett, ux. Thomas Attwood of London, Grocer.   Ann, ux. Robert Kyffin of Shrewsbury, co. Salop, Gent.

2. Richard Bestney=.... of St. Alban's.   Jane, mar. to .... Porter of co. Hertf.   3. Robert Bestney=Elyn, da. of of Wendover, co. Bucks.   .... Living.

James Bestney of Soame, co. Cambr.=....   John Bestney.

Edward Bestney of St. Edmond's Bury.=....

Elizabeth, da. and co-heir, ux. John Barker of Bilston in Suff.   Margerett, da. and co-heir, ux. Edward Berners of Some, co. Cambr.   Anne, da. and co-heir, ux. Robert Barker of Ipswich, co. Suff.   Joane, ux. Simon Steward of Cambridge.

Blakett of Tring.

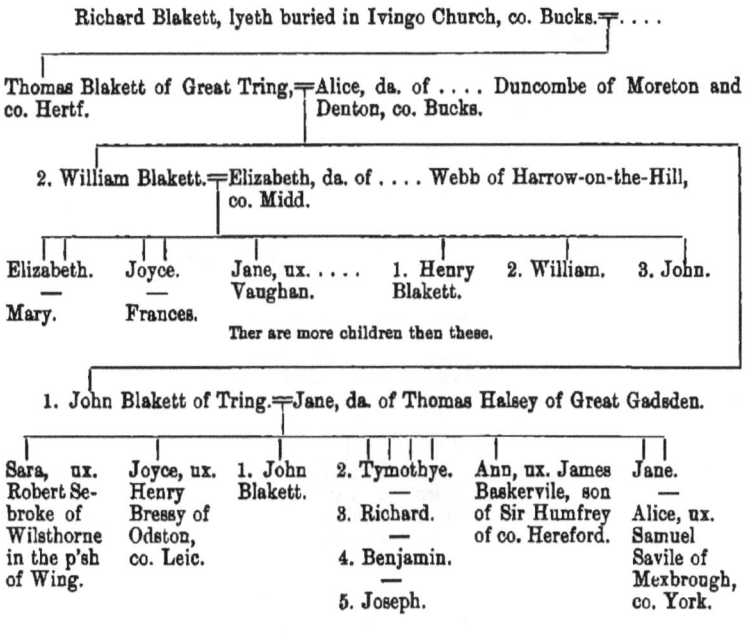

Blount of Tittenhanger.

ARMS.—Quarterly as at p. 29.

A note gives a sketch of the Arms quarterly as at p. 29, but without the bordure, and says "this uppon Sr Tho. Pope Blunt's coach."

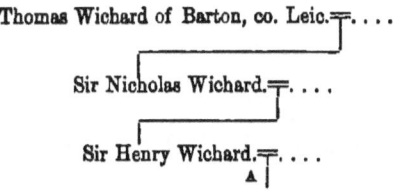

APPENDIX II.

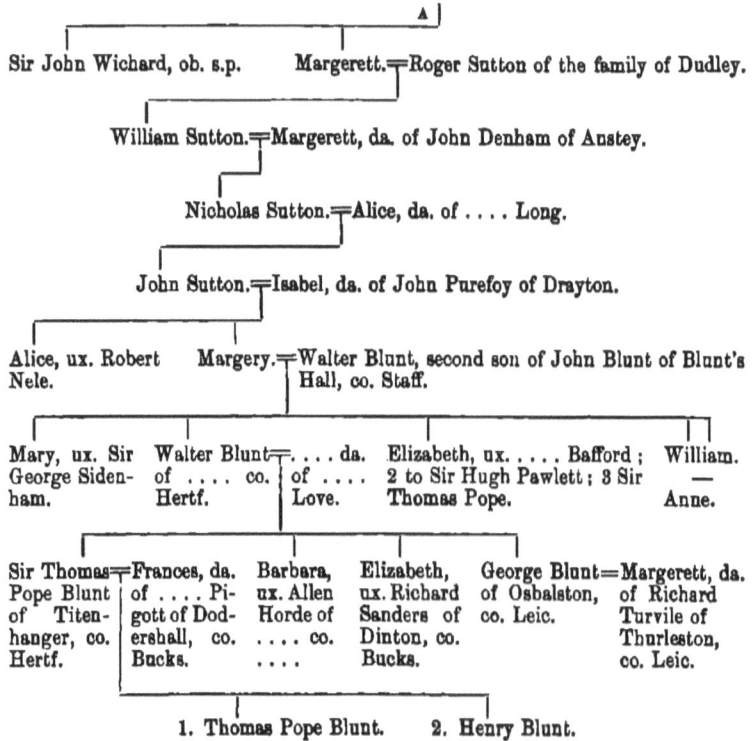

𝕭𝖗𝖆𝖉𝖇𝖊𝖗𝖞 of 𝕭𝖗𝖆𝖚𝖌𝖍𝖎𝖓.

ARMS.—*Quarterly*—1 and 4, *Sable, a chevron Ermine between three round buckles, points downwards, Argent;* 2 and 3, *Argent, a chevron between three chess-rooks Sable,* ROKELL.

Robert Bradbery of Olersett, co. Derby.=.... da. of .... Damport of Bramhall, co. Chesh.

William Bradbery of Braughing, co. Hertf.=Margerett, da. and heir of .... Rokell.

APPENDIX II.

A

- Robert Bradbery of Braughing. = ...
  - William.
- Sir Thomas Bradbery, Kt., Lord Maior of London. = Joane, da. of Denis Leech of Wellingborough, widow of Thomas Bodley of .... co. Devon, ob. in March 1623, and was bur. at St. Stephen's, Coleman Street.
- Henry.

Bristow of Sacomb.

ARMS.—*Ermine, on a fess cotised Sable, three crescents Or.*
CREST.—*Out of a crescent Or, a demi-eagle displayed Azure.*

Nicholas Bristow of Ayott St. Lawrence, Clarke of the Jewells to H. 8, E. 6, Q. Mary, and Q. Elizabeth, bur. at Ayott. = Lucey, da. of .... Barley, bur. at Ayott.

- 2. William Bristow. = ... da. of .... Battell.
- 3. Robert Bristow of Stoke, co. Northampton, *vide* Northampton.
  - Thomas.
  - Anthony.
- 4. Thomas Bristow. = ...

Nicholas Bristow of Ayott St. Lawrence, Clarke of the Jewells to Q. Elizabeth and K. James. = Margerett, da. of Sir John Botteler of Hatfield Woodhall, co. Hertf.

John Bristow, *vide* Visitation of Essex made 1634.

- Nicholas Bristow of Ayott. = Elizabeth, da. of .... Pynder.
  - 1. Nicholas Bristow.
  - 2. Edward. —
  - 3. Lytton.
- Anne, ux. John Epwell.
- Elizabeth, ux. George Clarke of Chysfeld.
  - Elizabeth, ux. Charles Thorold, son of Sir Edmond Thorold of Hough, co. Linc.
- Julian, ux. Thomas Colt of Lewes.
  - Hellen, ux. Richard Myn of Hartingfordbury.

- 2. Francis Bristow of Sacomb, co. Hertf. = Anne, da. of John Darnell of the Pipe Office, bur. at Hartingfordbury.
- Susan, ux. Thomas Langwith.
- Mary, ux. John Sell.
- 3. Philip Bristow. = Marcye, da. of .. Sell.
- Jane, ux. Nicholas Gardner.

Frances. Jane. 1. James. 2. Nicholas. 3. John. 4. Francis. Susan. Anne.

Brograve of Braughin.

ARMS.—*Quarterly of seven*—1, *Argent, three lions passant-gardant in pale Gules;* 2, *Argent, two lions passant-gardant in pale Gules,* LITLEBERY ; 3, *Barry of eight Gules and Ermine,* KIRKTON ; 4, *Quarterly Ermine and chequy Or and Gules,* WOODTHORPE ; 5, *Argent, a chevron Gules between three nails Sable,* ST. CLEERE ; 6, *Gules, a griffin segreant Or, within a bordure engrailed Argent,* BATTELL ; 7, *Argent, billitée and a chevron Sable,* LELHOLME. Over all *a crescent for difference.*
CREST.—*A demi-lion rampant-gardant Gules, ducally crowned Or.*
MOTTO.—GARDE TA FOY.

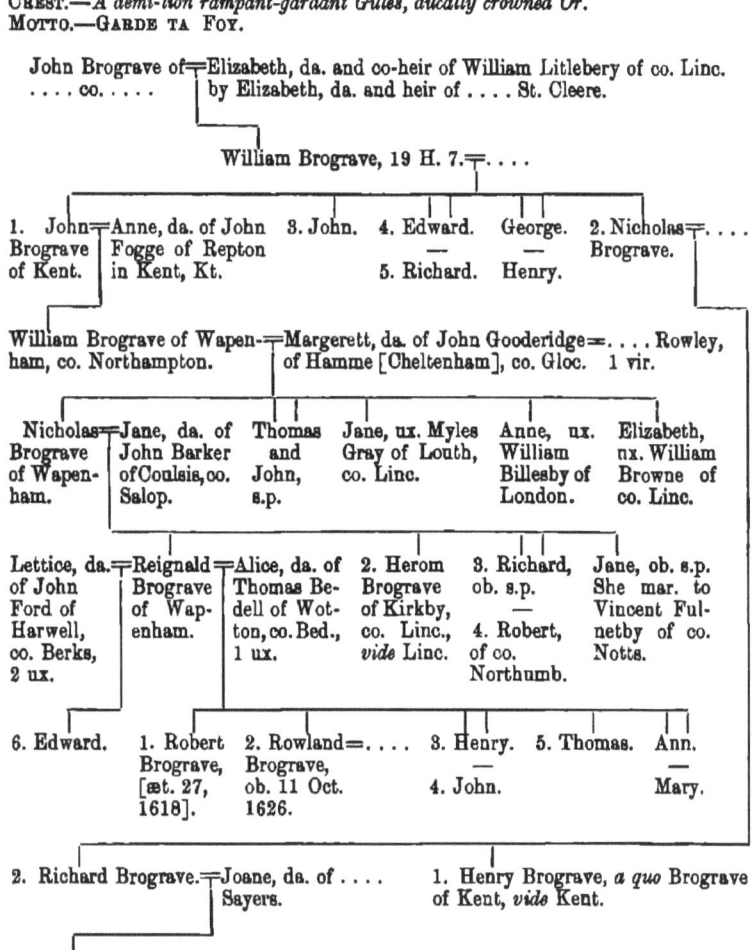

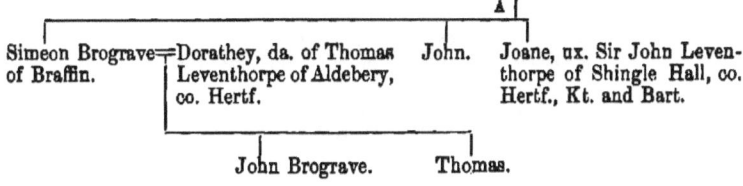

Bussye of Cheshunt.

ARMS.—*Quarterly of thirteen*—1, *Argent, three bars Sable*; 2, *Gules, three fusils in fess Argent within a bordure engrailed Or*, NEVILL; 3, *Gules, a fess dancettée Or between three escallops Ermine*, DYVE; 4, *Argent, three lions passant-gardant in pale Gules*, HUMPHYNES; 5, *Argent, billitée and a fess dancettée Sable*, DEYNCOURTE; 6, *Azure, billitée and a fess dancettée Or*, DEYNCOURTE; 7, *Ermine, five fusils in fess Gules*, EBDEN; 8, *Gules, a bend Ermine*; 9, *Gules, a chief Argent*, HERCYE; 10, *Ermine, a chief Azure*, ARCHES; 11, *Argent, on a saltire engrailed Sable nine annulets Or*, LEAKE; 12, *Sable, a castle triple-towered Or*, SOMERS; 13, *Argent, a chevron between three lozenges Sable*, STAVELEY.

CREST.—*A sea-dragon sans wings and legs, the tail nowed, all barry Argent and Sable.*

On each *an annulet for difference*.

(See the 'Visitation of co. Linc., 1562,' p. 27.)

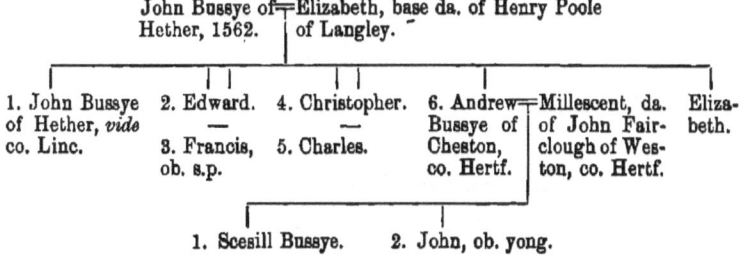

APPENDIX II.

Cade of King's Langley.

ARMS.—*Ermine, three piles engrailed Sable.*
CREST.—*A demi-cockatrice Or, combed and clawed Gules.*

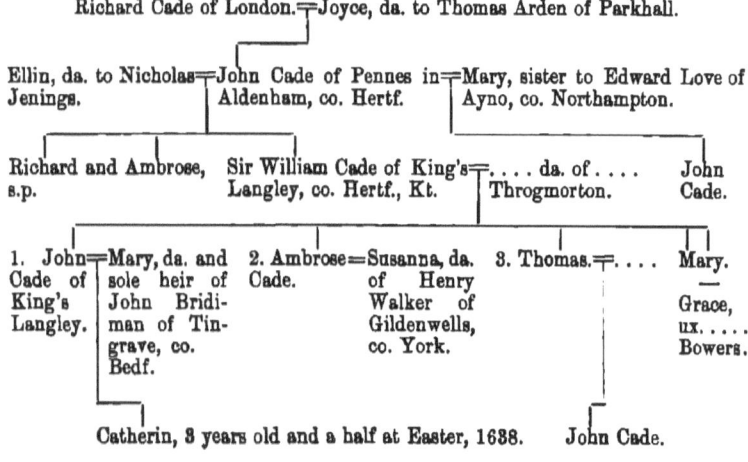

Richard Cade of London.=Joyce, da. to Thomas Arden of Parkhall.

Ellin, da. to Nicholas=John Cade of Pennes in=Mary, sister to Edward Love of
Jenings.   Aldenham, co. Hertf.   Ayno, co. Northampton.

Richard and Ambrose,   Sir William Cade of King's=. . . . da. of . . . .   John
s.p.   Langley, co. Hertf., Kt.   Throgmorton.   Cade.

1. John=Mary, da. and   2. Ambrose=Susanna, da.   3. Thomas.=. . . .   Mary.
Cade of   sole heir of   Cade.   of Henry   —
King's   John Bridi-   Walker of   Grace,
Langley.   man of Tin-   Gildenwells,   ux. . . . .
            grave, co.   co. York.   Bowers.
            Bedf.

Catherin, 3 years old and a half at Easter, 1638.   John Cade.

Caesar of Benington.

ARMS.—*Quarterly*—1 *and* 4, *Gules, three roses Argent, on a chief of the second as many more roses of the field;* 2, *Barry of six Sable and Argent, in chief three swans of the second,* ADELMAR ; 3, *Gules, three crescents Argent,* PERIENT.
CREST.—*On waves of water a dolphin naiant proper.*

Julius Cesar Delamare vel Seysar=Margery, da. of George=Michell Lock
Delamare, a Venetian by byrth,   Perient of . . . . co.   of London, 2
Docter and Phisitian to Q. Eliz.   Salop, and his heir.   vir.

Dorcas, da. of Sir Rich.=Sir Julius Cesar, Kt., M'r of the   Margerett, ux.
Martin, Kt., London,   Request to Q. Elizabeth, and M'r   Nicholas Wright
widow of Richard   of the Robes to K. James and K.   of East Mead, co.
Lusher, 1 ux.   Charles, dwelt at Totenham in 1593,   Southampton.
                    and at Hackney 1634.

A   B

APPENDIX II.

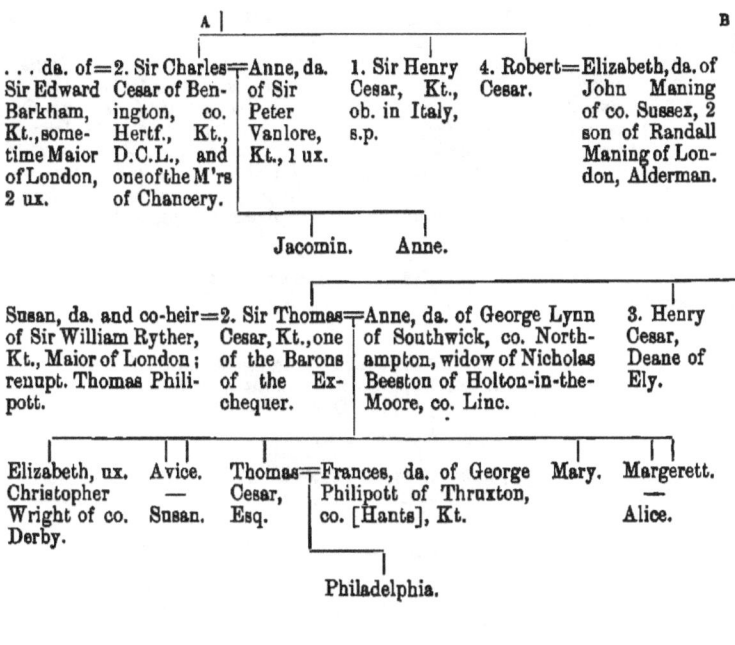

Cary of Aldenham.

ARMS.—*Quarterly of fifteen*—1, *Argent, on a bend Sable three roses of the field;* 2, *Sable, two bars nebulée Ermine;* 3, *France and England quarterly within a bordure gobony Argent and Or;* 4, *Azure, fleury and a lion rampant Gules;* 5, *Gules, three lions passant-gardant in pale Or, within a bordure Argent;* 6, *Or, two bars Gules, in chief three bezants;* 7, *Barry of ten Argent and Gules;* 8, *Gules, a fess between six cross-crosslets Or;* 9, *Chequy Or and Azure, a chevron Ermine;* 10, *Or, two bars Gules;* 11, *Lozengy Or and Azure within a bordure Gules bezantée;* 12, *Gules, a chevron between ten crosses patée Argent;* 13, *Gules, a lion passant-gardant Argent, ducally crowned Or;* 14, *Or, a fess between two chevrons Sable;* 15, *Argent, a chevron Gules.*

CREST.—*A swan, wings elevated Argent, legged Sable, beaked Gules.*
MOTTO.—FIDE ET AMICITIA.

Thus set out at the Funerall of Sir Adolphus Cary by *Clarenceux* Camden.

ANOTHER SHIELD.—*Quarterly of thirty-four*—1 *and* 34, 5, 6, 7, 8, 9, 12, 13, 15, 16, 17, 26, 27, 28, *and* 32, *as* 1, 2, 3, 4, 5, 6, 7, 8, 10, 11, 9, 12, 14, 13, *and* 15 *above;* 2, *Or, three piles Azure;* 3, *Gules, a fess between three crescents*

APPENDIX II. 135

Argent; 4, Azure, a chevron between three pears Or; 10, Barry of six Or and Azure, a bend Gules; 11, Gules, two bends wavy Or; 14, Per pale Or and Gules, three roundles counterchanged; 18, Argent, two bars Gules; 19, Quarterly Or and Gules, a bordure Vair; 20, Or, a cross Gules, a label of three points Azure; 21, Per pale Or and Vert, a lion rampant Gules; 22, Or, six lions rampant Sable, two, two, and two; 23, Sable, three garbs Argent; 24, Argent, a maunch Gules; 25, Argent, a lion rampant Azure, a chief Gules; 29, Argent, three eagles displayed Gules, beaked and legged Or; 30, Or, three bars Gules; 31, Argent, two lions passant in pale Argent, ducally crowned Or; 33, Argent, on a canton Azure a cinquefoil Or.
MOTTO.—IN UTROQUE FIDELIS.

Thus set out for Viscount Faulkland, when hee went Lord Deputy into Ireland, by *Clarenceux* Camden.

Thomas Cary of Chilton, co. Devon, Esq., 2 son of Sir William. =Margerett, da. and co-heir of Sir Robert Spencer by .... his wife, da. and heir of .... Duke of Somersett.

1. John Cary of Hackney, co. Midd. =Martha, da. of Edmond Denny of the City of Norwich, sister of Sir Anthony Denny, Kt. She was bur. at Hackney.

Wymond Cary of Hackney.=....

Sir Edward Cary, Kt.,=Catherin, da. of M'r of the Jewell Howse. Sir Henry Knevett, Kt., widow of Henry, Lord Pagett.

Elizabeth, ux. George Dacres of Cheshunt, co. Hertf.

Prudence, ux. Anthony Bridges of Westham in Essex.

Elizabeth, ux. John Savill of co. York.

Catherin, ux. Sir Henry Longvile of Wolverton, co. Bucks, Kt.

Muriell, ux. Sir Thomas Compton, Kt.

Anne, ux. Sir Francis Leeke of Sutton, co. Derby, Kt.

Frances, 1 ux. Rafe Bashe of Stansted, co. Hertf., Esq.; 2 to Sir George Manners of co. Derby, Kt., Erle of Rutland.

Anne, ux. Sir Edward Barrett of Avely, co. Essex, Kt., Lord Newburgh in Scotland.

Sir Adolphus Cary, Kt., ob. s.p., bur. at Aldenham. =Anne, da. and co-heir of Sir Robert Corbett of Morton Corbett, co. Salop, Kt.

Sir Henry Cary, Kt., Viscount Faulkland in Scotland, ob. at Theobalds, broke his leg by a fall. =Elizabeth, da. and co-heir of Sir Lawrance Tanfeld, Kt., Lord Chief Baron of the Exchequer.

Catherin.   Victoria.   1. Lucius Cary.   2. Lawrance.   Anne.   Elizabeth.
3. Edward.

APPENDIX II.

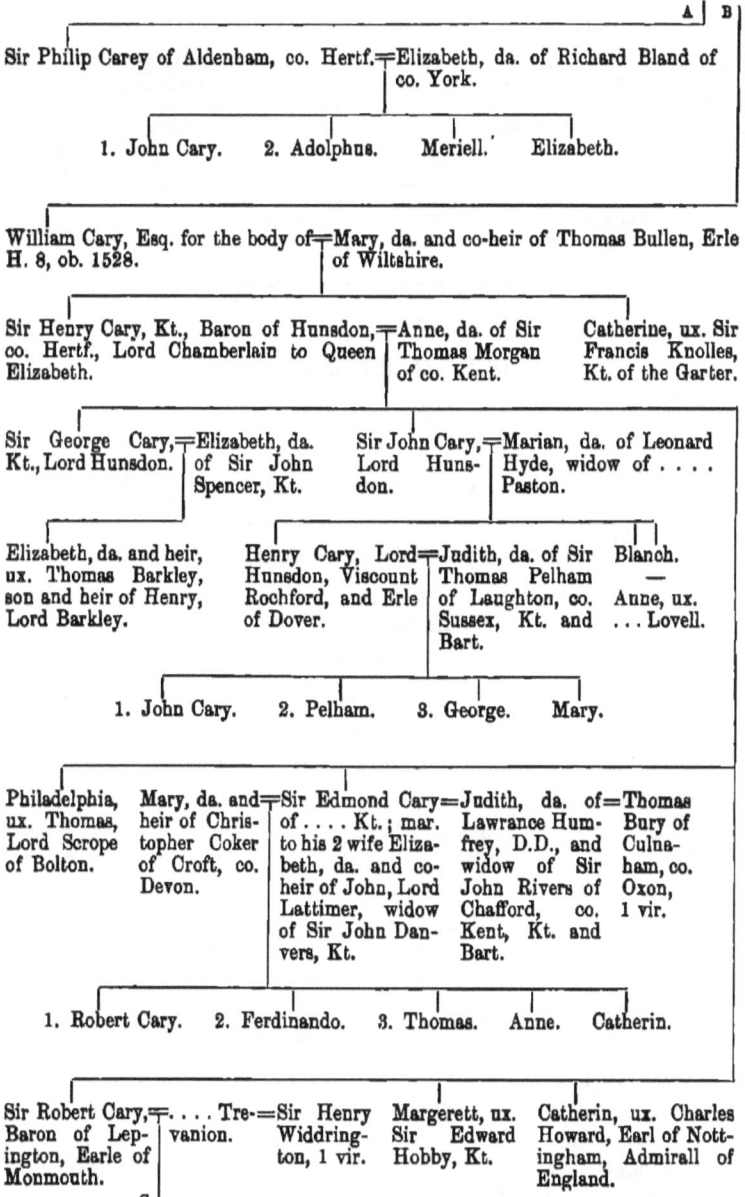

Sir Philip Carey of Aldenham, co. Hertf.=Elizabeth, da. of Richard Bland of co. York.

1. John Cary. 2. Adolphus. Meriell. Elizabeth.

William Cary, Esq. for the body of=Mary, da. and co-heir of Thomas Bullen, Erle
H. 8, ob. 1528. of Wiltshire.

Sir Henry Cary, Kt., Baron of Hunsdon,=Anne, da. of Sir   Catherine, ux. Sir
co. Hertf., Lord Chamberlain to Queen Thomas Morgan   Francis Knolles,
Elizabeth.   of co. Kent.   Kt. of the Garter.

Sir George Cary,=Elizabeth, da.   Sir John Cary,=Marian, da. of Leonard
Kt., Lord Hunsdon. of Sir John   Lord Huns-   Hyde, widow of ....
                Spencer, Kt.   don.   Paston.

Elizabeth, da. and heir, Henry Cary, Lord=Judith, da. of Sir   Blanch.
ux. Thomas Barkley,   Hunsdon, Viscount Thomas Pelham   —
son and heir of Henry,   Rochford, and Erle of Laughton, co.   Anne, ux.
Lord Barkley.   of Dover.   Sussex, Kt. and   ... Lovell.
                                           Bart.

1. John Cary. 2. Pelham. 3. George. Mary.

Philadelphia, Mary, da. and=Sir Edmond Cary=Judith, da. of=Thomas
ux. Thomas,   heir of Chris- of .... Kt.; mar. Lawrance Hum- Bury of
Lord Scrope   topher Coker to his 2 wife Eliza- frey, D.D., and Culna-
of Bolton.   of Croft, co. beth, da. and co- widow of Sir   ham, co.
               Devon.   heir of John, Lord John Rivers of Oxon,
                              Lattimer, widow   Chafford, co.   1 vir.
                              of Sir John Dan- Kent, Kt. and
                              vers, Kt.   Bart.

1. Robert Cary. 2. Ferdinando. 3. Thomas. Anne. Catherin.

Sir Robert Cary,=.... Tre-=Sir Henry   Margerett, ux. Catherin, ux. Charles
Baron of Lep-   vanion.   Widdring-   Sir Edward   Howard, Earl of Nott-
ington, Earle of   ton, 1 vir. Hobby, Kt.   ingham, Admirall of
Monmouth.   England.

APPENDIX II.

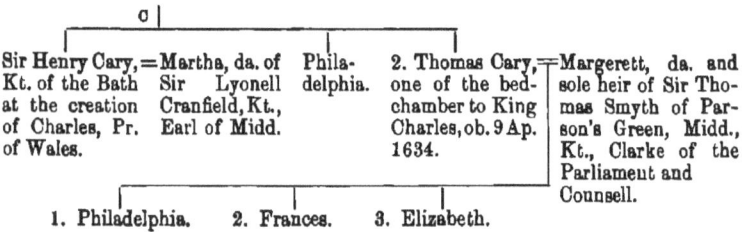

| Sir Henry Cary, Kt. of the Bath at the creation of Charles, Pr. of Wales. | = Martha, da. of Sir Lyonell Cranfield, Kt., Earl of Midd. | Philadelphia. | 2. Thomas Cary, one of the bedchamber to King Charles, ob. 9 Ap. 1634. | = Margerett, da. and sole heir of Sir Thomas Smyth of Parson's Green, Midd., Kt., Clarke of the Parliament and Counsell. |

1. Philadelphia.   2. Frances.   3. Elizabeth.

Chamber of Barkway.

William Chamber of Holme in Holdernes, *temp.* E. 1.=....

John Chamber, son and heir of William, 11 E. 2.=....

.... Chamber of Wolstie Castell, co. Cumb., 11 E. 3.=....

.... Chamber, *temp.* R. 2.=....

William Chamber of Wolstie Castell, 5 H. 4.=Margerett.

Richard Chamber of Milward and Wolstie Castell.=....

2. William Chamber of Royston, co. Hertf.,=....   Thomas Chamber of Wolstie
and had by 2 wives 22 children.   Castell, *vide* Cumberland.

Michell Chamber.=....   Richard Chamber of=Audrey, da. of Andrew Sterne
                      Barkway, co. Hertf. | of co. Cambr.

Simon=Catherin,   Jervas.   .... da. of=Robert Chamber=Ann, da. of
Chamber. da. of   .... Gost-   of Barkway.   Thomas Lee
       Thomas   wick of ....   of St. Julian's.
       Jervis of   co. Bedf., 1
       co. Leic.   ux.

Thomas Chamber=Anne, da. of Cornelius   Robert   Alexander and Richard,
of Barkway.   Harntals,   widdow of   and   ob. s.p.
                  Captaine Whitstock.   Frances,
                                           ob. s.p.

138   APPENDIX II.

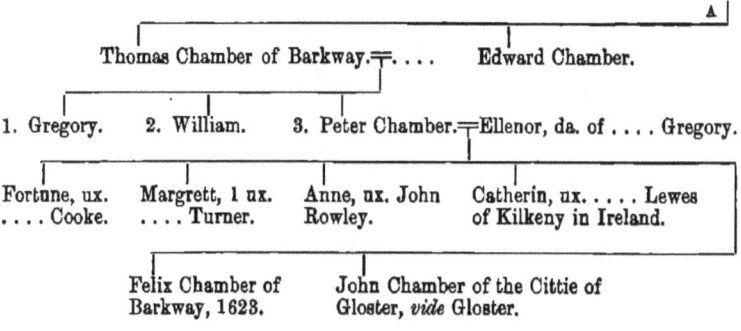

Childe of North Mims.

ARMS.—*Gules, a chevron engrailed Ermine between three eagles close Argent.*
CREST.—*On a mound Vert an eagle with wings expanded Argent, in the beak a snake proper.*

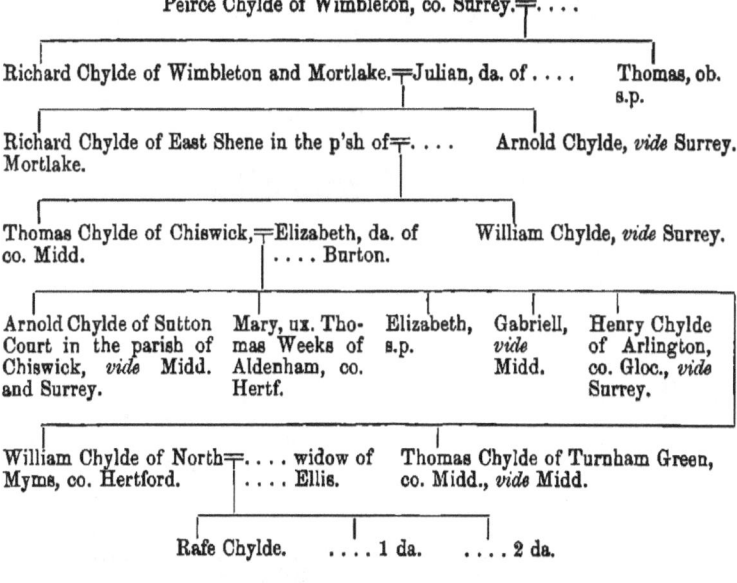

APPENDIX II.   139

Conyers of Barnet.

ARMS.—*Azure, a maunch or, in chief an annulet Argent for difference.*
CREST.—*A wing Gules.*

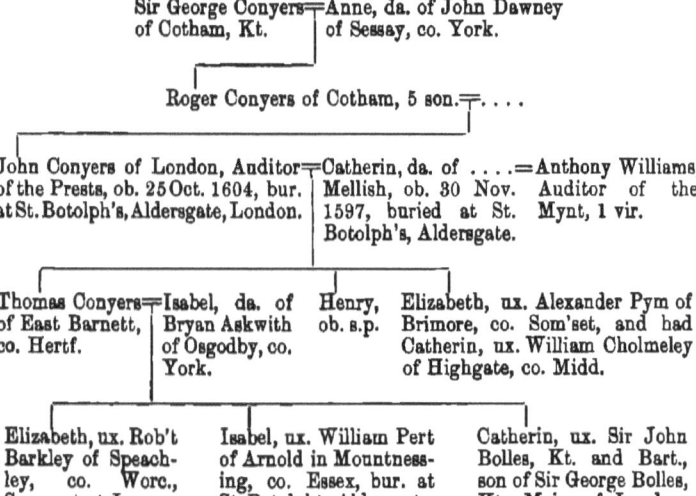

Sir George Conyers=Anne, da. of John Dawney
of Cotham, Kt.   of Sessay, co. York.

Roger Conyers of Cotham, 5 son.=....

John Conyers of London, Auditor=Catherin, da. of ....=Anthony Williams,
of the Prests, ob. 25 Oct. 1604, bur. Mellish, ob. 30 Nov. Auditor of the
at St. Botolph's, Aldersgate, London. 1597, buried at St. Mynt, 1 vir.
                                       Botolph's, Aldersgate.

Thomas Conyers=Isabel, da. of   Henry,   Elizabeth, ux. Alexander Pym of
of East Barnett, Bryan Askwith ob. s.p. Brimore, co. Som'set, and had
co. Hertf.   of Osgodby, co.   Catherin, ux. William Cholmeley
                  York.   of Highgate, co. Midd.

Elizabeth, ux. Rob't   Isabel, ux. William Pert   Catherin, ux. Sir John
Barkley of Speach-   of Arnold in Mountness-   Bolles, Kt. and Bart.,
ley,   co.   Worc.,   ing, co. Essex, bur. at   son of Sir George Bolles,
Sergeant-at-Law.   St. Botolph's, Aldersgate.   Kt., Maior of London.

Docwra of Putteridge.

ARMS.—*Sable, a chevron engrailed Argent, between three plates each charged with a pale Gules.*
CREST.—*A demi-lion rampant Sable, guttée d'eau, holding a plate charged with a pale Gules.*

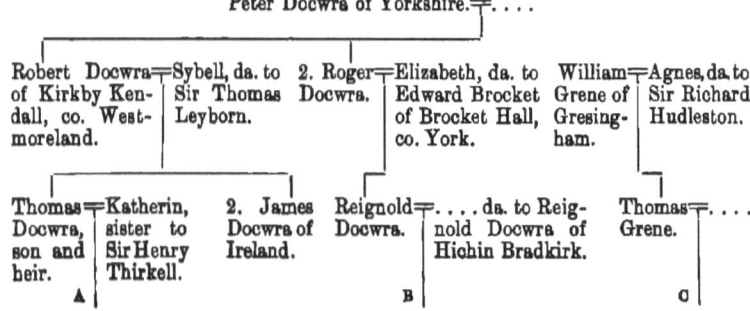

Peter Docwra of Yorkshire.=....

Robert Docwra=Sybell, da. to   2. Roger=Elizabeth, da. to   William=Agnes, da. to
of Kirkby Ken- Sir Thomas   Docwra. Edward Brocket   Grene of Sir Richard
dall, co. West- Leyborn.   of Brocket Hall,   Gresing- Hudleston.
moreland.   co. York.   ham.

Thomas=Katherin,   2. James   Reignold=....da. to Reig-   Thomas=....
Docwra, sister to Docwra of   Docwra. nold Docwra of   Grene.
son and Sir Henry Ireland.   Hichin Bradkirk.
heir.   Thirkell.
  A   B   C

APPENDIX II.

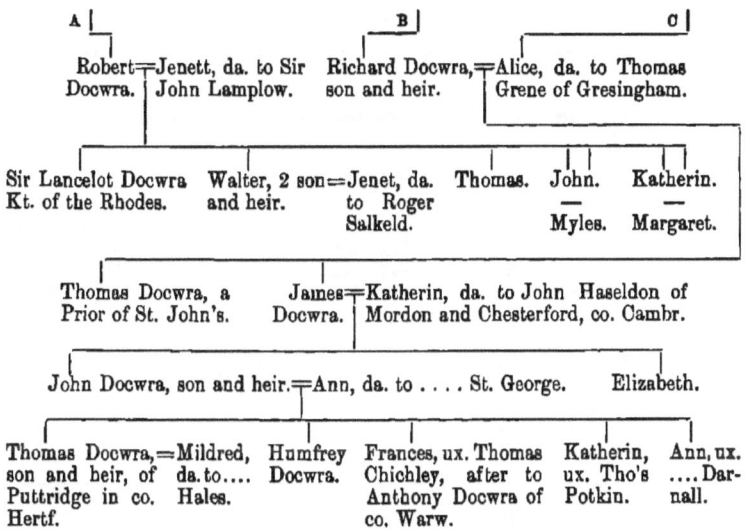

Dolman of Newnham.

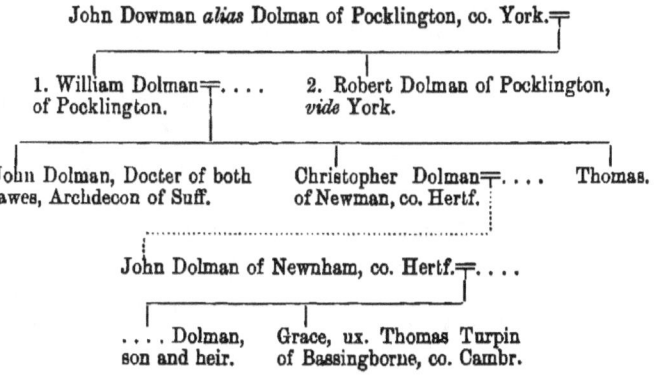

APPENDIX II. 141

Elmer alias Aylmer of Much Hadham.

ARMS.—*Argent, a cross Sable between three sea-aylets of the second, beaked and legged Gules.*

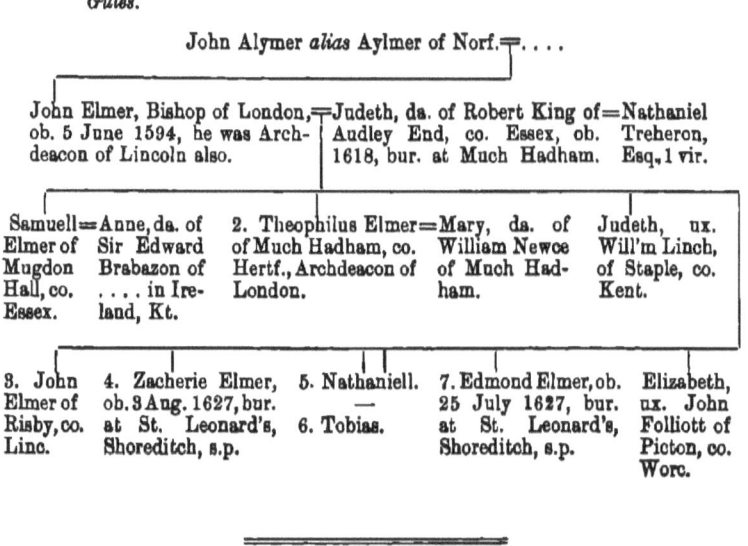

Ferrers of Punsborne.

ARMS.—*Quarterly—1, Gules, seven mascles conjoined, 3, 3, 1, Or, a label of three points Azure, bezantée ; 2, Vert, eight spears interlaced in saltire Or barbed Argent, BREAKSPEARE ; 3, Azure, three bars-gemelles Argent, BENSTED ; 4, Argent, two bars Azure, on a canton of the second a tun Gules, KNIGHTON.*
CREST.—*A unicorn trottant Ermine armed and maned Or, a label of three points as in the arms.*

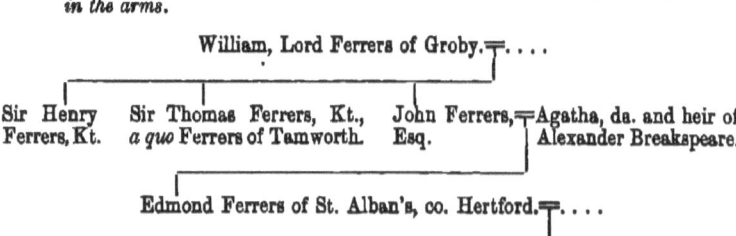

APPENDIX II.

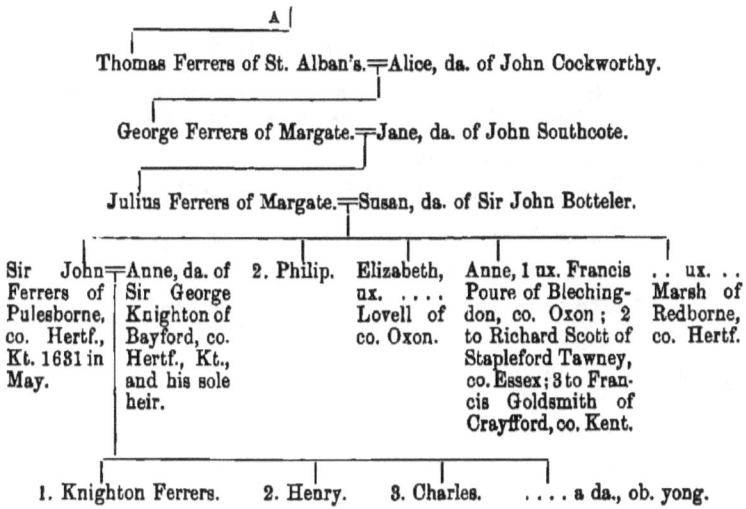

Thomas Ferrers of St. Alban's.=Alice, da. of John Cockworthy.

George Ferrers of Margate.=Jane, da. of John Southcote.

Julius Ferrers of Margate.=Susan, da. of Sir John Botteler.

| Sir John Ferrers of Pulesborne, co. Hertf., Kt. 1631 in May. | =Anne, da. of Sir George Knighton of Bayford, co. Hertf., Kt., and his sole heir. | 2. Philip. | Elizabeth, ux. .... Lovell of co. Oxon. | Anne, 1 ux. Francis Poure of Blechingdon, co. Oxon; 2 to Richard Scott of Stapleford Tawney, co. Essex; 3 to Francis Goldsmith of Crayfford, co. Kent. | .. ux. .. Marsh of Redborne, co. Hertf. |

1. Knighton Ferrers. 2. Henry. 3. Charles. .... a da., ob. yong.

Finch of St. Michael's.

This descent is entred in the Visitation of Surrey made in a° 1623.

John Finch of Redborne,=Christian, da. of .... Peacock of Finchley, co. Hertf. | co. Midd.

Thomas Finch of St. Michell's, neare St. Alban's, co. Hertf., 1623. =Dorathey, da. of .... Brewer of Markett, co. Hertf.   Richard Finch of Redborne.   Robert Finch of Redborne.

William Finch of St. Alban's.   Walter Finch of Croydon, co. Surrey, 1623.   Francis Finch of London.   Elizabeth.   Anne.

APPENDIX II.

Forster of Hunsdon.

ARMS.—*Quarterly*—1 and 4, *Argent, a chevron Vert between three bugle-horns Sable; 2 and 3, Argent, on a bend Sable three martlets Or; over all a crescent for difference.*
CREST.—*A buck statant Sable, attired Or.*
This Creast granted by W'm Camden, *Clarenceux*, 27 of Feb. 1604.

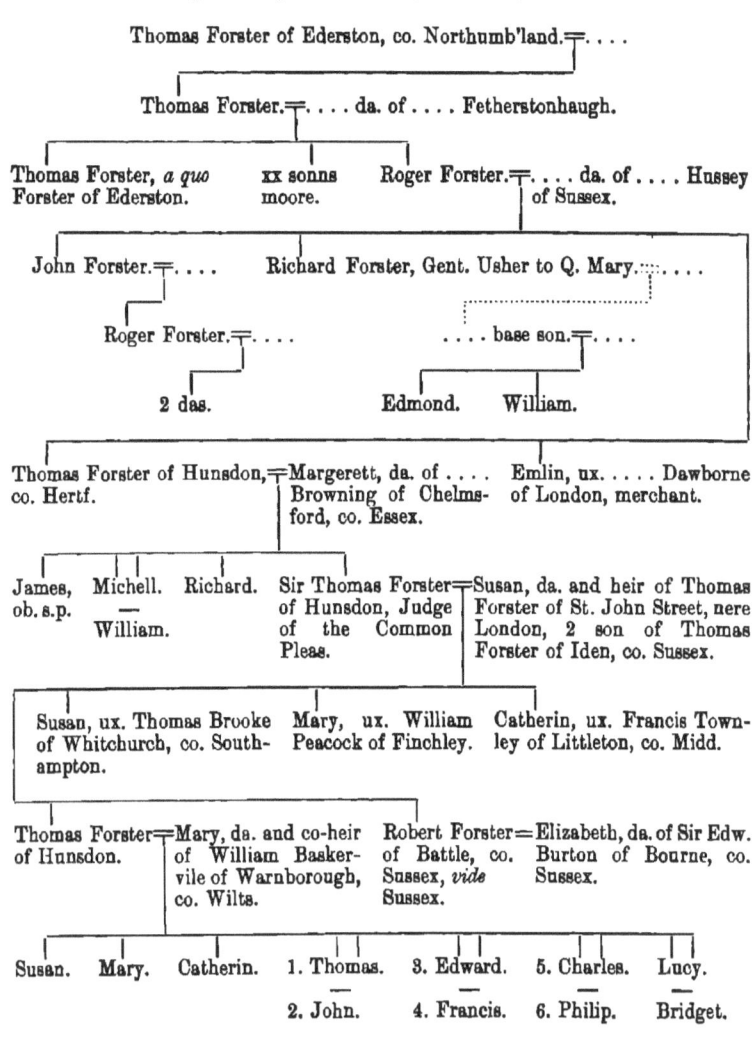

Thomas Forster of Ederston, co. Northumb'land.=....

    Thomas Forster.=.... da. of .... Fetherstonhaugh.

Thomas Forster, *a quo* Forster of Ederston.   xx sonns moore.   Roger Forster.=.... da. of .... Hussey of Sussex.

John Forster.=....   Richard Forster, Gent. Usher to Q. Mary.=....

Roger Forster.=....   .... base son.=....

2 das.   Edmond.   William.

Thomas Forster of Hunsdon,=Margerett, da. of ....   Emlin, ux. .... Dawborne
co. Hertf.   Browning of Chelms-   of London, merchant.
                       ford, co. Essex.

James, Michell. Richard.   Sir Thomas Forster=Susan, da. and heir of Thomas
ob. s.p.   —   of Hunsdon, Judge   Forster of St. John Street, nere
       William.   of the Common   London, 2 son of Thomas
                        Pleas.   Forster of Iden, co. Sussex.

Susan, ux. Thomas Brooke   Mary, ux. William   Catherin, ux. Francis Town-
of Whitchurch, co. South-   Peacock of Finchley.   ley of Littleton, co. Midd.
ampton.

Thomas Forster=Mary, da. and co-heir   Robert Forster=Elizabeth, da. of Sir Edw.
of Hunsdon.   of William Basker-   of Battle, co.   Burton of Bourne, co.
            vile of Warnborough,   Sussex, *vide*   Sussex.
            co. Wilts.   Sussex.

Susan.   Mary.   Catherin.   1. Thomas.   3. Edward.   5. Charles.   Lucy.
                               2. John.   4. Francis.   6. Philip.   Bridget.

Fotherley of Rickmansworth.

ARMS.—*Quarterly*—1 *and* 4, *Gules, a fess dancettée Or ;* 2 *and* 3, *Argent, a fess between three wolves' heads erased Sable,* HOUSE.
CREST.—*The two halves of a broken spear in saltire Or.*

A guifte of the crest to this coate by Pattent to Thomas Fotherley of Rickmansworth in com. Hertford, sonn of Thomas, dated the 6 of March 1623, p' Ri. St. George, *Clarenceux.*

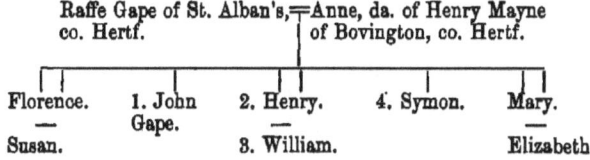

Thomas Fotherley of Rick-=Tabitha, da. and heir of Giles
mansworth, co. Hertf. | House of co. Essex.

Thomas Fotherley of Rickmansworth.

Gape of St. Alban's.

Raffe Gape of St. Alban's,=Anne, da. of Henry Mayne
co. Hertf. | of Bovington, co. Hertf.

| Florence. | 1. John Gape. | 2. Henry. | 4. Symon. | Mary. |
| Susan. | | 3. William. | | Elizabeth. |

Garrard of Wheathampsted.

ARMS.—*Quarterly*—1 *and* 4, *Argent, on a fess Sable a lion passant of the field ;* 2 *and* 3, *Argent, a chevron between three crescents Azure,* NETHERMYLL.
CREST.—*A leopard sejant proper.*

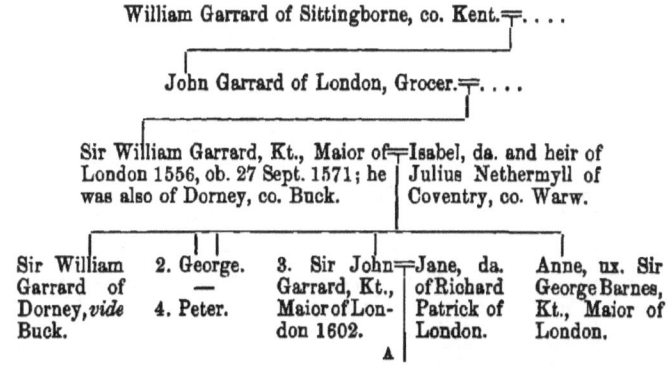

William Garrard of Sittingborne, co. Kent.=....

John Garrard of London, Grocer.=....

Sir William Garrard, Kt., Maior of=Isabel, da. and heir of
London 1556, ob. 27 Sept. 1571; he | Julius Nethermyll of
was also of Dorney, co. Buck. | Coventry, co. Warw.

| Sir William Garrard of Dorney, *vide* Buck. | 2. George. — 4. Peter. | 3. Sir John Garrard, Kt., Maior of London 1602. | =Jane, da. of Richard Patrick of London. | Anne, ux. Sir George Barnes, Kt., Maior of London. |

▲

APPENDIX II.

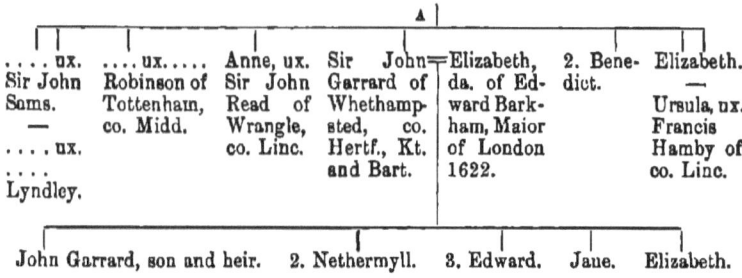

| .... ux. Sir John Soms. — .... ux. .... Lyndley. | .... ux. Robinson of Tottenham, co. Midd. | Anne, ux. Sir John Read of Wrangle, co. Linc. | Sir John Garrard of Whethampsted, co. Hertf., Kt. and Bart. | =Elizabeth, da. of Edward Barkham, Maior of London 1622. | 2. Benedict. | Elizabeth. — Ursula, ux. Francis Hamby of co. Linc. |

John Garrard, son and heir.   2. Nethermyll.   3. Edward.   Jane.   Elizabeth.

Goodman of Rushdon.

ARMS.—*Quarterly of six*—1, *Gyronny of eight Ermine and Sable, a spread eagle Or;* 2, *Azure, a chevron between three annulets Argent;* 3, *Argent, a chevron between three cross-crosslets Sable, a crescent for difference;* 4, *Gules, a fess and in chief three crescents Argent;* 5, *Azure, a fess dancettée between three martlets Or;* 6, *Sable, two lions passant in pale Argent.*

CREST.—*Out of a mural coronet a woman proper, habited Azure, crined Or, in the dexter hand a rose Gules stalked and leaved Vert.*

John Warton.=Agnes, da. of William de Millington.

Richard Warton.=....

Hugh Goodman of Chester, 31 H. 6.=Emme, da. and heir.

William Goodman, 31 H. 6.=....

Richard Goodman, 13 H. 7, 1497.=....

Hamlet Goodman,=.... da. and heir of John Southworth, Alderman of 1504.   Chester.

William Goodman of Chester, 1536.=Alice, da. of Rafe Grosvenor of Chester.   Rafe.

| 1. Adam Goodman, 1542.=.... | 2. John Goodman.=Alice, da. of .... Sampson. | 3. Rafe Goodman, 1550. |

| William Goodman, 1580. A | =Margerett, da. of Sir William Brereton, Kt. | Christopher Goodman, a Divine. B | =.... | William Goodman of Rushdon, co. Hertf. C | =Anne, da. and heir of .... Litlebery. |

U

APPENDIX II.

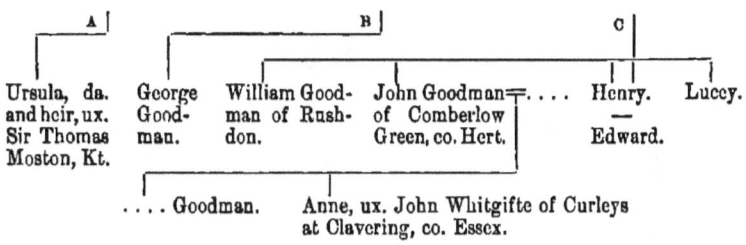

A		B		C	
Ursula, da. and heir, ux. Sir Thomas Moston, Kt.	George Goodman.	William Goodman of Rushdon.	John Goodman=.... of Comberlow Green, co. Hertf.	Henry. Edward.	Lucey.

.... Goodman.   Anne, ux. John Whitgifte of Curleys at Clavering, co. Essex.

Harvy of Shenley.

Richard Harvy of Kimolton, co. Hunt., 4 son=.... to John Harvy of Staffordshire.

Richard Harvy of Pottrels in the=Christian, cosin and sole heir to Sir John Turberp'sh of Shenley, co. Hertf., Esq. | vile, Kt., Treasurer of Callice.

| Catharin, ux. Charles Smyth, Grome of the Robes. | Jane, ux. John Redwood of Colney Street, co. Hertf. | Margery, ux. Denys Samors, Clerk of the Statute. | Isabel, ux. William Peacock of London, Lether Seller. | Elizabeth, ux. Francis Pigott, Master Cook to Q. Elizabeth. |

2. Richard=.... Harvy.

Ann, da. to ...=Thomas Harvy, Foot-=Kinbury, da. to ..
Webb of Mic- | man to Q. Elizabeth; | Cottington, relict
ham in Surrey, | mar. to his 3 wife | of Tho's Wheler of
relict of William | Agnes, widow to .... | London, 3 ux. [*sic*],
Steverton of | Prescot of co. Linc., | s.p.
Kingston, 1 ux., | s.p.
s.p.

Elizabeth, ux. John Huchin of London, Lether Seller.

John Harvey of Pottrels.=Margery, da. to John Coningsby of North Myms.

| Henry=Mary, da. to .... Harvy, | Bishop of London, 1597. | Linnen Draper. | 2. John. — 3. Dennys. | William Smyth,=Christian. co. Nott. | Elizabeth. |

Thomas.   Margerett, da. and heir, 1597.

APPENDIX II.

Jennings of Sandridge.

ARMS.—*Quarterly of nine*—1, *Argent, on a fess Gules three bezants*; 2, *Azure, two bars Or each charged with three martlets Gules, an annulet of the second for difference*, BURDETT; 3, *Gules, a bull's head cabossed argent armed Or*, DUSTON; 4, *Gules, on a chevron couple-closed Argent three lions rampant of the field*, ROWLETT; 5, *Paly of six Argent and Gules, a bordure engrailed Azure, on a canton of the second a spur Or*, KNIGHT; 6, *Quarterly per fess indented Argent and Sable, in the first and third quarters a bugle-horn Sable*, FOSTER; 7, *Azure, three peacocks' heads Argent beaked Or*, WARING; 8, *Gules, on a fess Or between three doves Argent beaked and legged Gules as many fleurs-de-lis Azure*, PENINGTON; 9, *Azure, a lion rampant Or within a bordure engrailed Gules, a canton of the second*, NEVILL.

[In the Visitation of 1634 the name of Sir John Jennings, Kt. of the Bath, occurs with these arms, marshalled thus: 1, 3, 4, 5, 6, 2, 7, 8, 9, but no pedigree is given.]

CREST.—*A demi-lion rampant erased Or, holding erect a mace Argent, the head bezantée.*

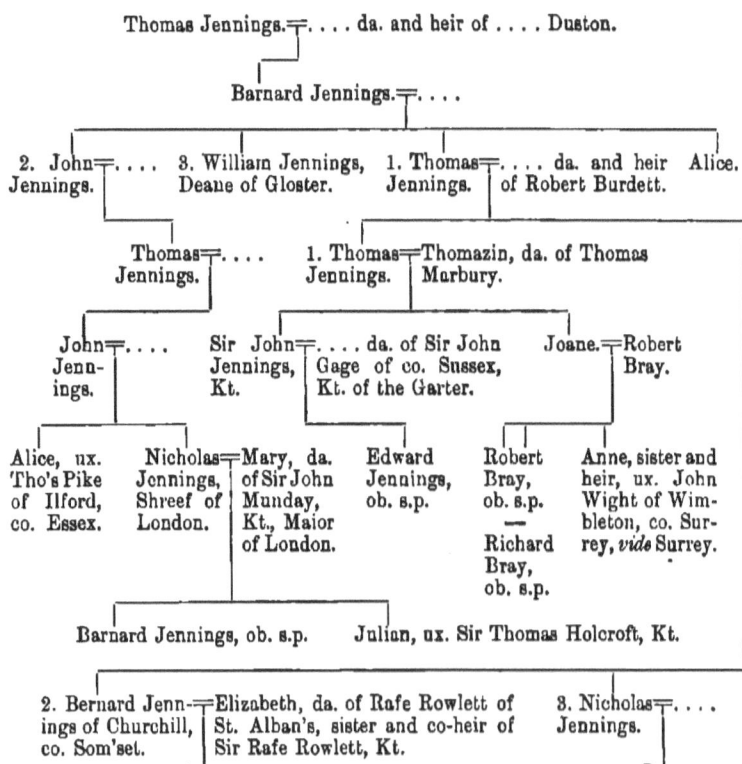

148   APPENDIX II.

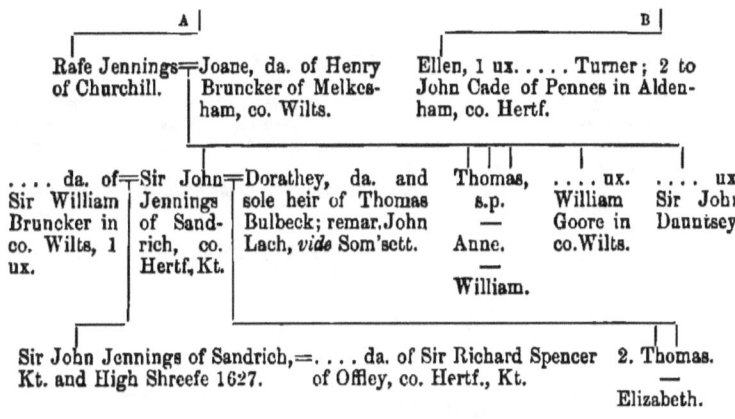

Kent of Aston.

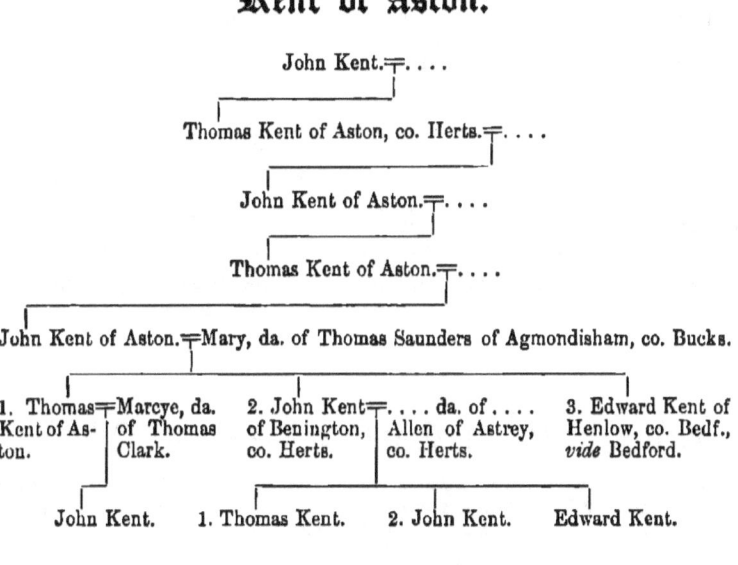

APPENDIX II.

Lee of Sopwell.

ARMS.—*Quarterly*—1 *and* 4, *Per chevron Or and Gules, in chief two lions combatant Sable* ; 2, *Gules, estoilée and three swords fessways in pale Or, the point of the middle sword toward the dexter side ;* 3, *Sable, three pales Ermine, on a canton Argent a lion rampant Azure.*
CREST.—*An arm in armour couped and embowed proper, the hand grasping a sword Or, the blade emitting " fier."*

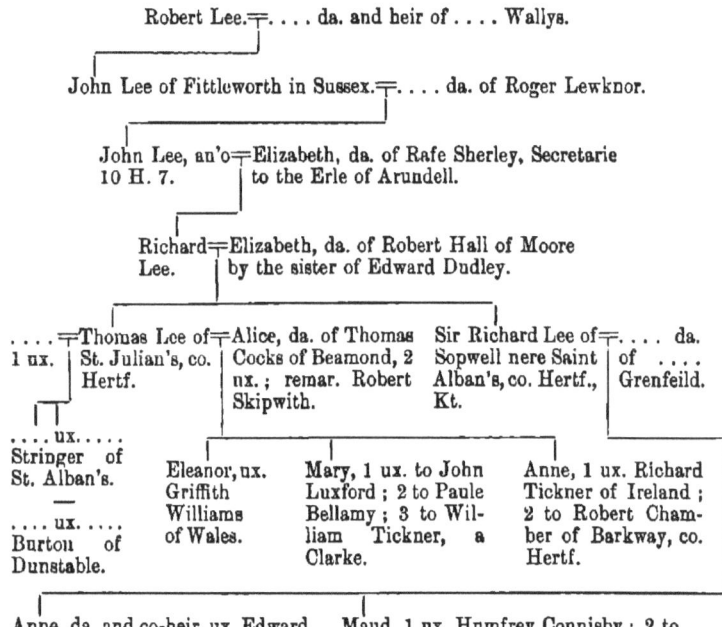

Robert Lee.=.... da. and heir of .... Wallys.

John Lee of Fittleworth in Sussex.=.... da. of Roger Lewknor.

John Lee, an'o=Elizabeth, da. of Rafe Sherley, Secretarie
10 H. 7. to the Erle of Arundell.

Richard=Elizabeth, da. of Robert Hall of Moore
Lee. by the sister of Edward Dudley.

....=Thomas Lee of=Alice, da. of Thomas Sir Richard Lee of=.... da.
1 ux. | St. Julian's, co. | Cocks of Beamond, 2 Sopwell nere Saint | of ....
      | Hertf. | ux.; remar. Robert   Alban's, co. Hertf., | Grenfeild.
                            Skipwith.   Kt.

.... ux. ....
Stringer of
St. Alban's.   Eleanor, ux.   Mary, 1 ux. to John   Anne, 1 ux. Richard
—   Griffith   Luxford ; 2 to Paule   Tickner of Ireland ;
.... ux. ....   Williams   Bellamy ; 3 to Wil-   2 to Robert Cham-
Burton of   of Wales.   liam Tickner, a   ber of Barkway, co.
Dunstable.   Clarke.   Hertf.

Anne, da. and co-heir, ux. Edward   Maud, 1 ux. Humfrey Connisby ; 2 to
Sadler of Temple, co. Hertf.   Raphe Pemberton, dyed s.p.

Leventhorpe of Shingle Hall and Albery.

ARMS.—*Quarterly*—1 *and* 4, *Argent, a bend gobony Gules and Sable, cotised of the second ;* 2, *Argent, a fess between three fleurs-de-lis Gules ;* 3, *Sable, a lion rampant Argent, ducally crowned Or, within a bordure engrailed of the last. On an inescutcheon the badge of Ulster.*
CREST.—*An old man's head side-faced proper, crined " Grey."*

John Leventhorpe.=[Mary], da. of [William] Clovell of Hanfield [West
                  Hanningfield], co. Essex.
A

APPENDIX II.

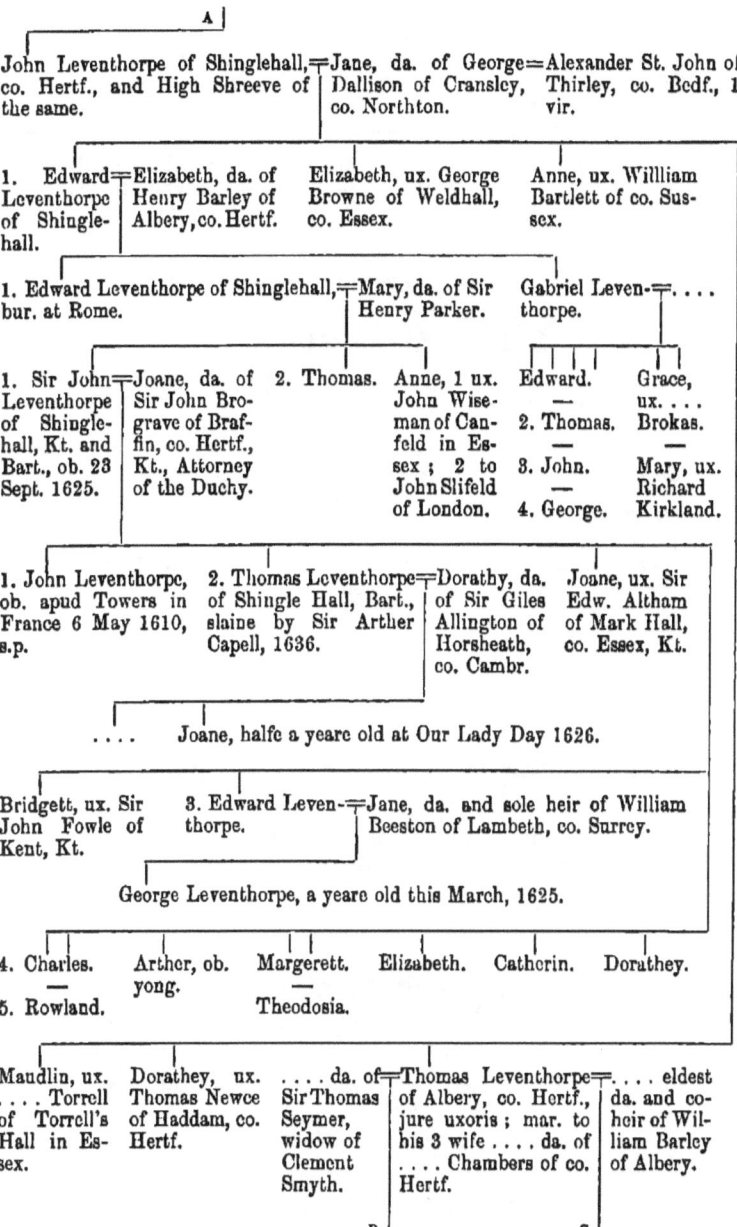

A |

John Leventhorpe of Shinglehall,⹀Jane, da. of George═Alexander St. John of
co. Hertf., and High Shreeve of | Dallison of Cransley, | Thirley, co. Bedf., 1
the same. | co. Northton. | vir.

1. Edward⹀Elizabeth, da. of | Elizabeth, ux. George | Anne, ux. Willliam
Leventhorpe | Henry Barley of | Browne of Weldhall, | Bartlett of co. Sus-
of Shingle- | Albery, co. Hertf. | co. Essex. | sex.
hall.

1. Edward Leventhorpe of Shinglehall,⹀Mary, da. of Sir | Gabriel Leven-⹀....
bur. at Rome. | Henry Parker. | thorpe.

1. Sir John⹀Joane, da. of 2. Thomas. Anne, 1 ux. Edward. Grace,
Leventhorpe | Sir John Bro- | John Wise- | — | ux. ...
of Shingle- | grave of Braf- | man of Can- | 2. Thomas. | Brokas.
hall, Kt. and | fin, co. Hertf., | feld in Es- | — |
Bart., ob. 23 | Kt., Attorney | sex ; 2 to | 3. John. | Mary, ux.
Sept. 1625. | of the Duchy. | John Slifeld | — | Richard
 | | of London. | 4. George. | Kirkland.

1. John Leventhorpe, 2. Thomas Leventhorpe⹀Dorathy, da. Joane, ux. Sir
ob. apud Towers in | of Shingle Hall, Bart., | of Sir Giles | Edw. Altham
France 6 May 1610, | slaine by Sir Arther | Allington of | of Mark Hall,
s.p. | Capell, 1636. | Horsheath, | co. Essex, Kt.
 | | co. Cambr.

.... Joane, halfe a yeare old at Our Lady Day 1626.

Bridgett, ux. Sir 3. Edward Leven-⹀Jane, da. and sole heir of William
John Fowle of | thorpe. | Beeston of Lambeth, co. Surrey.
Kent, Kt.

George Leventhorpe, a yeare old this March, 1625.

4. Charles. Arther, ob. Margerett. Elizabeth. Catherin. Dorathey.
— | yong. | —
5. Rowland. | | Theodosia.

Maudlin, ux. Dorathey, ux. ....da. of⹀Thomas Leventhorpe⹀.... eldest
.... Torrell | Thomas Newce | Sir Thomas | of Albery, co. Hertf., | da. and co-
of Torrell's | of Haddam, co. | Seymer, | jure uxoris ; mar. to | heir of Wil-
Hall in Es- | Hertf. | widow of | his 3 wife .... da. of | liam Barley
sex. | | Clement | .... Chambers of co. | of Albery.
 | | Smyth. | Hertf.

B | C

APPENDIX II.   151

```
                         B |                    C |
  ┌──────────────┬──────────┬────────┬──────────────────────────┐
Jane, ux. Thomas  Margerett.  1. John, s.p.  3. Rafe Leventhorpe, in Ireland
Allin of Braffin.    —           —           with my Lord Aungier.
                  Catherin.   2. Edward.
```

| Thomas, ob. s.p. | Anne, ux. Richard Frank of Hatfield in Essex. | Hellen, ux. John Longmer of Baddow in Essex; remar. John Capell. | Elizabeth, ux. Sir Francis Hubbert of co. Essex, Kt. | Dorathey, ux. Simon Brograve of Braffin, co. Hertf. |

Litton of Knebworth.

William=Audrey, da. and heir of Sir Philip Booth of
Lytton. | Shrubland, co. Suff.

Sir Robert Lytton of Shrubland.=. . . .   Rowland Lytton.=. . . .

| Elizabeth, ux. Edw. Barrett of Aveleigh, co. Essex. | Anne, ux. John Burlacey of Marlow, co. Bucks. | Ellen, da. and co-heir of Sir Robert, ux. 1 Gabriel Fowler; 2 Sir John Brocket of Brocket Hall, co. Hertf., Kt. | . . . . da. and co-heir. | Rowland=. . . . Lytton. |

William Lytton.=. . . .

. . . . da. of . . . . Carlton.=Rowland Lytton of Knebworth.=. . . . da. and heir of
                                                                  John Tate.

Sir Rowland Litton   Mary, ux. Edward Pulter of
of Knebworth.   Bradfeild Wymondly.

[*Continued as at* p. 73.]

Lockey of Ridge.

ARMS.—*Argent, a bend between two water-bougets Sable.*
CREST.—*An ostrich's head Argent, in the beak a key Sable.*

The antient coat of LOCKEY: *Argent, a chief Gules, over all a bend engrailed Azure charged with three annulets of the field.*

Richard Lockey of co. York.=. . . .

Bryan Lockey of co. York.=. . . .
A |

APPENDIX II.

Richard Lockey of St. Alban's, co. Hertf.=....da. of.... Fletcher of St. Alban's.

... da. of .... Fletcher, 1 ux. = John Lockey of St. Alban's. = Joane, da. of William Marston of Napsbury, nere St. Alban's. | Thomas. — James.

- Richard and Ralph, ob. s.p.
- Ellen, ux. Randall Dove.
- Dorothe, ux. Tho's Crane. — Joane ux. Thomas Inkersell, gent.
- Ellen.=John Sadler. | Ellen, ux. .... Keeling of Stafford towne.
- Elizabeth, ux. John Baulgye; 2 to Simon Wastell of co. Northampton.

William Lockey of Holmes in the p'sh of Ridge, co. Hertf., ob. 1 April 1622, by accident. = Anne, da. of Thomas Cartwright of Warwick, M'r of the Erle of Lester's Hospital there.

1. Anne, ux. Joseph Gastrell of co. Berks.   2. Mary.   3. Martha, ux. Jo. Grabrand of London, Mercer.   4. Elizabeth.

Jane, da. of Sir Thomas Ellis of Grantham, co. Linc., 2 ux. = John Lockey, son and heir, a Student in Cambr.; thirdly he mar. Abigail, the da. of Thomas Barnes of Alborough Hatch, co. Essex. = Margerett, da. of Sir Mathew Sanders of Shankton, co. Leic., Kt., ob. 10 Sept. 1633, s.p.

Mery of Hatfield.

ARMS.—*Gules, on a fess engrailed Argent between three water-bougets Or as many crosses patée Sable.*
CREST.—*A mast of a ship rompu and erect, thereto a yard with sail furled in bend sinister.*

Robert Mery.=....

Thomas Mery of Hatfield, co. Hertf.=....

- Robert Mery, Esq.=....
- William Mery, Grocer to H. 8.
- John Mery, Clerk of the Spicery to H. 8.=....
- Elizabeth, da. and after heir, ux. John Lewen of Coffley, co. Herts.

Joane, da. and co-heir, 1 mar. to Thomas Bowyer of London, and after to Alexander Nowell.   Elizabeth, da. and co-heir, ux. Thomas Norton.   Elizabeth, da. and heir, ux. Thomas Bacon.

APPENDIX II. 153

Mildmay of Sawbridgworth.

ARMS.—*Quarterly*—1 and 4, *Argent, three lions rampant Azure*; 2, *Azure, on a canton Argent a mullet Sable*, LE ROWSE; 3, *Sable, a chevron embattled Or between three roses Argent*, CORNISH.
CREST.—*A lion rampant-gardant Azure.*
On each *a crescent for difference.*

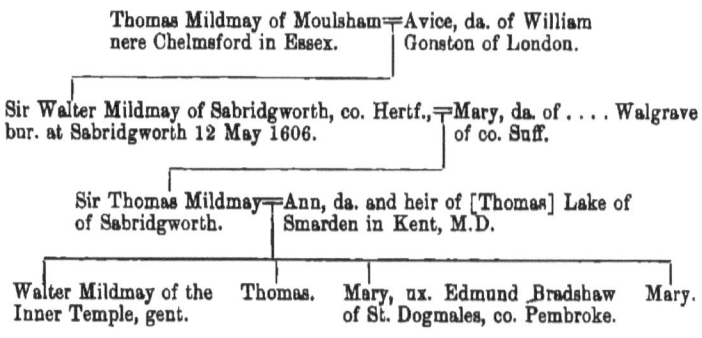

Moore of Hadham.

ARMS.—*Argent, guttée de sang and two chevrons Gules.*
CREST.—*Out of the top of a mural tower Gules, a lion rampant-gardant Or, supporting a banner Argent guttée de sang, thereon the Arms, the staff Sable.*

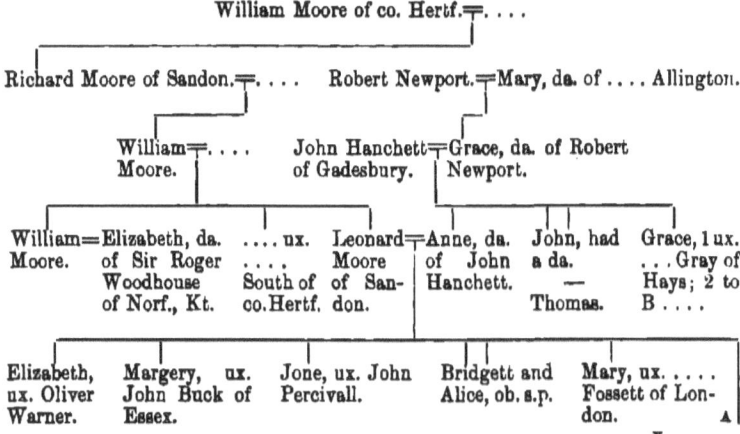

APPENDIX II.

▲

William Moore=Sarah, da. of Clement   Thomas=. . . .   Andrew
of Haddam.   Newce of co. Hertf.   Moore.   Moore.

Frances, ux. William   Adelina, ux. William Bill-   Mary, ux. Clement Pagenham
Roberts of London.   ingsley of co. Rutland.   of co. Linc.

Margerett, da. of=1. William Moore,=Hester, da. of Claus la Meere   2. John
Coun . . . . Torse   a Captain in the of Dunhage, widow of Sam-   Moore.
of Utrick, 1 ux.   Low Countries.   well Marlese.

Morley of Berkhampsted.

ARMS.—*Quarterly*—1 *and* 4, *Sable, a leopard's head Argent jessant-de-lis Or, a crescent of the last for difference;* 2 *and* 3, *Gules, a fess between three Catherine-wheels Argent,* MORLEY.
CREST.—*On a cap of maintenance Gules, turned up Ermine, a leopard's face Argent jessant-de-lis Or.*
    On each *a crescent for difference.*

S'r Henery Morley of Hertkeild in the County of Durham lived in the time of King Henery the 3'd, and was w'th the King at the Battaile of Lewes betwixt the King and S'r Simon Mountfort, Earle of Leicester.

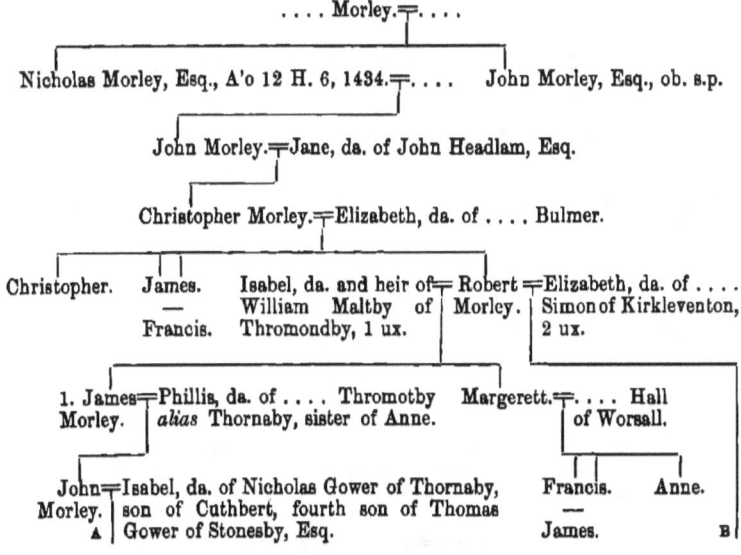

. . . . Morley.=. . . .

Nicholas Morley, Esq., A'o 12 H. 6, 1434.=. . . .   John Morley, Esq., ob. s.p.

John Morley.=Jane, da. of John Headlam, Esq.

Christopher Morley.=Elizabeth, da. of . . . . Bulmer.

Christopher. James.   Isabel, da. and heir of=Robert =Elizabeth, da. of . . . .
              —   William Maltby of | Morley. | Simon of Kirkleventon,
              Francis. Thromondby, 1 ux. | 2 ux.

1. James=Phillis, da. of . . . . Thromotby   Margerett.=. . . . Hall
Morley. | *alias* Thornaby, sister of Anne.   of Worsall.

John=Isabel, da. of Nicholas Gower of Thornaby,   Francis.   Anne.
Morley. | son of Cuthbert, fourth son of Thomas   —
▲ | Gower of Stonesby, Esq.   James.   B

APPENDIX II.   155

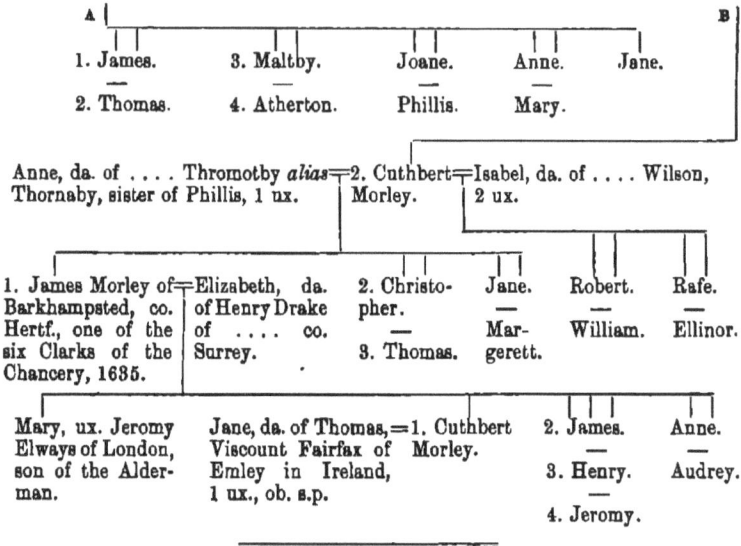

𝔑𝔢𝔴𝔭𝔬𝔯𝔱 𝔬𝔣 𝔓𝔢𝔩𝔥𝔞𝔪.

ARMS.—*Quarterly*—1 *and* 4, *Argent, a fess between three crescents Sable*; 2, *Quarterly Gules and Azure, a lion rampant Argent*; 3, *Argent, on a cross Sable five bezants.*

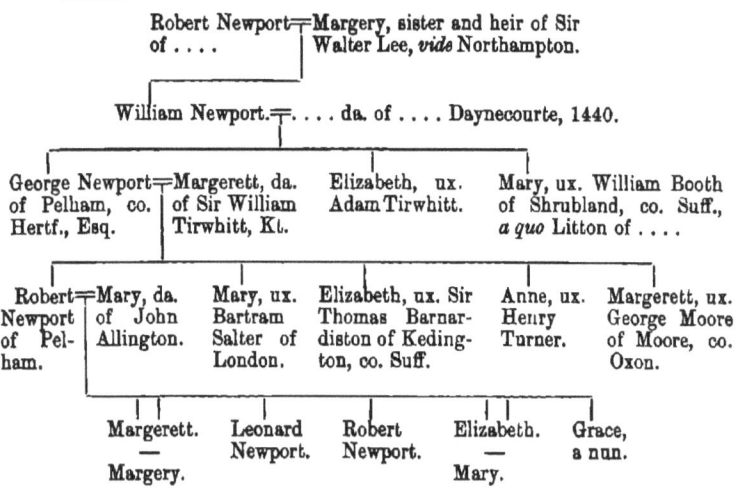

Peryent of Digswell.

ARMS.—*Quarterly*—1 *and* 4, *Gules, three crescents Argent, another for difference;* 2 *and* 3, *Azure, a lion rampant Argent guttée de sang,* FORSTER.
CREST.—*A lion rampant Argent guttée de sang.*

John Peryent, born =⊤= Joane, da. of Sir John Risam, Kt., ob. 3 H. 4 in Gascoigne, came [H. 5, Harl. MS. 6147]. *A pale indented between six cross-crosslets Sable.*
into England.

John Peryent, Esq., =⊤= Mary. Thomas Mansfeld, *temp.* =⊤= Maude, da. of .... Etton.
Lord of the Manor H. 4. *Azure, three cres-* *Barry of eight Argent*
of Digswell, co. Hertf. *cents between seven cross-* *and Gules, on a canton*
crosslets Or. *Sable a cross flory Or.*

John Peryent, Esq., Lord =⊤= .... da. of Thomas
of the Manor of Digswell. | Mansfeld.

1. John Peryent, under years =⊤= Hawis. Jane, a nun Margerett. 2. Thomas =⊤= ....
at the death of his father. at Darford. Peryent.

Mary, ux. Thomas Robinsonn of London, ob. George Peryent, born in =⊤= ....
1592 [*sic*]. *Argent, on a fess engrailed Gules* Salop, dyed in Ireland.
an annulet Or between six cinquefoils of the second.

Margery, da. and heir, ux. Cæsar Dalmare, Docter of Phissick
to Q. Elizabeth, commonly called Julius Cæsar.

Thomas =⊤= Mary, da. of .... Joyce, ux. William Roberts of London. He is bur.
Peryent, | Brockett of Whet- at Digswell. *Argent, three pheons Sable, on a chief*
Esq. hampsted, co. Hertf. *of the second a greyhound courant of the field.*

2. Sir John Peryent of Hatfield, co. =⊤= ....   3. George Peryent, =⊤= Agnes.
Hertf., Esq.; he was the first made his will 21
Auditor of the Court of Wards. H. 8.

.... da. .... da. and Elizabeth, ux. Henry =⊤= .... da. and Catherine,
and co- co-heir, ux. Humfrey Stile Peryent co-heir of .. ux. Will'm
heir, ux. Will'm Barley of Beckenham, of Birch Forster of Clopton of
.... Gill of Albery, co. co. Kent, Esq. Magna, Birch Magna. Kentwell,
of .... Hertf.   co. Es-   co. Suff.
co. Hertf.   sex.
A   B

APPENDIX II. 157

A | B |

Thomas Peryent=Anne, da. of John Browne of .... ux. .... Burton of co.
of Birch Magna, | Wickham Hall, co. Essex, 2 | Sussex. *Quarterly Gules and
co. Essex. | brother of Weston Browne. | Argent, four escallops counter-
                                                 changed.*

1. Sir Tho-=Anne, da. and co- 2. Hum-=Mary, da. and co-   Anne, ux. John
mas Peryent | heir of Sir Roger frey | heir of Sir Roger Taylor of Norf.
of   Birch | Aston, one of the Peryent.| Aston, Kt., widow ——
Magna, Kt. | gent. of the bed- | of Sir Samuel   Mary, ux. John
            | chamber to King | Payton of Kent, Soame, 4 son
            | James. She was | Kt. and Bart. She of Sir Stephen
            | sister of Mary. | was sister of Anne. Soame of Lon-
                                                             don.

1. Thomas Peryent of Digswell.=Alice.

1. Thomas=Anne, da. and heir   2. John   3. William=....   Alice, ux.
Peryent of | of Richard Drewell, Peryent,   Peryent   Richard
Digswell. | by Grace, da. and ob. in   of Aytenigh   Bowles of
           | heir of Richard   Lester-   Digswell.   Wallington,
           | Empsonn.   shire, s.p.   co. Hertf.

Dorathey, da. Anne, ux.   Elizabeth, Mary, ux.   Sir Geo.=Mary, da.   Ellenor,
and co-heir, Anthony   ux. ....   Affabell   Peryent | of John   ux. Tho-
ux. George   Carlton of   Ibgrave.   Rowlett   of Ayte,| Botteler of mas Hoo
Burgoyne of   Baldwin   of Saint   1619. | co. Hertf., of Hoo,
Quickswood,   Brightwell,   Alban's, | Kt.   co. Hertf.
co. Hertf.   co. Oxon;   co. Hertf.;
              she ob. 3   2 to Geo.
              Ap. 1562.   Horsey.

Philip   Mary, ux. Nicholas Trott   Anne, ux. Martin Trott   Elizabeth, ux.
Peryent. of Quixsott, co. Hertf., Esq. of Langridg, co. Essex. William Exbere.

𝔓lomer of 𝔎adwell.

ARMS.—*Vert, a chevron Or between three lions' heads erased Gules.*

William Plomer of Radwell,=Katherin, da. of .... Moore
co. Hertf., gent. | of Hampshire.

2. Thomas.   3. Edward.   Anne, mar. to George   Katherin, mar. to Robert
                          Cockain of Cockain   Audley of Gransen the
A   Hatley, co. Cambr.   Great, co. Hunt.

158   APPENDIX II.

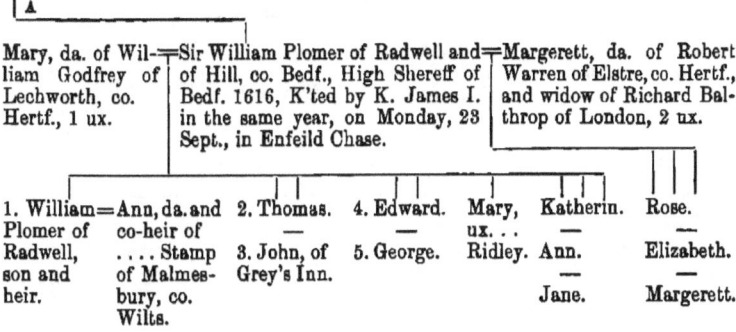

Potkin of Lilley and Rickmansworth.

ARMS.—*Argent, on a fess between three talbots Gules as many lozenges Or.*
CREST.—*A buck's head erased Sable, attired Or.*

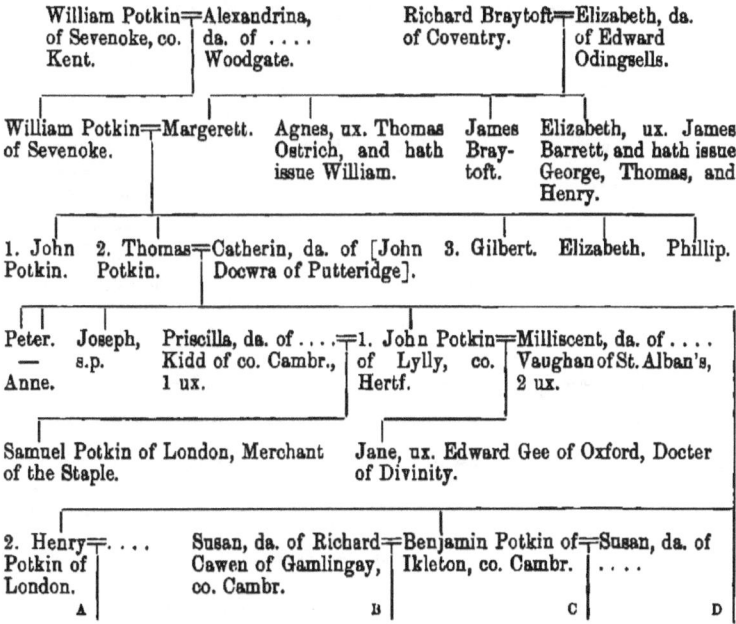

APPENDIX II.

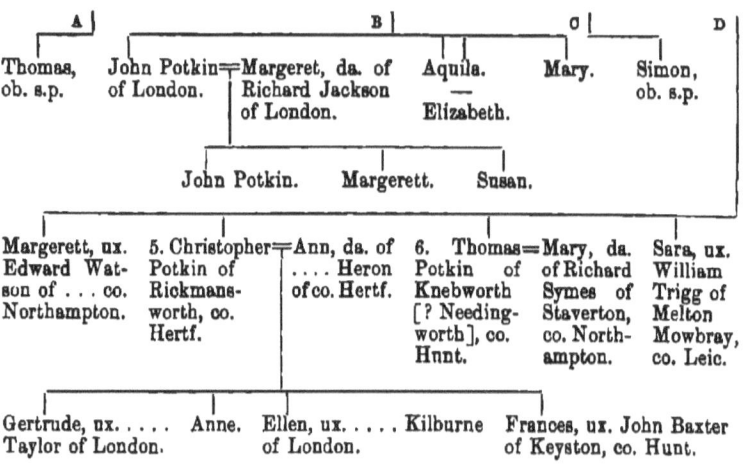

Pranell of Rushdenwell.

ARMS.—*Or, three bars Vert, over all an eagle displayed Sable.*
CREST.—*An eagle's head Or issuing out of rays of the last.*

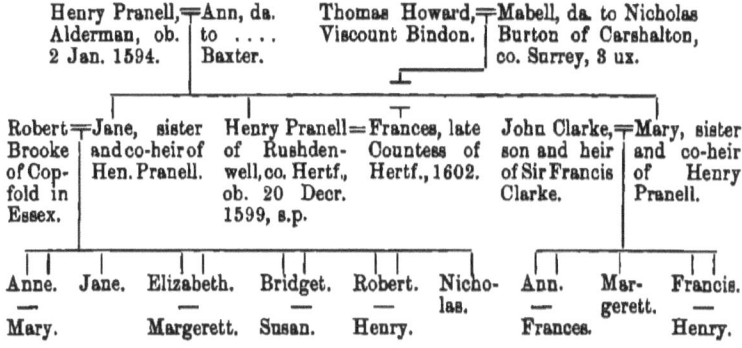

APPENDIX II.

Puckering of Weston.

ARMS.—*Quarterly of six*—1 *and* 6, *Sable, a bend of lozenges between two bendlets Argent;* 2, *Argent, on a mullet Sable an annulet of the field,* ASHTON; 3, *Ermine, on a fess Gules three annulets Or,* BARTON; 4, *Paly of six Argent and Vert,* LANGLEY; 5, *Argent, two bends the upper one engrailed Sable,* LEVER.
CREST.—*A buck salient Or.*

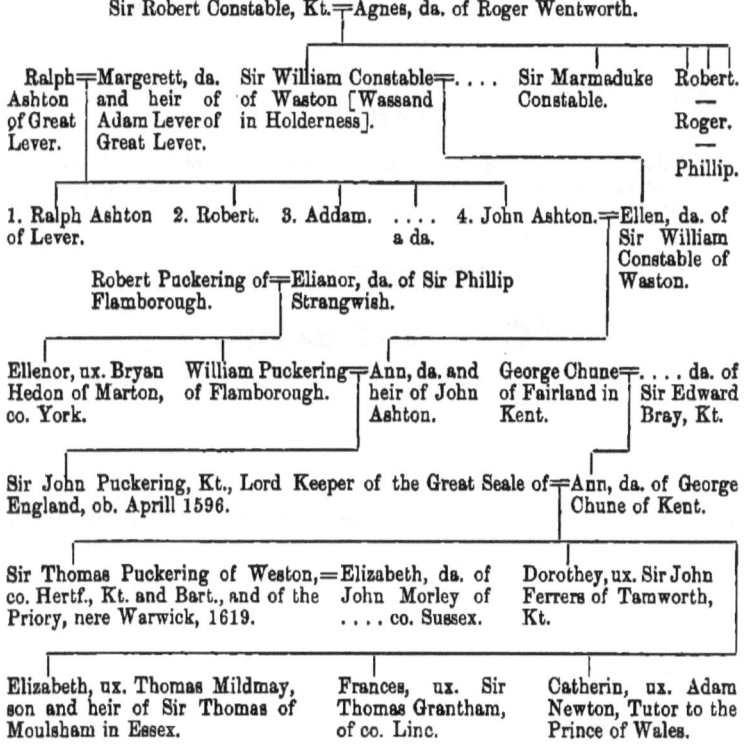

Sir Robert Constable, Kt.=Agnes, da. of Roger Wentworth.

Ralph Ashton of Great Lever. = Margerett, da. and heir of Adam Lever of Great Lever.

Sir William Constable of Waston [Wassand in Holderness]. = ...

Sir Marmaduke Constable.

Robert. — Roger. — Phillip.

1. Ralph Ashton of Lever. 2. Robert. 3. Addam. .... a da. 4. John Ashton.=Ellen, da. of Sir William Constable of Waston.

Robert Puckering of Flamborough.=Elianor, da. of Sir Phillip Strangwish.

Ellenor, ux. Bryan Hedon of Marton, co. York.

William Puckering of Flamborough.=Ann, da. and heir of John Ashton.

George Chune of Fairland in Kent.=.... da. of Sir Edward Bray, Kt.

Sir John Puckering, Kt., Lord Keeper of the Great Seale of England, ob. Aprill 1596.=Ann, da. of George Chune of Kent.

Sir Thomas Puckering of Weston, co. Hertf., Kt. and Bart., and of the Priory, nere Warwick, 1619.=Elizabeth, da. of John Morley of .... co. Sussex.

Dorothey, ux. Sir John Ferrers of Tamworth, Kt.

Elizabeth, ux. Thomas Mildmay, son and heir of Sir Thomas of Moulsham in Essex.

Frances, ux. Sir Thomas Grantham, of co. Linc.

Catherin, ux. Adam Newton, Tutor to the Prince of Wales.

Purvey of Wormley.

ARMS.—*Quarterly*—1 *and* 4, *Sable, three pairs of gauntlets clipping Argent;* 2, *Gules, three piles meeting at the base Or, on a canton Ermine a mullet Sable;* 3, *Argent, a lion rampant Sable, over all on a fess Azure three bezants,* WOODLIFF.
CREST.—*A demi-cockatrice Azure, combed beaked and wattled and with wings expanded Or.*

William Woodliff, Lord of the Manor of Wormley, co. Hertf. = Elizabeth, da. of .... Fisher of Longworth, co. York, Esq.; shee ob. last of May 1598. = Edward Saxilby, Baron of the Exchequer, 2 vir.

William Purvey of Wormleybury, co. Hertf., Auditor of .... = Anne, 1 da. and co-heir of William Woodliff. | Angelett, 2 da. and co-heir, mar. Walter Tooke.

William Purvey, Lord of the Manor of Wormley, ob. 23 Aug. 1617, s.p. = Dorathey, sister of Edward, Lord Denny; renupt. George Purefoy of Wadeley, co. Berks; shee ob. s.p.

Quarles of Cranes.

ARMS.—*Or, a fess dancetté Ermine between three sea-pewits Vert.*
CREST.—*A demi-eagle displayed Vert, beaked Or.*

William Quarles of Ely [*sic*], co. Norf. = ...

Alice, da. of Thomas Tulley of London, merchant, 1 ux. = John Quarles of London, draper, ob. 12 Nov. 1577; mar. to his 3 ux. Anne, da. of .... Greenway, and widow of John Holland of London, salter. = Dorothey, da. of .... Paule Darell of Lillingston, co. Buck., 2 ux., ob. 7 Jan. 1570. | Walter Yong, 1 vir.

Edward. | John. | Rafe, ob. s.p. | Judith, ux. William Beecher. | Francis, ob. s.p.

William Rickthorne of Cannonbury, co. Midd., ob. 10 Nov. 1582, s.p., 1 vir. = Ann. = Sir Arthur Atye of Cannonbury, 2 vir. | Margerett, ux. Robert Barker, mercer. | Benedict Quarles of Cranes, co. Hertf.

John Quarles of Grayc's Inn. = ... da. of .... Bradley. | William Quarles. = ... da. of Sir George Bond of London, Kt.

Y

Reade of Brockett Hall.

ARMS.—*Gules, a saltire between four garbs Or.*

Thomas Reade of Barton, co. Berks, Esq. === Mary, da. of George Stonehouse, Clerk of the Greene Cloth to K. Phillip and Q. Marye.

- Sir Thomas Read of Brockett Hall, co. Hertf., Kt., and of Barton nere Abingdon. === Mary, da. and heir of Sir John Brockett of Brockett Hall.
- John, s.p.
- Richard Read, mar. Ellen, da. of Alexander Cave of Bagrave, co. Leic.
- Mary, ux. ... Boulstred.

- Mary, ux. Robert Dormer of Dorney, co. Buck.
- Elizabeth. — Frances.
- Thomas Read, 17 yere old 1623.
- 2. Richard. — 3. John.
- Ellen. — Margerett.
- Anne.

Sapcotts of Tharfield.

John Sapcotts of Elton, co. Hunt. === ....

- 1. Sir John Sapcotts of Elton, *vide* Lincoln et Huntingdon.
- .... Sapcotts of the Town of Lester. === ....

- 1. Robert Sapcotts a Cannon of Lester, ob. s.p.
- 2. Henry Sapcotts of .... co. Linc. === Jane, da. and heir of Robert Smyth.
- 3. William Sapcotts, a Cannon of Lincoln, ob. s.p.

- 1. John Sapcotts of Tharfeld, co. Hertf. === .... da. of .... Shelton of .... co. Suff.
- 2. John Sapcotts, *vide* Lincoln.

  - 1. William Sapcotts.
  - 2. Robert Sapcotts.

Scroggs of Patmore.

ARMS.—*Argent, on a bend Azure between two greyhounds courant bendways Sable three pewits Or.*
CREST.—*A stork's head Argent collared Gules, wings endorsed bendy of four Or and Sable.*

Francis Scrogs of Patmore,=Jane, da. of John Newport of
co. Hertf. | Pelham, co. Hertf.

. . . . Scrogs of Patmore. . . . . .

Thomas Scroges of=Jane, da. of Weston Browne of=Walter Bridges of Patmore,
Patmore. | Abbess Rodinge, co. Essex. | 2 vir.

Alexander Scroges of Rainold, co. Bedf. Richard. William Bridges.

Shirley of Hertford Town.

ARMS.—*Paly of six Or and Azure, a canton Ermine, a crescent on a crescent for difference.*

John Shirley of the Towne of=Susan, da. of . . . .
Hertford, ob. 14 Sept. 1621. | ob. 18 June 1623.

John Shirley.   Elizabeth.

Shotbolt of Yardley.

Thomas Shotbolt.=Mary, da. of Sir Rafe Botteler of Woodhall, co. Hertf.

Sir John Shotbolt of Yardley, 1622.=Tony, da. of . . . .

Tony Shotbolt, 1622.   Alice, ux. Philip Botteler, son of Sir Philip.

Smyth of Annables.

ARMS.—*Quarterly*—1, *Per bend indented Or and Azure, two crosses moline counterchanged*; 2, *Gules, a cross Argent, over all a bend Sable*, WILLABY or WILLARBY; 3, *Gules, two bars Argent, in chief three plates*, OTEBY; 4, *Sable, a rose between three lions rampant Argent*.
CREST.—*Out of a ducal coronet Or a falcon volant proper.*
On each *a crescent for difference.*

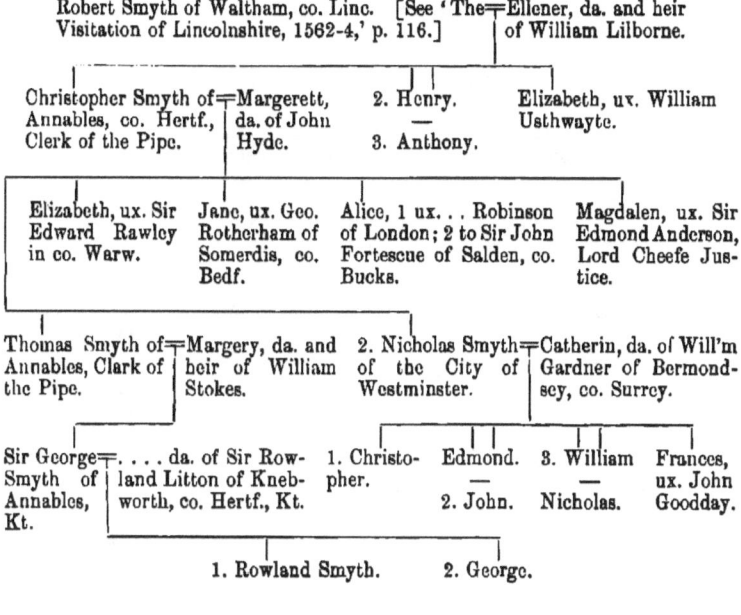

Robert Smyth of Waltham, co. Linc. [See 'The Visitation of Lincolnshire, 1562-4,' p. 116.] = Ellener, da. and heir of William Lilborne.

Christopher Smyth of Annables, co. Hertf., Clerk of the Pipe. = Margerett, da. of John Hyde.
2. Henry.
3. Anthony.
Elizabeth, ux. William Usthwayte.

Elizabeth, ux. Sir Edward Rawley in co. Warw.
Jane, ux. Geo. Rotherham of Somerdis, co. Bedf.
Alice, 1 ux. . . . Robinson of London; 2 to Sir John Fortescue of Salden, co. Bucks.
Magdalen, ux. Sir Edmond Anderson, Lord Cheefe Justice.

Thomas Smyth of Annables, Clark of the Pipe. = Margery, da. and heir of William Stokes.
2. Nicholas Smyth of the City of Westminster. = Catherin, da. of Will'm Gardner of Bermondsey, co. Surrey.

Sir George Smyth of Annables, Kt. = ... da. of Sir Rowland Litton of Knebworth, co. Hertf., Kt.
1. Christopher.
Edmond.
2. John.
3. William Nicholas.
Frances, ux. John Gooddsy.

1. Rowland Smyth.
2. George.

Snelling of St. Margaret's.

ARMS.—*Sable, three griffins' heads erased Or, a chief Ermine, in the fess point a bezant.*

This coate was used at buriall of Marke Snelling of Kingston Uppon Thames.

George Snelling of Kingston uppon Thames. = Rose, da. of . . . . Stephens.

APPENDIX II. 165

Marke Snelling=Anne, da. of   Elizabeth,   Thomas Snelling   Grace, ux.
of Kingston   Blase Carrell   ux. Stephen   of Kingston uppon   Rob't Hope
uppon Thames. of Kingston   Payne of   Thames, *vide* Sur- of .... co.
               uppon Thames.   London.   rey.   Derby.

John Snelling of St.=Anne, da. of .... Goodman   George Snelling of Thistle-
Margett's, co. Hertf.   of Hodsdon, co. Hertf.   worth, co. Midd.

Spencer of Offley.

Sir John Spencer of Worm-=Isabel, da. and heir
leighton 20 H. 7.   of Walter Graunt.

Sir William Spencer=Susan, da. of Sir Richard
of Althorpe 1 H. 8. | Knightley of Fawsley.

Sir John Spencer=Catherin, da. of Sir   Isabel.   Dorathey.   2. Anthony,
of Althorpe, Kt. | Thomas Kitson of   —   —   ob. s.p.
                   Hengrave, co. Suff., Kt. Jane.   Jane.

Sir John Spencer of   Thomas Spencer   Sir William Spencer   Other children,
Althorpe, Kt., *vide* of Clarendon, co. of Yarnton,co. Oxon, ob. in North'ton.
Northampton.   Warw.   Kt.

4. Sir Richard Spencer of=Hellen, da. and co-heir of Sir John Brockett
Offley, co. Hertf., Kt. | of Brockett Hall, co. Hertf., Kt.

Sir John Spencer of Offley,= .... da. of   .... ux. Sir   Ellen, ux. Sir   Anne,
Bart., mar. to his 1 ux.   Sir Thomas   John Jenings   .. Colepeper   ux. Sir
Sarah, da. of Sir Henry   Rotheram.   of Sandrich,   of co. Sussex. John
Anderson, Kt. and Alder-   co. Hertf.,Kt.   Boteler.
man of London.

Taylor of Furneux Pelham.

James Taylor of West Mele, co. Hertford, Doctor=Frances, da. of John
in Divinity and Prebend of Ely and Rector of West | Cutler of Springhall
Mele, ob. 19 March 1623, and there bur.   in Stanstead, co. Suff.

APPENDIX II.

A

| 1. Alice, ux. Edmond Betholl of Oxford. | 2. Mildred, ux. Henry Hancock of Furnes Pelham, co. Hertf., Clarke. | 3. Elizabeth, ux. Robert Sikes of Yardley, co. Hertf., Clarke. | 1. Richard = Tayler. | Frances, da. of William Vesey of Hintlesham, co. Suff. |

| 2. Andrew, ob. s.p. — 4. Henry. | 3. John = Taylor. | Elizabeth, da. of John Bragg of Stratford, co. Suff. | 4. Margerett, ux. William Crowe of Mutford, co. Suff., Clarke. | 5. Dorathey, ux. Nicholas Bodley of London, Fishmonger. |

Tooke of Essendon, Wormley, and Stanstead.

ARMS.—*Quarterly*—1 *and* 4, *Per chevron Sable and Argent, three griffins' heads erased counterchanged ;* 2, *Or, a cross engrailed Gules, thereon a crescent of the field for difference,* HAWTE ; 3, WOODLIFF.

CREST.—*A griffin's head erased Sable, holding erect in the beak a sword blade Argent, hilt and pommel Or.*

John Tooke of West Cliff, co. Kent.=.... da. of .... Malmains.

John Tooke of West Cliff.=Joyce, da. of .... Hoo, brother of the Lord Hoo.

| 2. Thomas Tooke of West Cliff, *vide* Kent. | 1. Rafe Tooke of Dover in Kent. = Jane, da. and co-heir of Roger Haute of Kent. *A mullet.* |

| 1. William=.... Tooke. | 2. Walter Tooke. = Mary, da. of ... Stanhop. | Jane. = James Isack of Kent. |

| .... da. and heir, ux. .... Roper of Kent. | Rafe Tooke of Goddingston in Kent. = Alice, da. of William Meggs of Canterbury. | James Isack. | Anne, ux. Sir John Darell, and had issue John Darell of Calehill. |

| 3. Richard Tooke of Donington, co. Cambr. = Christian, da. of Robert Burley of Andover. | Jane, ux. Thomas Cawthorne. | Elizabeth, ux. Thomas Bruse of Chatteris, co. Cambr. |

A   B

APPENDIX II.

A | | B

1. Christopher.   2. Lawrance=Elizabeth, da. of   Angelett,   Maudlyn.
                   Tooke.   Thomas Dent of   ux. Richard   —
                               Barwick.   Barker.   Petronell.

   1. Henry.   2. Edward.   Thomazin.   Mary.   Barbara.

2. Martin=Eunice, da. of   1. William Tooke=Alice, da. of   Mary, ux. James
Tooke of Richard Rey-   of Popes, co. Hertf., Robert Bar-   Parker of Don-
Donington noldsof Wick-   Auditor of the Court ley of Bibes- ington Parson-
in the Ile merhill in the of Wards and Live-   worth, co.   age.
of Ely.   Ile of Ely.   ryes.   Hertf.

   1. Henry=Anne, da. of ....=Walter Averell,   2. Rafe.   4. Martin.
   Tooke.   Spence of Lynn in 1 vir.   —   —
            Norf.   3. Thomas.   5. Richard.

      Cox Tooke, son and heir.   Angelett.

2. William Tooke=Mary, da. of   Angelett, 2 da.=Walter Tooke of=Jane, da.
of Hertford Town, Nicholas   and co-heir of Popes, Auditor of Richard
ob. 12 Feb. 1611. Tichborne of   William Wood-   of the Court of Goldstone,
                  Roydon, co.   liff, 1 ux.   Wards and Live- widow of
                  Essex, ob. 29   ryes 1588.   ... Threll
                  Aug. 1623.   of co. Essex.

1. William Tooke of=Judeth, da. of William   2. Christopher,   3. Nicholas.
Essendon, co. Hertf. Hartop of Burton, co.   ob. 19 Aug.
                     Leic.   1630, s.p.

   Elinor.   Judeth.   Frances.   1. Thomas,   2. Walter.   Ellinor.
                                  ob. s.p.   —
                                               3. Rafe.   Frances.

4. James Tooke of=Dorathey, da.   Dorathey,   Mary, ux. Edward
St. Alban's, co. Hertf., of John Gray ux. Edward   Darnell of Essen-
Feodarye of London of London.   Willon.   donbury.
and Middx.

   1. John.   2. James.   3. Nicholas.   4. Edward.   Mary.

1. Rafe   2. William,   3. John Tooke, Auditor   4. George,   5. Francis.
Tooke,   ob. Nov.   of the Court of Wards   a Captaine.
ob. s.p.   1630, s.p.   and Liveryes. He was
C   of Wormley; ob. s.p.   D

168   APPENDIX II.

C					D
6. Thomas Tooke, Auditor of the Court of Wards and Liveryes, of Wormley.	=Judeth, da. of John Trott of Conyhatch, co. Middx., widow of Lawrance Campe of London; ob. 8 July 1638.	Anne, ux. John Wyberd of co. Essex.	Joane, ux. Robert Lovelace of Eynsworth Castle in Kent.	Maudlyn, ux. Francis Earnley of Yatesbury, co. Wilts.	

1. John Tooke. = ... da. of Sir Thomas Dacres   2. Thomas.   Angelett.
of Cheshunt, co. Hertf.

3. Nicholas Tooke of Essendon Parsonage, co. Hertf.	=Alice, da. of Thomas Hickman of London.	Mary, ux. William Newce of Broxbourne, co. Hertf.	Petronell, ux. Edward Boughton of Plomsted in Kent.

Alice, ux. John Sheppard.	Angelett, ux. William Dighton, 2 s. of Henry Dighton of .... co. Linc.	1. Richard. — 2. George.	3. Tristram.	Martha, ux. .... Wilkinson.	Anne, ux. Philip Jennings.

Dorathey, ux. Nicholas Bash of St. Margerett's, alias Stansted Theale, co. Hertf.	4. Jasper Tooke	=Anne, da. and co-heir of Henry Rows of Rygate, co. Surrey.
of Stansted, co. Hertf.		

1. Edward Tooke of Boughton Malherbey, co. Kent.	=Elizabeth, da. of Arthur Anthony, widow of Humfrey Hayles, alias Yorke Herald.	Thomazin, ux. Gabriell Colford of Essex.	2. William Tooke.	=	Elizabeth, ux. Francis Cooke of London.

1. William.   2. Henry.   Anne.   Anthony.   Alice.

𝔙erney of 𝔓enley.

Sir Peter Carew, 1 vir.	=Audrey, da. to Will'm Gardner of Fulmer, near Chalfont, co. Buck.	=Sir Edmund Verney of Penley, co. Hertf. Mar. Frances, da. to John Hastings of co. Oxon, s.p.	=Mary, da. to John Blackney of Sparham.	=William St. Barb, 1 vir.

Francis Verney, eldest son. = Ursula, da. and co-heir.   Edmond Verney, 2 son.

APPENDIX II.

Warren of Harpenden.

ARMS.—*Chequy Or and Azure, on a canton Gules a lion rampant within a bordure Ermine.*

Exemplified and confirmed by *Clarenc.* Camden under his hand.

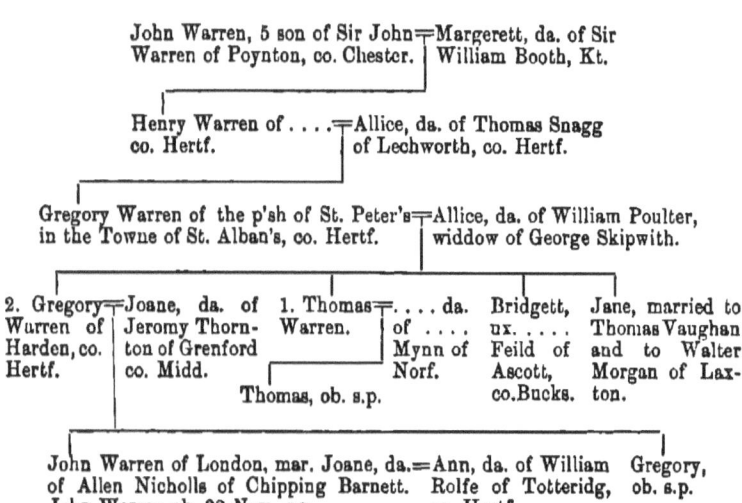

Williams of Abbot's Langley.

ARMS.—*Gules, a wolf issuing out of a rock from the sinister side of the escucheon all Argent, a crescent Or for difference.*

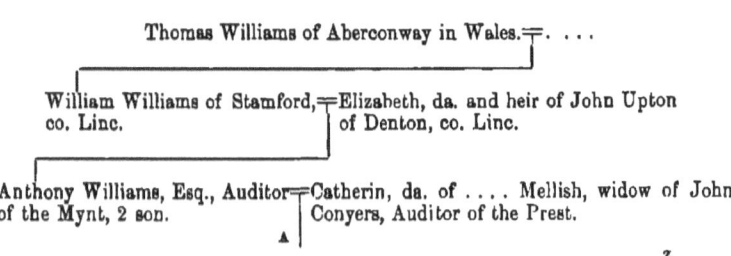

APPENDIX II.

```
                                    ▲
┌──────────────┬───────────────┬──────────────────┬──────────────────┐
1. Thomas=.... Catherin.   2. Alexander=Elizabeth, da.   Timothey [sic], ux.
Williams.                  Williams of   of Anthony      Nowell Sotherton
                           London, and   Carlton of      of London, one of
                           of the Pype   Baldwin         the Barons of the
                           Office, ob. 21 Brightwell,    Exchequer.
                           Aug. 1633.    co. Oxon.
```

Alexander.	Anthony Williams=Mary, da.	2. William Williams	3. Henry.
—	of Hertford Towne, of William	of London, merchant,	—
Elizabeth,	1629, and of Ab- Peere of	ob. s.p.	4. Thomas.
ob. s.p.	bot's Langley, co. Wadnoll,		
	Hertf., 1634. co. Kent.		

Elizabeth.	Catherin.	Alice.	1. Peere	2. Dudley.	Isabel.	Frances.
		—	Williams.	—		
		Bridgett.		3. Alexander.		

INDEX.

Pedigrees are printed in SMALL CAPITALS: Arms in *italics*.

A

Abnett, Br., 103; Wm., 103.
Adams, 5.
Adams, —, 5; Anne, 5.
Adelmar, 133.
Akeroyd, Jo., 30.
ALDEN, 25; *Alden*, 25.
Alderscy, Jo., 69, 87; Tho., 87.
Alfrey, Tho., 34.
Allen, —, 147; Anne, 39, 77; Fr., 77; Giles, 39; Sibell, 115; *Sir* Wm., 115.
ALLEY, 1; *Alley*, 1.
Alley, —, 118; Dor., 118.
Allin, Tho., 151.
Allington, —, 153; Dor., 150; *Sir* Giles, 150; Jo., 155; Mary, 153, 155.
Allway, Alwey, Jo., 3; Mary, 96; Raffe, 96.
Altham, *Sir* Edw., 150.
ANDERSON, 109; *Anderson*, 109.
Anderson, *Sir* Edm., 164; *Sir* Fr., 112; *Sir* Hen., 165; Sarah, 165.
Anderton, —, 109.
ANDREW, 123; *Andrew*, 123.
Andrew, Anne, 84; Jo., 75; Mary, 75; Tho., 84.
Andrewes, —, 120; Urs., 120.
Angell, Cath., 81; Wm., 81.
Anslow, —, 41; Hester, 41.
Anthony, Arthur, 168; Eliz., 168.
ANTROBUS, 123; *Antrobus*, 123.
Apleton, *Sir* Hen., 102.
Arden, Joyce, 133; Tho., 133.
ARNOLD, 1; *Arnold*, 1, 84.
Arnold, Alice, 84; Roger, 84; Wm., 115.
Arscot, —, 24.
Ashby, —, 18; Eliz., 18.
Arundell, *Sir* Jo., 113; Marg., 111; Rich. E. of, 111; *Sir* Tho., 113.
Ashton, 160.
Ashton, Adam, 160; Ann, 160; Jo., 160; Ralph, 160 *bis*; Rob., 160.
Ashwell, Fr., 34.
Askwith, Br., 139; Isab., 139.

Aston, Anne, 157; Mary, 157; *Sir* Rog., 157; Wm., 51; *Sir* Wm., 51.
Astry, Tho., 20.
Athill. *See* Lathill.
Atkinson, Joice, 69; Rob., 69.
Attin, Sam., 106.
Attwood, Tho., 127.
Atye, *Sir* Arthur, 161.
Aubrey, —, 111 *bis*; Chr., 11; Rob., 11.
Audley, —, 81; Eliz., 81; Rob., 157.
Averell, Walter, 167.
Awsiter, Anne, 60; Fr., 60.
Aylett, Sus., 41; Wm., 41.
AYLMER. *See* ELMER.

B

Babham, —, 123.
Bacon, Tho., 152.
Bafford, —, 129.
Bainbrig, Rob., 87.
Baker, 125.
Baker, —, 22, 125; Chr., 22; Edw., 79; Jane, 79; Tho., 125.
Baldock, —, 26.
BALDWIN, 125; *Baldwin*, 125.
Baldwin, Marg., 31; Tho., 31.
Ball, —, 5; Cic., 50; Tho., 50.
Bancroft, Ellin, 89; Tho., 89.
Banester, Geo., 32; Mary, 32.
Bankbrick, —, 17; Ann, 17.
BARBER, 25; *Barber*, 25.
Barber, Gabr., 107.
BARDOLF, 2, 26; *Bardolf*, 2.
Bardolph, —, 13, 67; Anne, 33; Edm., 33; Maud, 67.
Barker, Jane, 131; Jo., 127, 131; Rich., 167; Rob., 127, 161.
Barkham, —, 134; *Sir* Edw., 134, 145; Eliz., 145.
BARKLEY, 26; *Barkley*, 26.
Barkley, Hen. *Lo.*, 136; Rob. 139; Tho., 136.
BARLEY, 27; *Barley*, 27.
Barley, —, 33, 130, 150; Agnes, 23; Alice, 99, 167; Eliz., 150; Hen., 150; Jo., 23; Lucy, 130;

Mary, 2; Rob., 99, 167; Wm., 150, 156.
Barnardiston, Hanna, 33; *Sir* Tho., 33, 155.
Barnes, —, 69; Abig., 152; *Sir* Geo., 144; Hen., 15; Tho., 152.
Barnesdale, Eliz., 19; Jas., 19.
BARNWELL, 110; *Barnwell*, 110.
Barnwell, —, 121; Symon, 121.
Barr, —, 52, 116; Milliscent, 52.
Barret, —, 8; Edw., 151; Geo., 158; Hen., 158; Jas., 158; Tho., 158.
Barrington, *Sir* —, 29; Jane, 29; *Sir* Tho., 73.
Bartlett, Wm., 150.
Barton, 160.
BASH, 125; *Bash*, 125.
Bash, Edw., 89; Rafe, 135; Nich., 168.
Baskerville, *Sir* Humfr., 128; Jas., 128; Mary, 143; Wm., 143.
Bassett, Jo., 120.
Bathey, —, 37; Eliz., 37.
Battell, —, 131.
Baulgyes, Jo., 152.
Baxter, —, 159; Ann, 159; Jo., 159; Wm., 71.
BAYLY, 27 *bis*; *Bayly*, 27.
Bayly, —, 6; Jo., 31.
Baynard, 119.
Baynard, Hen., 119.
Rayning, Andr., 102; Mary, 102; Pawle, 102; Tho., 102.
Baywood, Geo., 28; Jud., 28.
Beamond, —, 115; Ann, 115.
Beauchamp, Alice, 111; Jo., *Lo.* Powick, 111.
Bedell, Alice, 131; Tho., 131.
Bedingfield, Edw., 96.
Bedle, *Sir* Tho., 36.
Beecher, Dor., 69; Hen., 69; Wm., 161; *Sir* Wm., 69.
Beeston, Jane, 150; Nich., 134; Wm., 150.
BELFELD, 3, 28; Belfeld, 3.
Bell, —, 53; Mary, 53.
Bellamy, Paul, 149.
Benjamin, —, 93; Ann, 93.
Bennett, —, 7; Ellen, 72; Hen., 72; Kath., 7.

Bensted, 141.
Bensted, —, 32; Cath., 141; *Sir* Edw., 141; Marg., 32.
Beriaford, *Dr.*, 56; Mary, 56.
BERKHAMPSTEAD, Town of, 107.
BERNERS, 28; *Berners*, 28.
Berners, Edw., 127; Jane, 103; Wm., 103.
Berven, Eliz., 126; Reig., 126.
Besford, —, 82; Joan, 82.
BESTNEY, 126; *Bestney*, 126.
Bethell, —, 21; Edm., 166.
Beverley, Jas., 49.
Bevill, Cath., 64; *Sir* Rob., 64.
Billesly, Wm., 131.
Billingsley, —, 78; Cic., 17, 78; Raufe, 92; Wm., 154.
Billington, —, 126; Jane, 127; Randall, 126; Tho., 127.
Birkenhed, 120.
Birkenhed, Ann, 120; Hen., 120.
Bishop, —, 146; Mary, 146.
Blackman, Mary, 93; Rich., 93.
Blackney, —, 126; Eme, 126; Jo., 168; Mary, 168.
BLAKETT, 128.
Bland, Eliz., 136; Rich., 136.
Blandon, Isab., 42; Jo., 42.
Blechenden, Mary, 37; Tho., 37.
Blewet, 119.
Blewet, Eliz., 119; Jo., 119.
BLOUNT, 29, 128; *Blount*, 29.
Blower, Eliz., 68; Rich., 68.
Bodley, Nich., 166; Tho., 130.
Bolar, Joan, 76; Jo., 76.
Bolle, Jane, 105, 122; Tho., 89, 105, 122, and *see* Bowles.
Bolles, *Sir* Geo., 139; *Sir* Jo., 139.
Bonas, —, 93; Beatr., 93.
Bond, —, 161; *Sir* Geo., 62, 161; Rose, 62.
Bonevyle, 119.
Bonevyle, Mary, 119; Nich., 119.
Bonwick, Benj., 105, 122.
Bouth, Bowth, 73.
Booth, Bowth, —, 126; Audr., 73, 151; Easter, 63; Marg., 169; *Sir* Ph., 73, 151; Wm., 63, 155; *Sir* Wm., 169.
BORASTON, 110; *Boraston*, 110.
Borne, Eliz., 71; Rich., 71.
Borough, Chr., 74; Sarah, 74.
Bostock, 8.
Bostock, —, 5, 8; Alice, 5; Ann, 8.
BOTELER, 29, 30, 111; *Boteler*, 30, 111.
Boteler, —, 77, 91; Anne, 80, 91; Beck, 77; Dor., 70; *Sir* Edw., 70; Helen, 80; *Sir* Hen., 37, 117; Jane, 37; Jo., 157; *Sir* Jo., 130, 165; Marg., 130; Mary, 157, 163; Ph., 163; *Sir* Rafe, 163; Tho., 80; Wm., 80, 122.
Boughton, Edw., 32, 168.

Boulstred, —, 162.
Bowers, —, 133.
Bowle, Eliz., 37; Tho., 37.
BOWLES, 112; *Bowles*, 112.
Bowles, —, 68; Jo., 77; Rich., 157, and *see* Bolle.
Bowyer, —, 7; Eliz., 109; Fr., 57, 109; Tho., 152.
Brabazon, Anne, 141; *Sir* Edw., 141.
BRADBERY, 129; *Bradbery*, 129.
Bradley, —, 161.
Bradshaw, —, 75; Edw., 153.
Bragg, Eliz., 166; Jo., 166.
Bray, —, 160; Anne, 147; *Sir* Edw., 160; Eliz., 23; Jo., *Lo.*, 23; Rich, 147; Rob., 147.
Braytoft, Agnes, 158; Eliz., 158; Jas., 158; Marg., 158; Rich., 158.
Breakspeare, 141.
Breakspeare, Ag., 141; Alex., 141.
Breche, —, 19.
Brereton, Hen., 69; Marg., 145; *Sir* Wm., 145.
Bresay, Hen., 128.
Brett, —, 18.
Brewer, —, 142; Dor., 142.
Bridges, —, 15; Eliz., 15; Walter, 163.
Bridiman, Jo., 133; Mary, 133.
BRIGGS, 30.
BRISCO, 31 *bis*; *Brisco*, 30.
Brisco, Edw., 52; Joan, 52.
BRISTOW, 130; *Bristow*, 130.
Bristow, Eliz., 42; Fr., 42; Nich., 42.
BROCKETT, 32, 33; *Brockett*, 26, 33.
Brockett, —, 13, 65, 156; Edw., 3, 26, 139; Eliz., 139; Helen, 165; Jane, 6; Jo., 6; *Sir* Jo., 151, 162, 165; Lucy, 13, 65; Mary, 26, 156, 162; Wm., 2.
BROGRAVE, 33, 131; *Brograve*, 33, 131.
Brograve, —, 58; Jane, 80; Joan, 150; *Sir* Jo., 150; Marg., 58; Sim., 80, 151.
Brokas, —, 150.
BROMLEY, 34; *Bromley*, 34.
Brooke, — 69; Anne, 159; Br., 159; Cath., 69; Edw., 68; Eliz., 159; Hen., 159; Jane, 159; Marg., 68, 159; Mary, 91, 159; Nich., 159; Rob., 91, 159; Sus., 159; Tho., 143; Wm., 34, 103.
Brown, Browne, Anne, 123, 157; Chr., 107; Eliz., 61; Geo., 150; Humfr., 61, 72; Jane, 113, 163; Jo., 72, 157; Weston, 157, 163; Wm., 123, 131.
Browning, —, 143; Marg., 143.
Bruncker, —, 148; Hen., 148; Joan, 148; *Sir* Wm., 148.

Bruse, Tho., 166.
Buck, Jo., 153.
Buckland, —, 20; Joan, 20.
Buffkyn, Raffe, 28.
Bulbeck, Dor., 148; Tho., 148.
BULL, 3, 34.
Bull, Hen., 107.
Bullen, Mary, 136; Tho., *E.* of Wilts, 136.
BULLER, 35; *Buller*, 35.
Bulmer, —, 154; Eliz., 154.
Burdett, 147.
Burdett, —, 147; Rob., 147.
Burgoyne, Geo., 157; Jo., 112.
Burlacey, Jo., 151.
Burley, Chr., 166; Rob., 166.
Burne, Marg., 101; Tho., 101.
Burrell, Eliz., 86; Rich., 86.
Burton, —, 113, 138, 149, 157; *Sir* Edw., 143; Eliz., 138, 143; Mabel, 159; Nich., 159; Rowland, 91.
Bury, Jas., 5; Tho., 136; Urs., 5.
BUSSYE, 132; *Bussye*, 132.
Butcher, Helen, 103; Rose, 103.
Butler, —, 43; Eliz., 45; *Sir* Jo., 45; Sus., 43.
Buttery, Fulke, 83.
Button, —, 45; Wm., 45.

C

CADE, 133; *Cade*, 133.
Cade, Jo., 148.
CÆSAR, 25, 133; *Cæsar*, 133.
Cæsar, *Sir* Chas., 109; Jacom., 109.
CAGE, 35; *Cage*, 35.
Cage, Dan., 92; Eliz., 92.
Caldwell, Dan., 75.
Calfeld, Geo., 97; *Sir* Wm., 97.
Calton, —, 21; Eliz., 21.
Campe, —, 99, 105; Lawr., 99 *bis*, 168.
Cannon, —, 58; Eliz., 34; Geo., 58; Jo., 34; Marg., 58.
CAPELL, 36, 113; *Capell*, 113.
Capell, *Sir* Arthur, 86, 117; Anne, 40; Hen., 8; Jo., 151; Pen., 85, 117.
Capet, Jo., 118.
Carew, —, 47; *Sir* Peter, 168; *Sir* Wym., 47.
Carlton, —, 151; Anne, 73; Anth., 157, 170; Eliz., 170; Geo., 73; *Sir* Jo., 32.
Carpenter, —, 37, 49; Eliz., 49.
Carrell, Anne, 165; Blasc, 165.
CARTER, 37; *Carter*, 37.
Carter, Fr., 48; Rob., 48.
Cartwright, Anne, 152; Tho., 152.
CARY, 134; *Cary*, 134.
Cary, *Sir* Edw., 125; Fr., 125.
CASON, 37; *Cason*, 37.

INDEX. 173

Cason, Edw., 112, 117 ; Ellen, 117.
Casey. —, 59 ; Mary, 59.
Castell, Joane, 119 ; *Sir Jo.,* 119 ; Rob., 90.
Castle, Jas., 81.
Catlin, *Sir Rob.,* 112.
Cave, Alex., 162 ; *Sir* Alex., 32 ; Edm., 116 ; Ellen, 162 ; Julian, 116.
Cawen, Rich., 158 ; Susan, 158.
Cawthorn, Tho., 166.
Cecil, *Sir* Tho., 37.
CHAMBER, 38, 137 ; *Chamber,* 38.
Chamber, Rob., 149.
Chambers, —, 150 ; Abr., 76.
CHAPMAN, 4 ; *Chapman,* 4.
Charge, Hen., 82 ; Marg., 82.
CHAUNCEY, 4, 38, 39 ; *Chauncey,* 4.
Chaworth, Dor., 91 ; *Sir* Geo., 91.
Chedder, 113.
Chedder, Mabell, 113 ; Tho., 113.
Cheesman, 18.
Cheesman, Edw., 19 ; El., 19.
Cherry, — 53 ; Marg., 53.
CHESTER, 39 ; *Chester,* 39.
Chester, —, 113 ; Anne, 85 ; *Capt.,* 113 ; *Sir* Rob., 85.
Chevall, 82.
Cheyne, —, 20 ; Edm., 116 ; Jo., 20 ; Lucy, 116.
Chichley, Tho., 140.
Chidioke, *Sir* Jo., 113 ; Kath., 113.
CHILDE, 138 ; *Childe,* 40, 138.
Childe, Tho., 40.
Chissell, Wm., 112.
Cholmeley, Wm., 139.
CHUNE, 40.
Chune, Ann, 160 ; Geo., 160.
Churchman, Alice, 95 ; Rob., 95.
CLARKE, 41, 42 ; *Clarke,* 41.
Clarke, —, 14, 52, 91, 116, 117 ; Anne, 159 ; Cath., 38 ; Eliz., 52 *bis* ; Fr., 159 ; *Sir* Fr., 159 ; Geo., 52, 130 ; Hen., 159 ; Jane, 91 ; Joan, 14 ; Jo., 55, 84, 159 ; Josepha, 56 ; Marcye, 148 ; Marg., 159 ; Mary, 55 ; Tho., 122, 148 ; Wm., 38, 52, 56.
Clitherow, —, 21 ; Bennet, 14, 21 ; Hen., 14.
Clopton, Jo., 75 ; Wm., 156.
Clovell, Mary, 149 ; Wm., 149.
COCK, 5 ; *Cock,* 5.
Cock, Anne, 87 ; Wm., 87.
Cockain, Geo., 157.
Cocks, Alice, 149 ; Tho., 149.
Cockworthy, Alice, 142 ; Jo., 142.
Coe, Edw., 39.
COGHILL, 42 ; *Coghill,* 42.
Coker, Chr., 136 ; Mary, 136.
COLE, 42 ; *Cole,* 42.

Cole, Ab., 95 ; Wm., 95.
Colepeper, *Sir* —, 165.
Colford, Gabr., 168.
COLLES, 43 ; *Colles,* 43.
Colles, Marg., 88 ; Wm., 88 *bis.*
COLLEY, 5 ; Colley, 5.
Collins, —. 12 ; Lettice, 12.
Collman, Edw., 61.
Colshill, —, 47.
Colt, Tho., 130.
COLTE, 43 ; *Colte,* 43.
COMBE, 6, 44 ; *Combe,* 6, 120.
Combe, Combes, —, 95 ; Fr., 33, 52 ; Marg., 95 ; Mary, 33 ; Rob., 120.
Compton, *Sir* Tho., 135.
CONEY, 44 ; *Coney,* 44.
Coney, Conny, Jo., 49 ; *Sir* Rich., 49.
CONINGSBY, 45 ; *Coningsby,* 45.
Coningsby, Conisby, —, 44, 111 ; Ann, 30, 111 ; Eliz., 75 ; *Sir* Hen., 75, 91 ; Humfr., 30 ; *Sir* Humfr., 149 ; Jane, 31 ; Jo., 10, 111, 146 ; Marg., 146 ; Mary, 10, 91 ; *Sir* Rafe, 31, 44.
Conniswell, —, 121.
Constable, Ellen, 160 ; *Sir* Marm., 160 ; Ph., 160 ; Rob., 160 ; *Sir* Rob., 160 ; Rog., 160.
Constantyne, 123.
Constantyne, —, 123 ; Felix, 123.
CONYERS, 139 ; *Conyers,* 139.
Conyers, Jo., 169.
Cooke, —, 8, 9, 138 ; Anne, 8 ; Chas., 117 ; Fr., 168 ; Jo., 79 ; Mary, 56 ; Wm., 56.
Cooper, Chr., 118.
COPPIN, 45 ; *Coppin,* 45.
Coppin, Anne, 16, 77 ; Wm., 16, 77.
COPWOOD, 6 ; *Copwood,* 6.
Corbett, —, 115 ; Anne, 135 ; Jo., 36 ; Rob., 73 ; *Sir* Rob., 135.
Core, Eliz., 9 ; Tho., 9.
Cornish, 153.
Cornwall, Jane, 39 ; Jo., 39.
Cottington, —, 146 ; Kinb., 146.
COTTON, 46 ; *Cotton,* 18.
Cotton, —, 18 ; *Sir* Tho., 116.
Coventry, —, 70 ; Tho., *Lo.,* 107.
Cowley, Tho., 107, 109.
Cox, 7, 46 ; *Cox,* 7.
Crane, —, 83 ; Anne, 95 ; Tho., 152.
Cranfield, *Sir* Lionel, *E.* of Midd., 137 ; Martha, 137.
Cranmer, Marg., 81 ; Tho., *Abp.,* 81.
Crawley, Rich., 84.
Cray, 25.
Cray, Eliz., 25 ; Jo., 25.
CRESSY, 2 ; *Cressy,* 2.

Croftes, —, 30 ; Mary, 30.
Crooke, —, 127 ; Marg., 127.
CROSBY, 47.
Crosfield, Gavin, 107.
Croston, 31.
Crouch, 121.
Crouch, —, 121 ; Marg., 80 ; Tho., 80.
Crowe, Wm., 166.
Cutler, Fr., 165 ; Jo., 165 ; Tho., 58.
Cutts, *Sir* Jo., 32.

D

DACRES, 47 ; *Dacres,* 47.
Dacres, —, 168 ; Eliz., 61 ; Prud., 48 ; *Sir* Tho., 48, 61, 168.
Dallison, Geo., 150 ; Jane, 150.
Dalyson, Edw., 21.
Damport, —,129 ; Anne, 119 ; Jo., 119 ; Tho., 119.
Danvers, *Sir* Jo., 136.
Darell, Dor., 161 ; Eliz., 91 ; Jo., 55, 91, 166 ; *Sir* Jo., 166 ; Mary, 55 ; Paul, 161.
Darkenold, Eliz., 2, 26 ; Rob., 2, 26.
Darnell, —, 140 ; Anne, 72, 120 ; Edw., 167 ; Eliz., 72, 100 ; Jo., 72, 83, 100, 120 ; Josian, 83 ; Mary, 72 ; Sus., 72.
Daubenie, El., 113 ; *Lo.,* 113.
Dauntsey, *Sir* Jo., 148.
Davies, Nich., 65.
Davy, Jo., 17, 78 ; Mary, 17, 78.
Dawborne, —, 143.
Dawney, Anne, 139 ; Jo., 139.
Dawson, Rob., 107.
Day, Rose, 124 ; Tudor, 124.
Dayle, Jo., 34.
Daynecourte, —, 155.
Delamott, Joyce, 95 ; Rich., 95.
Delmare, Cæsar, 156.
Denham, Jo., 129 ; Marg., 129.
Denny, *Sir* Anth., 135 ; Edm., 135 ; Martha, 135.
Dent, Eliz., 167 ; Tho., 167.
Denton, Anne, 78 ; Math., 78.
Derham, Tho., 109.
Devenish, —, 112 ; Ann, 112.
DEWHURST, 48 ; *Dewhurst,* 48.
Deyncourte, 132.
Dicons, Eliz., 22 ; Tho., 22.
Dighton, —, 121 ; Hen., 168 ; Wm., 168.
Dillon, —, 50 ; Anne, 50.
Dimock, Jo., 17.
Diper, *Mr.,* 63.
DIXON, 48 ; *Dixon,* 48.
DOCWRA, 48, 139 ; *Docwra,* 139.
Docwra, Anne, 83 ; Anth., 140 ; Cath., 158 ; Edw., 80 ; Ellen, 80, 114 ; Fr., 96, 105 ; Jo., 83, 158 ; Tho., 96, 114.

INDEX.

Dod, 50; *Dod*, 50.
DOLMAN, 140.
Dormer, Rob., 162; Wm., 48.
Dove, Randall, 152.
Dover, Abig., 95; Rob. *bis*, 95; Seb., 95.
Downes, Dor., 62; Nath., 38; Wm., 62.
Downhall, —, 21.
Drake, Eliz., 155; Hen., 155; Sir Jo., 112.
Draper, —, 62; Jone, 62.
DREW, 50; *Drew*, 50.
Drewell, Anne, 28, 157; Rich., 157; Rob., 28.
Driver, —, 69.
Drury, Sir Drew, 112; Fr., 112.
Drywood, Wm., 48.
Dudley, —, 149; Edw., 149; Lo. North, 32.
Duncombe, —, 128; Alice, 128; Faith., 71; Hen., 20; Sus., 92, 123; Tho., 123; Wm., 71, 92.
Dunen, —, 97.
Duston, 147.
Duston, —, 147.
Dye, Anne, 148; Rog., 48.
DYER, 7; *Dyer*, 7.
Dyer, Jo., 107.
Dynes, Jo., 48.
Dynham, Sir Jo., 113; Kath., 113.
Dyve, 132.

E

EAKINS, 51.
Eakins, Alice, 54; Jo., 54.
Eames, Edw., 167.
Earle, —, 118; Eliz., 118.
Earnley, Fr., 168.
Earlesman, Eliz., 31; Tho., 31.
East, Dor., 118; Tho., 49.
Ebbet, —, 56.
Ebden, 132.
Edlin, —, 100.
Edmondson, Rob., 12.
Edolfe, —, 85; Martha, 85.
Edwards, —, 5, 37; Heath, 56.
Eedes, Fr., 106; Marg., 106.
Eldrington, —, 8; Julian, 8.
Ellis, —, 138; Jas., 89; Jane, 152; Sir Tho., 152.
Eliot, —, 121.
Elsden, Geo., 13.
ELMER, 141; *Elmer*, 141.
Elmes, Martha, 47; Tho., 47.
Elrington, Edw., 89.
Elwayes, Jeromy, 155.
Emery, Tho., 27.
Emes, Jo., 74.
Empson, Grace, 157; Rich., 157.
Enifre, Jo., 33.
Epwell, Jo., 130.
Eton, Wm., 6.
Etton, 156.
Etton, —, 156; Maude, 156.

Evans, Geo., 35; Mary, 35.
Evelin, —, 49.
Everard, Anne, 79; Tho., 79.
Everley, —, 68, 90; Gilb., 90.
Ewen, —, 7.
EWER, 51; *Ewer*, 51.
Ewer, Abel, 46; Barb., 44; Hen., 44; Jo., 74; Mary, 46; Sibill, 74.
Exbere, Wm., 157.

F

Fabian, —, 77.
FAIRCLOUGH, 52; *Fairclough*, 52.
Fairclough, —, 60; Dor., 60; Jo., 132; Nich., 132.
Fairfax, Jane, 155; Tho., *Visc.*, 155.
FANSHAW, 114; *Fanshaw*, 114.
Fanshaw, Sir Jo., 78; Mary, 78.
Farington, 119.
Farington, Eliz., 119; Tho., 119.
Farrant, Humfr., 55; Jane, 55.
FARRAR, 53; *Farrar*, 53.
Feld, Jo., 7.
Felton, —, 94; Eliz., 94.
Fenne, 23.
Fenne, Ann, 24; Hugh, 24.
Ferne, Chr., 92; Jo., 92; Sir Jo., 77, 92.
Fernefold, —, 10; Eliz., 10.
Fereby, —, 45.
FERRERS, 141; *Ferrers*, 141.
Ferrers, Sir Jo., 160; Rob., 111.
Field, —, 169.
Filmere, Rob., 40.
Finch, 142.
Fincham, —, 89.
Finning, —, 56; Marg., 56.
FISH, 54 *bis*; *Fish*, 54.
Fish, Jo., 117; Mary, 51; Wm., 51.
Fisher, —, 161; Eliz., 161; Lawr., 118.
Fitz Andrew, 119.
Fitz Andrew, Joan, 119; Jo., 119.
Fitz Gerrard, *Lo.*, 30.
Fitzherbert, —, 6.
Fitzhugh, 119.
Fitzhugh, Alice, 112; Rich., 112; Tho., 119.
Fitz Rafe, —, 47.
Fitzwalter, 123.
Fitzwalter, Mary, 123; Rich., 123.
Fletcher, —, 31, 152 *bis*.
Fludd, —, 38.
Fogg, Anne, 131; Sir Jo., 131.
Folliott, Jo., 141.
Fordam, Eliz., 98; Jo., 131; Wm., 98.
FORSTER, 143; *Forster*, 143, 156.
Forster, —, 156.
Forte, Jo., 40.

Fortescue, Sir Jo., 164.
Fortherby, Mary, 25; Tho., 25.
Fossett, —, 153.
Foster, 20.
Foster, —, 5, 147; Fr., 22; Joane, 5; Jo., 22.
FOTHERLEY, 144; *Fotherley*, 144.
FOWKE, 54; *Fowke*, 54.
Fowle, Sir Jo., 150.
Fowler, —, 32; Gabr., 151; Tho., 91.
FRANCES, 55; *Frances*, 55.
Frank, Rich., 151.
Frankes, 99.
Frankes, Anne, 72; Tho., 72.
Franklin, Geo., 62; Hen., 112; Tho., 61; Wm., 112.
Fransham, Agatha, 1; Geff., 1.
Freak, Eliz., 115; Sir Tho., 115.
Freer, —, 97; Sir Edw., 97.
Frodsham, —, 32; Eth., 32.
Frowick, Eliz., 45; Hen., 45.
Fryar, Wm., 12, 85.
Fryer, Sir Wm., 87.
Fulnetby, Vincent, 131.
Fulwell, Alice, 127; Rob., 127.
Furnyvall, —, 21; Ellen, 21.

G

Gaddesden, Jo., 107.
Gage, —, 147; Sir Jo., 147.
GAPE, 144.
Gape, Hen., 107.
Garaway, —, 109; *Ald.*, 62; Mary, 32; Eliz., 62; Sir Paul, 35; Tho., 35; Sir Wm., 109.
GARDENER, 56; *Gardener*, 56.
Gardener, —, 9.
GARDINER, 57 *bis*; *Gardiner*, 57 *bis*.
Gardiner, Edw., 103; Leon., 15; Mary, 103; Tho., 3.
Gardner, Audr., 168; Cath., 164; Nich., 130; Wm., 164, 168.
Garland, —, 4.
Garnett, Jasper, 65; Mary, 65.
Garnon, Dionis, 66; Jas., 66.
GARRARD, 144; *Garrard*, 144.
Garton, 98.
Garton, Fr., 98; Jane, 63; Sir Peter, 63; Rob., 98.
Gascoigne, —, 121; Alice, 79; Jo., 79.
Gastrell, Jos., 152.
Gates, —, 41; Br., 41.
Gaynsford, —, 22; Sir Jo., 22.
Gee, Edw., 158.
Gent, Geo., 61; Thom., 94; Wm., 94.
Gentilis, Alb., 44; Ann, 44.
Gibson, Fr., 15; Rich., 15.
Gifford, —, 61; Dyon., 61.
Giles, —, 92; Marg., 92.
GILL, 58; *Gill*, 58.

INDEX.

Gill, —, 156; Br., 94; Geo., 94; Grace, 59; Jo., 90; Rafe, 59; Urs., 90.
Gladman, 8.
Gladman, —, 8; Jo., 37; Rich., 8.
Glascock, Eliz., 67; Marg., 101; Rich., 67, 101.
Glover, Wm., 75; *Sir* Wm., 75.
Gobion, 111.
Gobion, Hawise, 111; Hugh, 111; Rich., 111.
Godfrey, —, 20; Mary, 83, 158; Wm., 83, 158.
Godman, —, 97.
Goldsmith, Fr., 17, 142.
Goldstone, Jane, 167; Rich., 167.
Goldwell, Marg., 105, 122; Wm., 105, 122.
Gomershall, Eliz., 103; Jo., 103.
Gonston, Avice, 153; Wm., 153.
Goodday, Jo., 164.
GOODERE, 8, 58; *Goodere*, 8.
Goodere, —, 20, 77; Alice, 77; Ann, 5; Tho., 5.
Gooderidge, Jo., 131; Marg., 131; Sarah, 93; Tho., 93.
GOODMAN, 145; *Goodman*, 145.
Goodman, —, 165; Anne, 165.
Goodwin, —, 83; Anne, 83; Jo., 83.
Goore, Wm., 148.
Gore, *Sir* Jo., 30; Sarah, 30.
Gostwick, —, 137.
GOURNEY, 58; *Gourney*, 58.
Gower, Cuthbert, 154; Isabel, 154; Nich., 154; Tho., 154.
Grabrand, Jo., 152.
Grace, Marg., 87; Rich., 87.
Granado, Cath., 40; Jas., 40.
Grant, —, 35; Alice, 35.
Grantham, *Sir* Tho., 160.
Graunt, Isab., 165; Walter, 165.
Grave, —, 5.
GRAVELEY, 8; *Graveley*, 8.
Graveley, —, 28; Eliz., 28; Hen., 121; Jo., 121; Tho. *bis*, 121.
Graves, —, 54; Cic., 34; Emme, 54; Geo., 34; Tho., 41.
Gray, —, 153; Dor., 167; Jo., 167, Jo., *Lo.*, 36; 113; Marg., 36, 101, 114; *Marq.* of Dorset, 113; Miles, 131; Tho., 101.
GREENE, 59; *Greene*, 59.
Greene, —, 7, 50, 79, 121; Bennett, 34; Lawr., 34; Marg., 50.
Greenway, —, 161; Anne, 161.
Gregory, —, 138; Ell., 38, 138; Tho., 38.
Grene, Alice, 140; Tho., 139; Wm., 139.
Grenfield, —, 149.
GREVE, 9; *Greve*, 9.
Grigge, Tho., 3.

GRIMESDICH, 17.
Grimston, —, 96; Marg., 80; Tho., 80.
GROSVENOR, 10; *Grosvenor*, 10.
Grosvenor, Alice, 145; Rafe, 145.
GRUBBE, 59; *Grubbe*, 59.
Grubbe, Jo., 84.
Grundy, Ralph, 63.
Grymbold, —, 12.
Grymbold, Joan, 12; Nich., 12.
GULSTON, 60; *Gulston*, 60.
Gunter, Const., 9; Jo., 9.
Gwynne, —, 18; Eliz., 18.

H

Hackett, Rog., 84.
Haileharte, —, 59; Alice, 59.
HALE, 61 *bis*, 62; *Hale*, 61.
Hale, —, 47.
Hales, —, 97, 140; Jo., 48; Lucy, 97; Mildred, 48, 140.
Halfhead, Mary, 94; Rich., 94.
Hall, —, 14, 154; Anne, 14, 45; Eliz., 149; Jo., 45; Rob., 149.
Halley, —, 106; Kymb., 106.
HALSEY, 62; *Halsey*, 62.
Halsey, Jane, 128; Mary, 47; Rob., 47; Tho., 128.
Halswell, Anne, 61; *Sir* Nich., 61; Rob., 61.
HALTON, 62; *Halton*, 62.
Halton, Jos., 107.
Hamby, Fr., 145.
Hamond, 5.
Hamond, —, 5, 16 *bis*, 101; Anne, 16; Eliz., 5, 101; Tho., 87.
Hampton, 121.
Hampton, Marg., 121; Wm., 121.
Hanby, —, 54; Jud., 54.
HANCHETT, 63; *Hanchett*, 63.
Hanchett, Anne, 153; Grace, 153; Jo., 153 *bis*; Tho., 153, and *see* Hanshott.
Hancock, Hen., 166.
Hanger, Geo., 103.
Hanlow, —, 111.
Hansacre, —, 111; Ella, 111.
Hanshott, —, 116; Grace, 120; Jo., 120, and *see* Hanchett.
Harbert, —, 7.
Harcourt, —, 19, 96; *Sir* Jo., 96.
Hare, Anne, 81; Rob., 81.
Harfett, Eliz., 98; Jo., 98.
Harlakenden, —, 120; Deb., 120.
Harleston, Jo., 65.
Harman, Alice, 25; Jo., 25.
Harmer, Geo., 34; Jo., 44.
Harntals, Anne, 137; Corn., 137.
HARRIS, 63; *Harris*, 63.
Harris, Jo., 47.
Harrison, —, 24, 71; Ellen, 24.

Harthill, 18.
Harthill, —, 18; Marg., 18.
Hartley, Marg., 15; Tho., 15.
Hartop, Jud., 167; Wm., 167.
HARVEY, 146.
Harvey, —, 97; Cath., 97.
HARVY, 10.
Harvy, Jo., 53; Mary, 53.
Haseldon, Kath., 140; Jo., 140.
Hastings, 119.
Hastings, —, 23; Fr., 23, 168; Jo., 119, 168; Jone, 119.
Hatton, *Sir* Chr., 114.
Haute, 166.
Haute, Jane, 166; Rog., 166.
Haward, 57.
Haward, Anne, 57; Hen., 57; Mary, 57; Mich., 57.
Hawes, —, 6; Dor., 75; *Sir* Jas., 102; Jo., 75; Jud., 41; Marg., 102; Tho., 41.
HAYDON, 11 *bis*; *Haydon*, 11.
HAYES, 64; *Hayes*, 64.
Hayles, Humfr., 168.
Hayward, Alex., 7.
Haywood, Cath., 26; Tho., 26.
Headlam, Jane, 154; Jo., 154.
Hedon, Bryan, 160.
Helder, *alias* Spicer, —, 88; Joane, 88.
Hemington, Edith, 102; Wm., 102.
Henage, —, 17; Isab., 17.
Henmarsh, Jane, 104; Wm., 104.
Henson, Edw., 118.
Hercye, 132.
Herdson, Barb., 78; Edw., 78.
Heron, —, 159; Ann, 159; Nich., 68.
HERTFORD, Town of, 107.
Hewes, Alex., 5; Eliz., 5.
HEWETT, 64; *Hewett*, 64.
Hewett, Tho., 73.
Hewson, —, 32; Dor., 32.
Heyton, —, 96; Fr., 96.
Hickman, Alice, 168; Hen., 76; Marg., 100; Tho., 100, 168.
Hicks, —, 116; *Sir* Baptist, 116; Ellis, 45; Susan, 45; Wm., 45.
HIDE, 64; *Hide*, 64.
Hide, —, 121; Mary, 121.
Higham. *See* Hyem.
Highnowe, —, 21.
Higmore, Nich., 106.
HILL, 12; *Hill*, 110.
Hill, —, 55; Alice, 46, 51; Agnes, 121; Edm., 51; Eliz., 51; Jo., 110; *Mr.*, 46; Rich., 50, 110; Rob., 48; Tho., 110, 121.
Hillersden, Tho., 73.
Hills, —, 7, 97; Edm., 97.
Hinde, *Sir* Wm., 36.
Hinton, Sam., 60.
Hobby, *Sir*, Edw., 136.
Hobson, Jo., 118.
Hodgson, —, 127; Hen., 127.
Holcroft, *Sir* Tho., 147.

Holdich, Tho., 118.
Holland, Jo., 161.
Hollingshead, Eliz., 124 ; Tho., 124.
Hollingworth, —, 9 ; Eliz., 9.
Honywood, Joyce, 89; Rob., 89.
Hoo, 12, 65 ; *Hoo*, 12.
Hoo, —, 166 ; Joyce, 166 ; Marg., 32 ; Rich., 94 ; Rob., 94 ; Tho., 2, 32, 157.
Hope, Rob., 165.
Hoper, Rich., 56.
Hoppie, Geo., 107.
Hopton, —, 109.
Hor, Anne, 30 ; Sam., 30.
Horde, Allen, 129.
HORSEY, 114; *Horsey*, 114.
Horsey, Geo., 49, 157 ; *Sir* Geo., 89 ; Helen, 49 ; Jasper, 49 ; *Sir* Jerom, 32 ; *Sir* Rafe, 49.
Horton, Eliz., 55 ; Jer., 55.
Hoskins, Chas., 62 ; Dor., *Lady*, 36 ; *Sir* Tho., 62.
House, 144.
House, Giles, 144 ; Tab., 144.
How, Benj., 34 ; Jo., 66, 115 ; Martha, 66.
Howard, Chas., *E.* of Notts, 136 ; Fr., 159 ; Tho., *Visc.* Bindon, 159.
Howell, Marg., 95 ; Rich., 95.
HOWLAND, 65.
Howse, *Ald.*, 64 ; Marg., 64.
Hubbert, *Sir* Fr., 151.
Huchin, Jo., 146.
Hudleston, Agnes, 139 ; *Sir* Rich., 139.
Hughes, —, 58 ; Fr., 58.
HUMBERSTON, 66 ; *Humberston*, 66.
Humfrey, Judith, 136 ; Lawr., 136 ; Wm., 107.
Humphynes, 132.
Hungate, —, 35 ; Ann, 35 ; *Sir* Hen., 35.
Hunt, —. 3, 34 ; Alice, 3, 34.
HURST, 66, 67 ; *Hurst*, 66.
Hurst, —, 26.
Hussey, —, 143 ; Br., 116 ; Jo., *Lo.*, 116.
Hutton, Jo., 36 ; Tho., 9 ; Thom., 9.
HYDE, 67 *bis* ; Hyde, 67 *bis*.
Hyde, —, 105, 54, 69 ; Jo., 164 ; Leonard, 136 ; Lucy, 69 ; Marg., 164 ; Marian, 105, 136 ; Ralfe, 113.
Hyem, Rich., 44.
Hynd, —, 23.

I

IBGRAVE, 13 ; *Ibgrave*, 13.
Ibgrave, —, 157 ; Giles, 21.
Ingleby, —, 27 ; Aune, 27.
INKERSALL, 68 ; *Inkersall*, 68.
Inkersall, Tho., 152.
Ireland, —, 88 ; Dor., 88.

IRONSIDE, 68 ; *Ironside*, 68.
Isack, Anne, 166 ; Jas., 166.
Ivory, Jo., 68 ; Rob., 107.
Iwardby, 23.
Iwardby, —, 23 ; Marg., 23.
Izod, —, 14 *bis* ; Agnes, 14.

J

Jackson, —, 41 ; Hen., 84 ; Jo., 69, 117 ; Marg., 159 ; Martha, 84 ; Rich., 159.
Jacob, *alias* Bredclaughe, —, 12 ; Marg., 12.
JAMES, 69.
Jenkinson, Anth., 105, 122 ; Lucy, 105, 122.
Jenks, Jo., 72.
Jennens, —, 20.
JENNINGS, 147 ; *Jennings*, 147.
Jennings, Anne, 48 ; Ellen, 133 ; *Sir* Jo., 165 ; Nich., 133 ; Ph., 168 ; Tho., 48.
Jermy, —, 1, 75 ; *Sir* Tho., 75.
Jervis, Cath., 137 ; Tho., 137.
Jesson, Jo., 31.
Jobson, —, 16 ; *Sir* Fr., 16 ; Marg., 16.
Johnson, —, 83 ; Fr., 118 ; Marg., 83.
JOSCELIN, 14, 69 ; *Joscelin*, 69.
Joscelin, —, 41.
Jurdeyne, *alias* Langley, Jane, 13 ; Joan, 13 ; Jo., 13 *bis* ; Tho., 13 ; Wm., 13.

K

Keeling, —, 152.
Kelinge, Jo., 107.
Kelk, Sia, 53 ; Wm., 53.
Kell, —, 118 ; Br., 118.
Kemis, —, 76 ; Edw., 36 ; Joan, 76.
Kempe, Fra., 81 ; Fr., 81.
KENT, 148.
Kent, Edw., 53 ; Jane, 41 ; Jo., 41.
Kerbie, —, 18.
Ketridg, Jane, 60 ; Rich., 60.
Keys, —, 37.
Kidd, —, 158 ; Priscilla, 158.
Kilburne, —, 159.
Kildare, Gerrard, *E.* of, 112.
Kilpeck, —, 111 ; Kath., 111.
KIMPTON, 69 ; *Kimpton*, 69.
Kimpton, —, 41, 105 ; Edm., 105, 121 ; Eliz., 121 ; Marian, 41 ; Tho., 41.
King, Alis., 15 ; Jo., 15, 61 ; Jud., 141 ; Rob., 141.
KINGSLEY, 70 ; *Kingsley*, 70.
Kirkby, 120.
Kirkby, Jo., 120 ; Mary, 120.
Kirkland, Rich., 150.
Kirkton, 131.
KITCHIN, 70; *Kitchin*, 70.
Kitson, Cath., 165 ; *Sir* Tho., 165.

Knevett, Cath., 135 ; *Sir* Hen., 135.
KNIGHT, 14 ; *Knight*, 14, 20, 147.
Knightley, *Sir* Rich., 165 ; Sus., 165.
KNIGHTON, 70 ; *Knighton*, 70, 141.
Knighton, Anne, 142 ; *Sir* Geo., 142 ; Jane, 3, 34 ; Tho., 3, 34.
Knolles, Knowles, *Sir* Fr., 30, 112, 136 ; Kath., 30, 112.
Kyffin, Rob., 127.

L

Lach, Jo., 148.
Lacon, Edw., 32 ; Jane, 32.
Lacy, —, 7 ; Eliz., 13 ; Joan, 7 ; Jo., 53 ; Marg., 53 ; Wm., 13.
LAKE, 71.
Lake, Ann, 153 ; Tho., 153.
LAMBERT, 121 ; *Lambert*, 62, 121.
Lambert, —, 61, 62 ; Alice, 82 ; Eliz., 105 ; Freeman, 105 ; Marg., 96 ; Mary, 61, 62 ; *Sir* Oliver, *Lo.*, 96 ; Simon, 82 ; Walter, 96.
La Meere, —, 126 ; Claus, 154 ; David, 126 ; Hester, 154.
Lamplow, Jenett, 140 ; *Sir* Jo., 140.
Lane, —, 68 ; Eliz., 120 ; *Sir* Wm., 120.
Langdall, 120.
Langdall, —, 120.
LANGHORNE, 71 ; *Langhorne*, 71.
Langhorne, Rob., 77 ; Wm., 78.
Langley, 160.
Langley, Eliz., 43 ; *Sir* Jo., 43.
Langwith, Tho., 130.
Latham, —, 20.
Lathill or Athill, —, 9 ; Agnes, 9.
Latimer, Eliz., 136 ; Jo., *Lo.*, 136.
LAVENDER, 72 ; *Lavender*, 72.
LAWRENCE, 72 ; *Lawrence*, 99.
Lawrence, —, 36 ; Edw., 107 ; Jane, 45 ; *Sir* Jo., 45.
Lawson, Mary, 46 ; Wm., 46.
Leake, 132.
LEE, 149 ; *Lee*, 149.
Lee, Anne, 89, 137 ; Marg., 155 ; *Sir* Rich., 89, 90 ; Tho., 137 ; *Sir* Walter, 155.
Leech, Denis, 130 ; Joane, 130.
Leeke, *Sir* Fr., 135.
Lelholme, 131.
Lenthorp, —, 126.
Le Rowse, 153.
LEVENTHORPE, 149 ; *Leventhorpe*, 149.
Leventhorpe, —, 17 ; Dor., 132 ; Jo., 17 ; *Sir* Jo., 132 ; Tho., 132.
Lever, 160.

INDEX.

Lever, Adam, 160; Marg., 160.
Levison, Wm., 87.
LEWEN, 115; *Lewen*, 115.
Lewen, Jo., 152; *Sir Just.*, 36.
Lewes, —, 138.
Lewknor, —, 149; Rog., 149.
Ley, Hester, 85; Jas., *E.* of Marlborough, 85.
Leyborn, Syb., 139; *Sir Tho.*, 139.
Lilborne, Ell., 164; Wm., 164.
Lilly, Michell, 126; Philad., 126.
Linch, Wm., 141.
Littlebery, 131.
Littlebery, —, 145; Anne, 145; Eliz., 131; Wm., 131.
LITTON, 73, 115, 151; *Litton*, 73.
Litton, —, 32, 117, 164; Mary, 85, 117; *Sir Rob.*, 12, 32; Rowl., 85; *Sir Rowl.*, 164.
Living, —, 127; Elyn, 127.
Lock, Michell, 133.
LOCKEY, 151; *Lockey*, 151.
Lodges, Hen., 28; Joan, 28.
Long, —, 129; Alice, 129; Jo., 100; Martha. 100.
Longevale, de, Isab., 119; Jo., 119.
Longmer, Jo., 151.
Longvile, Arthur, 11; Fr., 11; *Sir Hen.*, 135.
Love, —, 29, 129; Edw., 133; Joan, 29; Mary, 133.
Lovelace, Rob., 65, 168.
Lovell, —, 136, 142.
Lovett, Rich., 3.
LOWE, 74; *Lowe*, 74.
Lowe, Roynes, 75.
Lucas, —, 69; Anne, 14, 69; Tho., 14.
Luckin, Prud., 79; Rob., 79.
Lumley, Scis., 27; Rich., 27.
Lunsford, —, 46; Br., 7, 46; Wm., 7.
Lusher, Rich., 133.
Loxford, Jo., 149.
Lyndley, —, 145.
Lynn, Anne, 134; Geo., 134.

M

Machelafeld, 124.
Machelafeld, Eliz., 124; Jo., 124.
Maddison, Edw., 91.
Malmaynes, 12.
Malmaynes, —, 12, 166; *Sir Nich.*, 12.
Maltby, Isab., 154; Wm., 154.
Man, *Sir Chr.*, 104; Wm., 104.
Manesty, Rob., 118; Wm., 118.
Manners, Anne, 113; *Sir Geo., E.* of Rutl., 135; Kath., 113; Tho., *E.* of Rutl., 113 *bis.*
Manning, Maning, Eliz., 134; Jo., 134; Randall, 134; Wm., 60.
Mannock, —, 47; Ann, 4; Eliz., 47; Hen., 4.
Mansfield, 156.

Mansfield, —, 156; Tho., 156.
Mainwaring, Arth., 70; Tho., 70.
Marbury, Tho., 147; Thom., 147.
Mardock, 4.
Mardock, Ann, 4; Jo., 4.
Markham, Fr., 13; Gertr., 90; Rob., 90.
Marlborough, Hen., *E.* of, 36.
Marmion, Maude, 111; *Sir Ph.*, 111.
Marsh, Eliz., 5; Jo., 5, 123; Joan, 51; Rand., 51.
MARSHALL, 15; *Marshall*, 15.
Marshall, —, 19, 85; Eliz., 6, 19, 44, 80, 85; Rob., 80; Wm., 6, 44.
MARSTON, 74; *Marston*, 74.
Marston, Alice, 31; Anne, 86; Ellen, 31; Giles, 31; Jane, 51; Joan, 152; Tho., 86; Wm., 31, 51, 152.
Martin, Anne, 38; Dorcas, 133; *Sir Rich.*, 133; Steven, 38.
Mascall, Eliz., 70; Jo., 70.
Mathew, Const., 55; Fr., 28; Jo., 55; Wm., 28.
Mathews, Dor., 59; Wm., 59.
Maudit, Cath., 56; Tho., 56.
MAYNARD, 15.
Maynard, —, 20.
MAYNE, 75; *Mayne*, 75.
Mayne, —, 43; Anne, 144; Hen., 144; Jas., 123; Susan, 43.
Mayott, Tho., 115.
Meade, Rich., 34.
MEAUTIS, 75; *Meautis*, 75.
Medcalf, 119.
Medcalf, Chr., 119.
Mellish, —, 139, 169; Cath., 139, 169.
Merry, —, 16; Alice, 16; Eliz., 80; Rob., 80.
MERY, 152; *Mery*, 152.
Methwold, Anne, 127; Tho., 127.
Michell, —, 66, 67, 89; Edw., 58; Eliz., 66, 67, 80; Marg., 89; Mary, 58; Tho., 80.
Micklefield, —, 33.
Midleton, —, 35; Jo., 40.
MILDMAY, 153; *Mildmay*, 153.
Mildmay, Humfr., 113; Tho., 160; *Sir Tho.*, 160.
Millington, 124.
Millington, —, 124; Jane, 124.
Millington, de, Agnes, 145; Wm., 145.
Min, Myn, —, 169; Eliz., 67; Geo., 67; Jo., 62; *Sir Jo.*, 62; Rich., 130.
MOHUN, 16; *Mohun*, 16.
Mohun, Edith, 114; *Sir Reig.*, 114.
Mollington, Tho., 111.
Monck, Jo., 38.
MONOX, 76; *Monox*, 76.
Montague, Edw., *Lo.*, 36; Theo., 63.

Montford, Eliz., 77; Fr., 77.
Montjoy, —, 79; Cath., 79.
MOORE, 153; *Moore*, 153.
Moore, —, 83, 151; Cath., 83, 157; Geo., 155.
Mordaunt, Edm., 32; Eliz., 32, 35; Geo., 35; Lewis, 77.
More, Eliz., 81; Jo., 24; Rafe, 81.
Moreigh, Dor., 68; Rich., 68.
MORGAN, 76; *Morgan*, 76.
Morgan, Anne, 136; *Sir Tho.*, 136; Walter, 169.
Morles? Morley, —, 3; Euph., 3.
MORLEY, 154; *Morley*, 154.
Morley, Eliz., 160; Jo., 160.
MORRISON, 76, 115; *Morrison*, 76, 116.
Morrison, *Sir Chas.*, 36; Eliz., 36, 104; Tho., 104, 117.
Mortimer, 2.
Mortimer, —, 2.
Morton, —, 7; Elenor, 7.
Moston, *Sir Tho.*, 146.
Moyne, —, 76.
Munday, *Sir Jo.*, 147; Mary, 147.
Munne, Jo., 27.
Muschampe, —, 120.
Mychell, Br., 127; Jo., 127.
Myn. *See* Min.

N

Neale, Rob., 29.
NEEDHAM, 16, 77; *Needham*, 16, 77.
Needham, Eustace. 71, 96, 105; Geo., 96; Jane, 96; Lettice, 71; Rob., 109.
Nethermyll, 144.
Nethermyll, Isab., 144; Jul., 144.
Nevill, 20, 132, 147.
NEWCE, 17 *bis*, 78; *Newce*, 17 *bis*, 78.
Newce, Clement, 154; Mary, 141; Sarah, 154; Tho., 150; Wm., 107, 141, 168.
NEWCOMEN, 79; *Newcomen*, 79.
Newcomen, —, 97.
Newdigate, *Sir Rob.*, 68.
Newgate, —, 97.
NEWPORT, 79, 155; *Newport*, 155.
Newport, Grace, 79, 153; Jane, 163; Jo., 163; Mary, 20; Rob., 20, 79, 153.
Newton, —, 11, 113; Adam, 160; Alex., 11; Alice. 11 *bis*; *Sir Jo.*, 113; Tho., 113.
Newman, —, 13; Jacob, 118; Lawr., 117; Rob., 76.
Nicholls, Allen, 169; Joane, 169.
Nicholson, Fr., 20; Wm., 20.
Nicoll, Eliz., 70; Wm., 70.
Nightingale, Blanch, 66; Rob., 40; *Sir Tho.*, 40; Wm., 66.
NODES, 18, 80; *Nodes*, 80.

A A

178　INDEX.

Nodes, Noades, Edm., 54; Geo., 49; Mary, 54.
Norris, —, 98; Mary, 98.
North, —, 82; Jane, 82.
NORTON, 80; *Norton*, 80.
Norton, Anne, 46, 78; Eliz., 124; Luke, 28, 46, 78, 88; Martha, 46; *Sir* Rich., 124; Susan, 28; Talbot, 88; Tho., 46, 152.
Norwood, —, 12.
Norwood, —, 13; Dor., 13; Wm., 112.
Nowell, Alex., 152.
Nutting, —, 120.

O

Odingsells, Edw., 158; Eliz., 158.
Offley, Edw., 107
Onslow, Cath., 58; Geo., 58.
Osborne, Edw., 22; *Sir* Rob., 68.
Ostrich, Tho., 158; Wm., 158.
Oteby, 164.
Oxenbridge, *Sir* Rob., 37; Sus., 37.
Oxton, Tho., 107.

P

Packington, —, 43; *Ald.*, 43.
Padgett, —, 87.
Page, —, 92; Sicilly, 92.
Pagenham, Clement, 154.
Pagett, Hen., *Lo.*, 135.
Pakenham, *Sir* Hen., 49.
PALMER, 18; *Palmer*, 18.
Palmer, —, 37.
Pantulph, 111.
Pantolph, Maude, 111; Wm., *Lo.* of Wemme, 111.
Parell, Anne, 71; Wm., 71.
Parker, —, 38; Anne, 39; *Sir* Hen., 150; Jas., 167; Jane, 28; Jo., 28; Peter, 39.
Parr, Eliz., 3; Gilb., 28; Helen, 28; Rich., 3.
Parratt, —, 20.
Pascall, Andrew, 122.
Paston, —, 136.
Patrick, Jane, 144; Rich., 144.
Pawlett, Geo., 83; *Sir* Hugh, 129; Wm., *Marq.* of Winchester, 113.
Payne, Stephen, 165.
Paynter, Hen., 84.
Payton, *Sir* Sam., 157.
Peacock, —, 142; Chr., 142; Wm., 143, 146.
Peck, —, 100; Alice, 100.
Peckham, Anne, 113; *Sir* Wm., 113.
Pedley, Wm., 93.
Pelham, Judith, 136; *Sir* Tho., 136.
Peere, Mary, 170; Wm., 170.
PEMBERTON, 81; *Pemberton*, 81.

Pemberton, Raphe, 107, 149.
Pembridge, Wm., 115.
PENNE, 82, 116; *Penne*, 82.
Penne, Dor., 33; Rob., 33.
Pennington, 20, 147.
Pennington, Isab., 15; Rob., 15.
Pennyall, Jo., 55.
Percivall, Jo., 153.
Percye, Susan, 86; Tho., 86.
Perian, Jane, 49; *Sir* Wm., 49.
PERIENT, 156; *Perient*, 156.
Perient, Geo., 133; Gert., 58; Helen, 65; *Sir* Jo., 58; Marg., 133; Wm., 65.
Perkins, Rich., 33.
Perrey, Mary, 76; Math., 76.
Pert, Tyndall, 117; Wm., 139.
Pettitt, —, 96.
Pettiward, Martha, 57; Rog., 57.
Pettus, Chr., 90; *Sir* Jo., 90.
Petty, *Sir* Aug., 95; *Sir* Jo., 95.
Peyton, *Sir* Jo., 109; Rob., 109.
Philipott, Fr., 134; *Sir* Geo., 134; Tho., 134.
Phillips, Eliz., 40; Hen., 7; Mary, 115; Rich., 115; Tho., 40.
Phipps, Tho., 71.
PICHFORD, 82; *Pichford*, 82.
Pichford, Eliz., 66; Pen., 87; Rob., 66; Wm., 87.
Pigeon, —, 19.
Pigott, 29.
Pigott, —, 3, 120, 129; Benj., 77; Dor., 47; Fr., 29, 129, 146; Jo., 40; Reb., 34; Tho., 29, 34, 47; Val., 120.
Pike, Tho., 147.
Pinarake, —, 27; Jane, 27.
Pinchpole, 23.
Pinchpole, Eliz., 24; Jo., 24.
Pipe, Marg., 99; *Sir* Rob., 99.
Piss, 43.
Piss, —, 43; Eliz., 43.
PLOMER, 83, 157; *Plomer*, 83, 157.
Plomer, —, 115; Jane, 115.
Plumsted, —, 93.
Pointz, —, 90; *Sir* Gabr., 90; *Sir* Nich., 23; Sus., 90.
Pole, Tho., 16.
Pollard, Rafe, 47.
Poole, Eliz., 132; Ell., 126; Hen., 132; Jane, 118; *Sir* Tho., 126; Wm., 118.
Pope, Jane, 44; Jo., 32, 44; *Sir* Tho., 129.
Porter, —, 127; Ambrose, 39; Mary, 74; Tho., 74.
POTKIN, 158; *Potkin*, 158.
Potkin, Tho., 140.
Poure, Fr., 142.
POWELL, 83; *Powell*, 83.
Powell, Jo., 49; Sam., 49; Sarah, 87; Tho., 87.
Poynter, —, 6; Ellin, 74; Wm., 74.
PRANELL, 159; *Pranell*, 159.
Pratt, Eliz., 57; Rafe, 57.
Prescot, —, 146; Agnes, 146.

PRESTON, 84; *Preston*, 84, 119.
Preston, Mary, 60; Maude, 119; Roger, 119; Wm., 60.
Price, Edm., 26; Pris., 26.
Proby, *Sir* Peter. 118.
Procter, Sam., 35.
PUCKERING, 160; *Puckering*, 160.
Pudifoote, —, 74; Alice, 74.
PULTER, 85, 116; *Pulter*, 85.
Pulter, —, 29; Alice, 29, 111, 169; Edw., 77, 105, 111, 122, 151; Ellen, 77; Litton, 36; Lucy, 110; Marg., 122; Mary, 105; Wm., 110, 169.
Purdey, Wm., 118.
Purefoy, Isab., 129; Jo., 129.
PURVEY, 161; *Purvey*, 161.
Puttenham, Edw., 90; Eliz., 90; *Sir* Geo., 90.
Pye, *Sir* Walter, 91.
Pym, Alex., 139.
Pynder., 130; Eliz., 130.

Q

QUARLES, 161; *Quarles*, 161.

R

RADCLIFFE, 19, 85; *Radcliffe*, 19, 59.
Radcliffe, Edw., 40; Joane, 59; Jo., 59; *Sir* Rich., 59.
Rainsford, *Sir* Fr., 52.
Ramston, Jo., 2.
Randolfe, —, 75; Alice, 75.
Rawley, *Sir* Edw., 164.
Raymond, Bridget, 4, 38; Jo., 4, 38; Mary, 4.
READE, 162; *Reade*, 162.
Reade, —, 12; Jo., 28; *Sir* Jo., 145; Symon, 12; Theod., 40; Tho., 12, 117; *Sir* Tho., 32.
Redwood, Jo., 146.
Reeve, Marg., 34; Wm., 34.
Revell, Rog., 114.
Reynolds, —, 76; Eunice, 167; Geo., 38; Jane, 76; Lucy, 38; Rich., 167.
RICH, 86; *Rich*, 86.
Richold, Nich., 118.
Rickthorne, Wm., 161.
Ridley, —, 158.
Rigby, —, 115.
Riley, Anne, 79; Jas., 79.
Risam, 156.
Risam, Joane, 156; *Sir* Jo., 156.
Risley, —, 52.
Rivers, *Sir* Jo., 136.
Roberts, 156.
Roberts, Jo., 107; Marg., 3; Tho., 3; Wm., 154, 156.
ROBINSON, 86; *Robinson*, 86, 156.
Robinson, —, 50, 145, 164; Geo., 71; Jo., 109; Tho., 156.
ROBOTHAM, 87; *Robotham*, 87.
Robotham, Grace, 88; Jo., 88.
Rochdale, Grace, 93; Rich., 93.

INDEX. 179

Roche, 111.
Roche, —, 111; Grisell, 111.
Rochford, —, 3.
ROGERS, 87.
Rokell, 129.
Rokell, —, 129; Marg., 129.
ROLFE, 88; Rolfe, 88.
Rolfe, Ann, 169; Jas., 43, 87; Mary, 43; Wm., 169.
Rose, —, 1.
ROTHERAM, 88; Rotheram, 88.
Rotheram, Geo., 2, 164; Sir Tho., 165.
Rowlett, 20, 147.
Rowlett, —, 20; Affabell, 157; Eliz., 147; Joan, 20; Marg., 15, 20; Ralph, 15, 20; Sir Ralph, 15, 20, 112, 147.
Rowley, —, 131; Jo., 138.
Rows, Anne, 168; Hen., 168.
Rushton, Wm., 84.
Russell, —, 96.
Ruthe, Rich., 107.
Rutland, Hen., E. of, 116.
Ryther, Sus., 134; Sir Wm., 134.

S

SADLER, 89 bis; Sadler, 89.
Sadler, Anne, 114; Edw., 149; Ellen, 152; Jane, 125; Jo., 152; Sir Rafe, 49, 114, 125.
ST. ALBAN'S, Town of, 107.
St. Barbe, Urs., 168; Wm., 168.
St. Cleere, —, 131; Eliz., 131.
St. George, —, 140; Anne, 83, 140; Tho., 83.
St. John, Alex., 150; Anne, 73, 115; Martha, 49; Oliver, 49; Oliver, Lo., 73, 115.
St. Leger, 12.
St. Leger, Isab., 12; Sir Jo., 12.
St. Omer, 12.
St. Omer, Alison (? Ellinor), 12; Lo., 12.
Salisbury, Wm., E. of, 107.
Salkeld, Jenett, 140; Rog., 140.
Salter, Bartram, 155; Sir Edw., 32.
SALTONSTALL, 90; Saltonstall, 90.
Saltonstall, Jud., 86; Sir Rich., 86.
Samors, Denys, 146.
Sampson, 145; Alice, 145.
Sams, Sir Jo., 145.
SAPCOTTS, 162.
Sanders, —, 55; Chr., 55; Marg., 152; Sir Mathew, 152; Rich., 129.
Sandis, Br., 67; Miles, 67.
SAUNDERS, 90.
Saunders, —, 86; Fr., 30; Marg., 82, 116; Mary, 148; Sus., 30; Tho., 82, 116, 148.
Savill, Jo., 135; Sam., 128.
Sawell, Anne, 125; Rich., 125.
Saxilby, Edw., 161.
Sayers, —, 131; Joane, 131.

Scargill, Dor., 43; Fr., 43.
Scott, Rich., 142.
SCROGGS, 163.
Scroggs, —, 79.
Scrope, Tho., Lo. of Bolton, 136.
Sebroke, Rob., 128.
SEDLEY, 91.
Segrave, Jo., 127.
Sele, Marg., 15; Rich., 15.
SELIOKE, 91; Selioke, 91.
Sell, —, 130; Jo., 130.
Selyard, 124.
Selyard, Dor., 124; Nich., 124.
SENNOKE, 92; Sennoke, 92.
Seymer, —, 150; Sir Tho., 150.
Shakerley, —, 45.
Shambrooke, Sus., 27; Wm., 27.
Sheeres, Arthur, 57.
Shelley, Jo., 27.
Shelton, —, 63, 162; Alice, 14, 69; Sir Jo., 14, 69.
Sheppard, —, 60; Const., 60; Jo., 21, 168.
SHIRLEY, 163; Shirley, 163.
Sherburne, Sir Edw., 126; Jud., 126.
Sherington, —, 90; Sir Jo., 90; Wm., 115.
Sherley, Eliz., 149; Rafe, 149.
Sherwood, —, 64; Cath., 64.
Shipley, Wm., 27.
Shirley, —, 114.
SHOTBOLT, 163.
Shotbolt, —, 112; Alice, 30, 112; Jo., 30.
Shouldham, Anne, 94; Humf., 94.
Shukborough, Jo., 6, 44.
Shute, Nath., 77.
Sidenham, Sir Geo., 129.
Sikes, Rob., 166.
Silvester, Alice, 95; Rob., 95.
Simon, —, 154; Eliz., 154.
SIMPSON, 92; Simpson, 92.
Simpson, —, 65; Marg., 65.
Skevington, Lettice, 27; Wm., 27.
SKINNER, 93; Skinner, 93.
Skinner, —, 86; Jone, 86.
SKIPWITH, 20; Skipwith, 20.
Skipwith, —, 3, 34; Helen, 3; Joan, 123; Jo., 16; Ralfe, 7; Rob., 149; Wm., 123.
Slaney, Anne, 73, 115; Steph., 73, 115.
Slifield, Jo., 153.
Smartfoote, Rich., 58.
Smith, Geo., 115; Sir Geo., 73; Sir Nich., 115; Wm., 55.
SMITHWICK, 21; Smithwick, 21.
Smithwick, Rob., 14.
SMYTH, 164; Smyth, 119, 164.
Smyth, —, 2, 22, 97; Chas., 146; Eliz., 114; Godfrey, 34; Jane, 114, 162; Jo., 119; Marg., 2, 146; Mary, 46, 119; Rich., 38, 119; Rob., 57, 162; Tho., 114; Wm., 46, 146.
SNAGG, 21; Snagg, 21.
Snagg, Alice, 169; Mary, 32; Tho., 32, 169.

SNELLING, 164; Snelling, 164.
Soame, Jo., 157; Sir Steph., 157.
Somers, 132.
Somerset, D. of, 135.
Songer, 121.
Songer, Jas., 121; Jo., 121; Marg., 121.
Sonings, 121.
Sonings, Joan, 122; Rob., 122.
Sotherton, Nowell, 170; Tim., 176.
South, —, 153.
Southcote, Jane, 142; Jo., 142.
Southworth, —, 145; Jo., 145.
Sparke, 119.
Sparke, —, 120; Anne, 120.
Specott, Humfr., 24.
Spence, —, 167; Anne, 167.
SPENCER, 22, 165; Spencer, 22.
Spencer, —, 148; Anne, 52; Chas., 63; Eliz., 136; Jo., 109; Sir Jo., 136; Marg., 109, 135; Nich., 52, 87; Sir Rich., 32, 148; Sir Rob., 135; Rob., Lo. Wormleighton, 109; Tho., 63.
Spenlow, Agnes, 127; Edw., 126; El., 126.
Spicer, Tho., 120.
Spilman, —, 120; Marg., 120.
Spring, Mary, 57; Tho., 57.
Squire, Jo., 3.
Stamp, —, 158; Anne, 83, 158; Cath., 83; Eliz., 83; Jo., 83.
Stanhope, —, 166; Mary, 166.
Staveley, 132.
Staynes, —, 70; Abigail, 70.
Stephens, —, 164; Rose, 164.
Stermont, Geo., 65; Sus., 65.
STERNE, 93, 94; Sterne, 93.
Sterne, Andr., 137; Audr., 137.
STEWARD, 94.
Steward, Marg., 131; Simon, 127, 131.
Stile, Edw., 77; Humfr., 156; Marg., 77.
Stocker, Anth., 36.
Stokes, Marg., 164; Wm., 164.
Stoner, Cath., 40; Jo., 40.
Stonehouse, Geo., 162; Mary, 162.
Stoner, Jo., 34.
Strangwish, El., 160; Sir Ph., 160.
STRATFORD, 95; Stratford, 95.
Streete, Humfr., 30; Reb., 30.
Stringer, —, 149; Hen., 62; Lettice, 62.
Stuart, —, 33; Humfr., 33; Marg., 33.
Stuke, Anne, 98; Eliz., 98; Ellen, 98; Fr., 98; Geo., 98; Jo., 98; Mary, 98.
Stutevile, —, 68; Sir Martin, 68.
Sudley, Joan, 111; Jo., Lo., 111.
Suliard, Mary, 29; Tho., 79.
Sunings, Joane, 105; Rob., 105.

INDEX.

Sussex, Rob., *E.* of, 116.
SUTTON, 29; *Sutton*, 29.
Sutton, Alice, 129; Faith, 42; Jo., 42, 129; Marg., 129; Roger, 129; Wm., 129.
Swifte, —, 9 *bis*; Dor., 9; Marg., 9.
Swindlehurst, —, 76; Jone, 76.
Symes, Mary, 159; Rich., 159.

T

Tanfield, Eliz., 135; *Sir* Lawr., 135.
Tate, —, 151; Jo., 151.
TAVERNER, 95; *Taverner*, 95.
Taverner, Marg., 105; Peter, 49, 105.
TAYLOR, 165.
Taylor, —, 159; Alice, 110; Jo., 157; Raphe, 110; Reb., 42; Tho., 42.
Tempest, Alis, 119; Edw., 119.
Temple, Cath., 127; Wm., 127.
Tendring, —, 4, 38; Joan, 4, 38.
Thirkell, *Sir* Hen., 139; Kath., 139.
THOMPSON, 97; *Thompson*, 97.
Thompson, —, 54, 63, 115; Eliz., 54; Hen., 89.
Thornborough, Edw., 40.
Thornton, Eliz., 36; Jeremy, 169; Joan, 169; Rob., 36.
THOROGOOD, 98, 117; *Thorogood*, 117.
Thorogood, —, 115; Ann, 115; *Sir* Jo., 75.
Thorold, Chas., 130; *Sir* Edm., 130.
Threll, —, 167.
Throgmorton, —, 133; Cath., 39; Jo., 39.
Thromotby *alias* Thornaby, —, 154, 155; Anne, 155; Phillis, 154.
Thurston, *Mr.*, 63.
Tichborne, Mary, 167; Nich., 167.
Tickner, Rich., 149; Wm., 149.
Tirringham, Dor., 37; *Sir* Tho., 37.
Tirwhitt, Marg., 155; *Sir* Wm., 155.
Toenson, Jo., 15.
TOOKE, 98, 99, 166; *Tooke*, 98, 166.
Tooke, Dor., 126; Wm., 126.
Torrell, —, 150.
Torse, —, 154.
Townley, Fr., 143.
Tracye, Marg., 95; Rob., 95.
Treheron, Nath., 141.
Trevanion, —, 136.
Trigg, Wm., 159.
Trott, —, 99; Jo., 168; Jud., 168; Martin, 157; Nich., 157.
Tucke, Mary, 18; Wm., 18.
Tucker, Eliz., 91; Fr., 91; Geo., 91 *bis*; Rob., 91; Wm., 115.

Tuke, —, 120.
Tulley, Alice, 167; Tho., 161.
Turbervile, Chr., 10, 146; *Sir* Jo., 10, 146.
Turk, Fr., 41; Wm., 41.
Turner, —, 118, 138; Eliz., 26; Hen., 120, 155; Jo., 26; Marg., 120.
Turpin, Tho., 140.
Turvile, Marg., 129; Rich., 129.
Twyford, Eliz., 101; Rob., 101.
Twyneho, —, 11 *bis*; Anne, 11; Edw., 11.
Tyler, Judith, 72; Tho., 72.

U

Umfrevile, 119.
Umfrevile, Anne, 119; Tho., 119.
Underhill, 70.
Underwood, —, 14; Edw., 52; Rob., 52.
Upton, Eliz., 169; Jo., 169.
Usthwayte, Wm., 164.

V

Van Hulst, Hans, 69; Mary, 69.
Vanlore, Anne, 134; *Sir* Peter, 134.
Vaughan, —, 128, 158; Eliz., 70; Milliscent, 158; Steph., 70; Tho., 169.
Vavasor, —, 102; Eliz., 102.
VERNEY, 23, 168; *Verney*, 23.
VERNON, 99; *Vernon*, 99.
Vernon, Chr., 72.
Vesey, Fr., 166; Wm., 166.
Viel, Dennis, 42; Sus., 42.
Villiers, Eliz., 112, 120; Geo., *E.* of, 112.
Vinton, Eliz., 118; Tho., 118.

W

Wad, Chr., 56; Eliz., 56.
Wade, Alice, 36; *Sir* Wm., 36.
Wake, 119.
Wake, Eliz., 119; Hen., 119.
Walcott, Eliz., 118; Humfr., 49; Wm., 118.
Walgrave, —, 153; Mary, 153.
Walkden, Tho., 8.
Walker, Alice, 100; Hen., 100, 133; Sus., 133; Tho., 100.
Waller, —, 21, 29, 111; Geo., 38.
Wallis, Hen., 82; Susan, 82.
Wallop, —, 88; Eliz., 88.
Wallys, —, 149.
WALTER, 23; *Walter*, 23.
Ward, 48; Anne, 48; Jas., 3; Jo., 50; Rich., 94.
Waring, 20, 147.
Warner, Eliz., 31; Hen., 31; Oliver, 153.
WARREN, 100, 169; *Warren*, 100, 169.

Warren, —, 21; Marg., 158; Rob., 158.
Warren *alias* Bygrave, Wm., 77.
WARREN *alias* WALLER, 101.
Warren alias *Waller*, 101.
Warton, Emme, 145; Jo., 145; Rich., 145.
Wastell, Simon, 152.
WATERHOUSE, 119; *Waterhouse*, 119.
Waterhouse, Agnes, 6; Jo., 6.
WATHE, 101; *Wathe*, 101.
Watson, —, 77; Edw., 159; *Sir* Lewis, 77.
WATTS, 102 *bis*; *Watts*, 102.
Watts, Jo., 57.
Waynman, *Sir* Rich., 97; Tho., 97.
Webb, —, 3, 53, 128, 146; Abr., 84; Alice, 50; Anne, 146; Eliz., 53, 128; Martha, 84; *Sir* Rich., 115; Tho., 50; *Sir* Wm., 73.
Weeks, Tho., 138.
WELD, 103; *Weld*, 103.
Weldisbe, —, 16, 77; Jane, 16, 77.
Welsh, —, 35; Anne, 39; Eliz., 35.
Wentworth, —, 2, 96; Agnes, 160; Jo., 113; Rog., 160.
Westcot, —, 56.
Westerne, Hen., 72.
Weston, —, 23.
Wetherall, —, 106.
Whaddon, Andrew, 120.
Whalley, Rich., 114.
Wheeler, *Mr.*, 63; Tho., 146.
Whethill, Marg., 45; Rich., 45.
Whinne, 31.
WHITAKER, 103; *Whitaker*, 103.
White, —, 70; Steph., 118; Sus., 70.
Whitehead, —, 96; *Sir* Hen., 98.
Whitgift, Jo., 146.
Whitstock, *Capt.*, 137.
Whittaker, Jer., 28; Jo., 127.
Whittingham, 23.
Whittingham, Mary, 23; Rob., 23.
Wichard, *Sir* Hen., 129; *Sir* Jo., 129; Marg., 129; *Sir* Nich., 129; Tho., 129.
Wichingham, 12.
Widdrington, *Sir* Hen., 136.
Wight, Jo., 147.
Wilcox, 85.
Wilcox, —, 85.
Wilde, Anne, 104; *Sir* Jo., 104.
Wilkinson, —, 168.
Willaby, 164.
Willey, —, 7.
WILLIAMS, 169; *Williams*, 169.
Williams, *Sir* Abr., 63; Anth., 139; Grif., 169.
WILLIMOTT, 104; *Willimott*, 104.
WILLIS, 104; *Willis*, 104.

Willon, Edw., 167.
Wilmot, *Sir* Chas., 109.
WILSON, 105, 121; *Wilson*, 105, 121.
Wilson, —, 155; Isabel, 155; Rafe, 117.
Winch, Annis, 66; Edw., 118; Wm., 66.
WINGATE, 105; *Wingate*, 105.
Wingate, Edw., 78, 96; Fr., 78, 96; Geo., 3; Jane, 96.
Wingfield, Geo., 31.
Wise, —, 49.
Wiseman, Jo., 150; Wm., 36.
Woodcock, Eliz., 124; Fr., 44; Ralph, 44, 124.
Woodford, Eliz., 70; Judith, 70; Mary, 70; Rob., 70.

Woodgate, —, 158; Alexandrina, 158.
Woodhouse, Eliz., 153; *Sir* Rog., 153.
Woodliff, 161.
Woodliff, Ang., 99, 167; Wm., 99, 167.
Woodthorpe, 131.
Woodward, Jo., 53; *Sir* Jo., 53; Martha, 53.
Wright, —, 126; Chr., 134; Fr., 126; Nich., 133.
WROTH, 106.
Wrottesley, Dor., 72; Walter, 72.
Wyberd, Jo., 168.
Wyburd, Mary, 104; Tho., 104.

Wychard, 29.
Wychard, *Sir* Hen., 29; *Sir* Jo., 29; Marg., 29.
Wykes, —, 1; Amy, 1.
WYNDOWT, 106; *Wyndowt*, 106.
Wythe, Anne, 52; Walter, 52.

Y

Yong, Walter, 161.
Yoxhall, Nath., 92.

Z

Zouch, *Lo.*, 113.

ERRATA.

Page 39, *for* Parkes *read* Parker.
  ,, 47, *for* Halsby *read* Halsey.
  ,, 57, *for* Walls *read* Watts.
  ,, 89, *for* Rash *read* Bash.

The Harleian Society,

INSTITUTED FOR THE

PUBLICATION OF INEDITED MANUSCRIPTS

RELATING TO

Genealogy, Family History, and Heraldry.

The Harleian Society,

INSTITUTED FOR THE

PUBLICATION OF INEDITED MANUSCRIPTS

RELATING TO

GENEALOGY, FAMILY HISTORY, AND HERALDRY.

COUNCIL ROOM—140 WARDOUR STREET, W.

President.

HIS GRACE THE DUKE OF MANCHESTER, K.P.

Vice-Presidents.

HIS GRACE THE DUKE OF WESTMINSTER, K.G.
THE MOST NOBLE THE MARQUIS OF BUTE, K.T.
THE RIGHT HON. VISCOUNT MIDLETON.
THE RIGHT HON. LORD MONSON.
THE HON. HENRY ROPER-CURZON.
SIR HENRY M. VAVASOUR, Bart., F.S.A.
RALPH ASSHETON, Esq.

Council.

W. AMHURST TYSSEN AMHERST, Esq., F.S.A.
GEORGE W. MARSHALL, Esq., LL.D., F.S.A.
J. PAUL RYLANDS, Esq., F.S.A.
GRANVILLE LEVESON GOWER, Esq., F.S.A.
GEORGE J. ARMYTAGE, Esq., F.S.A.
JOSEPH JACKSON HOWARD, Esq., LL.D., F.S.A.
THOMAS BROOKE, Esq., F.S.A.
THE REV. F. T. COLBY, D.D., F.S.A.
CAPT. EDWARD ARTHUR WHITE, F.S.A.
W. PRIDEAUX COURTNEY, Esq.
DUDLEY G. CARY ELWES, Esq., F.S.A.
SIR JOHN MACLEAN, F.S.A.

Honorary Treasurer.

JOSEPH JACKSON HOWARD, Esq., LL.D., F.S.A.,
3 Dartmouth Row, Blackheath, S.E.

Honorary Secretaries.

GEORGE J. ARMYTAGE, Esq., F.S.A.,
Clifton Woodhead, near Brighouse.
*J. PAUL RYLANDS, Esq., F.S.A.,
Heather Lea, Claughton, Birkenhead.

Bankers.

THE LONDON AND COUNTY BANK, 21 Lombard Street, E.C.

Auditors.

HENRY WAGNER, Esq., F.S.A.
THE REV. C. J. ROBINSON, M.A.

Hon. Local Secretary for Washington (U.S.A.) and District.

WILLIAM H. UPTON, Esq.

Hon. Local Secretary for Connecticut (U.S.A.).

THE HON. DANIEL C. EATON.

* To whom all communications are to be addressed relative to the Society.

Rules.

1. This Society shall be called the HARLEIAN SOCIETY.

2. It shall have for its chief object the publication of the Heraldic Visitations of Counties, and any manuscripts relating to Genealogy, Family History, and Heraldry, selected by the Council.

3. The Council shall consist of a President, nine Vice-Presidents, and twelve Members of Council, two of whom shall hold the posts of Secretary and Treasurer; and any four, including the Treasurer or Secretary, shall form a quorum. In case of equality of votes, the Chairman to have a casting vote. Any Candidate may be elected with the consent in writing of one Member of the Council, the Treasurer, and the Secretary.

4. Three Members of the Council shall retire in rotation annually, but shall be eligible for re-election.

5. The Annual Subscription shall be One Guinea, paid in advance, and due on the 1st day of January in each year; and new Members shall pay an Entrance Fee of 10s. 6d. in addition to their first Annual Subscription.

6. Members may at their option subscribe Two Guineas per annum, in which case they will be entitled to the publications of the Register Section of the Society.

7. The funds raised by the Society shall be expended in publishing such works as are selected by the Council; but no payment in money shall be made to any person for editing any work for the Society.

8. One volume at least shall be supplied to the Members every year.

9. An Annual Meeting shall be held in the month of January every year, at such time and place as the Council may direct; and due notice shall be sent to the Members of the Society at least a fortnight previously.

10. No work shall be supplied to any Member unless his Subscription for the year be paid; and any Member not having paid his Subscription for two years, having received notice thereof, shall cease to belong to the Society.

11. No copies of the publications of the Society shall be supplied to persons not actually Members, and each Member shall be restricted to a single Subscription.

12. An account of the receipts and expenses of the Society to be made up to the 31st of December in each year, and published with a list of the Members and the Rules of the Society in the following Volume.

13. These Rules shall not be altered except at the Annual Meeting, and three clear weeks' notice must be given to the Secretary of any such intended alteration.

Report for the Year 1885.

DURING the year twenty-one Members have joined the Society; twelve have resigned, nine have died, and the names of seven have been removed under Rule X.

Three hundred and sixty-two remain on the Roll of Members, of whom one hundred and seventy-eight are subscribers to the Register Section.

The Volumes which have been issued for the year are—The "Visitation of Dorsetshire in 1623," and the "Visitation of Gloucestershire in 1623."

The "Visitations of Hertfordshire in 1572 and 1634," now in the Press, are almost completed, and will be issued to the Members very shortly.

The Shropshire Pedigrees, comprising the Visitations of 1569, 1584, and 1623, are fully transcribed, and will, it is anticipated, form Two Volumes.

In the Register Section, the Second Volume of the "Registers of St. James, Clerkenwell," has been issued.

The "Register of Marriages at St. George, Hanover Square," Volume I., is in the Press, and in a forward state. The Second Volume is now being transcribed.

The "Registers of Christ Church, Newgate Street," are ready for the Press.

The Accounts for the year are appended to this Report.

The retiring Members of the Council are Messrs. COURTNEY and ELWES, and Sir JOHN MACLEAN.

Harleian Society.

ACCOUNTS FOR THE YEAR ENDING 31ST DECEMBER, 1885.

ORDINARY ACCOUNT.

Dr.

	£	s.	d.
Balance to 31st December, 1884	492	6	8
Subscriptions	363	12	0
Books purchased by Members	61	8	6
Dividend on Stock (£632 : 8s.)	18	7	7
Interest on Deposit (£150)	2	14	2
	£938	8	11

Cr.

	£	s.	d.
Messrs. Mitchell and Hughes:—			
Balance of Bedford Visitation, etc.	67	19	7
General Printing, etc.	13	16	6
Balance of Gloucester and Dorset Visitations	202	9	0
Payment on account of General Printing, etc., including £100 for Hertfordshire Visitation	130	7	11
Cabinet for Woodblocks	7	10	0
Bookshelves	8	10	0
Insurance	8	8	0
Rent of Room	5	0	0
Advertisements	2	12	0
Incidents, Honorary Secretary and Treasurer	20	0	0
Tracings from British Museum (Birch)	1	11	6
Transcript of Shropshire Visitation (J. Eedes)	22	0	0
	£490	4	6
Balance	448	4	5
	£938	8	11

REGISTER SECTION.

Dr.

	£	s.	d.
Balance to 31st December, 1884	70	4	8
Subscriptions	183	15	0
Sale of Books	28	16	6
	£282	**15**	**9**

Cr.

Messrs. Mitchell and Hughes:—

	£	s.	d.
On account of St. James's Registers	63	0	9
Balance of St. James's Registers and General Printing, etc. (including cost of Index)	114	17	7
Transcript of Bath Abbey Registers	8	0	0
	185	18	4
Balance	96	17	5
	£282	**15**	**9**

GENERAL BALANCE.

	£	s.	d.
To Balance, Ordinary Account	448	4	5
" Register Section	96	17	5
	£545	**1**	**10**

	£	s.	d.
Net Balance in Bank	545	1	10
	£545	**1**	**10**

Examined and found correct,

HENRY WAGNER,
CHARLES J. ROBINSON, } *Honorary Auditors.*

JOSEPH JACKSON HOWARD, *Honorary Treasurer.*

7th January, 1886.

List of Members, with the Dates of their Election.

CORRECTED TO JANUARY 1ST, 1886.

Those marked (*) are Subscribers to the Register Section.

27 Sept. 1876.	*F. WILLIAM ALINGTON, 13 Mitre Court Chambers, Temple, E.C.
20 Oct. 1885.	ROWLAND CREW ALSTON, Harrold Hall, Bedford.
24 Nov. 1869.	*REGINALD AMES, 2 Albany Terrace, Park Square East, N.W.
29 Apr. 1869.	*W. AMHURST TYSSEN AMHERST, M.P., F.S.A. (*Council*), Didlington Hall, Brandon.
31 Dec. 1875.	*JOHN AMPHLETT, Clent, Stourbridge.
24 Nov. 1869.	FRANK ANDREW, Chester Square, Ashton-under-Lyne.
1 July, 1870.	WILLIAM SUMNER APPLETON, Boston, U.S.A.
27 Mar. 1869.	*GEORGE J. ARMYTAGE, F.S.A. (*Hon. Secretary*), Clifton Woodhead, near Brighouse.
12 Apr. 1869.	*RALPH ASSHETON (*Vice-President*), Downham Hall, Clitheroe.
6 Dec. 1870.	JOHN ASTLEY, Stoneleigh Terrace, Coventry.
5 Oct. 1872.	ATHENÆUM, Liverpool (W. ROSCOE JONES, Librarian).
4 Sept. 1880.	*Captain F. W. T. ATTREE, R.E., Springfield House, Worthing.
9 Aug. 1884.	T. A. CARLESS ATTWOOD, The Cliff, Malvern Wells.
21 Jan. 1882.	FRANCIS JOSEPH BAIGENT, Winchester.
28 July, 1869.	JOSEPH GURNEY BARCLAY, 54 Lombard Street, E.C.
14 Jan. 1879.	*The Rev. C. W. BARDSLEY, Vicarage, Ulverston, Lancaster.
7 May, 1885.	EVERARD BARTON, Summerdyne, Bewdley.
1 Jan. 1883.	*Captain H. BATHURST, Springhill, Frome, Somerset.
4 Nov. 1870.	JOHN BATTEN, F.S.A., Aldon, Yeovil.
12 June, 1871.	*FRANCIS BAYLEY, F.S.A., 66 Cambridge Terrace, Hyde Park, W.
7 June, 1877.	EDWIN J. BEDFORD, 37 Elmore Road, Broomhill, Sheffield.
21 Sept. 1876.	BEDFORD ARCHÆOLOGICAL SOCIETY, Bedford (D. G. C. ELWES, Hon. Secretary).
23 Jan. 1885.	CHARLES L. BELL, Chesterton Road, Cambridge.
11 Aug. 1877.	WALTON GRAHAM BERRY, Broomfield, Fixby, near Huddersfield.
17 June, 1875.	SAMUEL BIRCHAM, 46 Parliament Street, S.W.
13 Dec. 1878.	THOMAS BIRD, Canons, Romford.
9 Mar. 1871.	*BIRMINGHAM LIBRARY, Union Street, Birmingham (C. E. SCARSE, Librarian).
24 July, 1883.	*BIRMINGHAM CENTRAL FREE LIBRARY, Ratcliffe Place, Birmingham (J. MULLINS, Librarian).
24 Apr. 1869.	F. A. BLAYDES, Shenstone Lodge, Ashburnham Road, Bedford.
1 June, 1869.	*The Rev. CHARLES W. BOASE, Exeter College, Oxford.
22 Oct. 1874.	*REGINALD STEWART BODDINGTON, 15 Markham Square, S.W.
20 Jan. 1871.	*BODLEIAN LIBRARY, Oxford.

16 Feb. 1884.	CHARLES NEWPORT BOLTON, Brook Lodge, Waterford.
27 July, 1871.	*WILLIAM EDWARD BOOLS, 7 Cornhill, E.C.
26 Jan. 1871.	Lieut.-Colonel HAWORTH-BOOTH, Hullbank House, Hull.
25 Apr. 1877.	*R. C. BOSTOCK, Little Langtons, Lower Camden, Chislehurst.
8 Sept. 1874.	*BOSTON ATHENÆUM, Boston, U.S.A. (per Trübner and Co., 57 Ludgate Hill, E.C.).
15 Oct. 1875.	*BOSTON FREE PUBLIC LIBRARY, Boston, U.S.A. (per Trübner and Co., 57 Ludgate Hill, E.C.).
20 Jan. 1877.	*C. E. B. BOWLES, M.A., 34 Richmond Terrace, Clifton, Bristol.
3 Apr. 1877.	*Miss JULIA BOYD, Moor House, Leamside, Durham.
12 Sept. 1872.	EDWARD W. BRABROOK, F.S.A., 28 Abingdon Street, Westminster, S.W.
18 May, 1870.	*The Rev. WILLIAM BREE, The Rectory, Allesley, Coventry.
26 Aug. 1882.	*WILLIAM ERNEST BRENNAND, Blandford, Dorset.
13 Aug. 1878.	*The Hon. and Rev. Canon BRIDGEMAN, Wigan Hall, Wigan.
24 Nov. 1869.	*The Hon. and Rev. JOHN R. O. BRIDGEMAN, 89 Harley Street, W.
1 Jan. 1886.	WILLIAM BRIGG, Woodville, Far Headingley, Leeds.
24 Nov. 1869.	*THOMAS BROOKE, F.S.A. (*Council*), Armitage Bridge, Huddersfield.
29 Apr. 1869.	*FRANCIS CAPPER BROOKE, Ufford Place, Woodbridge.
4 Nov. 1870.	*The Rev. FREDERICK BROWN, F.S.A., Fern Bank, Beckenham, Kent.
28 Nov. 1876.	*J. R. BROWN, F.R.G.S., 14 Hilldrop Road, Camden Town, N.
19 June, 1869.	*PERCY C. S. BRUERE, Rockville, Lansdown, near Bath.
12 June, 1871.	C. G. PRIDEAUX-BRUNE, 10 Grosvenor Gardens, S.W.
21 May, 1869.	*Colonel W. E. G. LYTTON-BULWER, Quebec House, East Dereham.
11 June, 1869.	*Sir BERNARD BURKE, C.B., LL.D., Ulster King-of-Arms, The Castle, Dublin.
2 May, 1871.	*The Most Noble the MARQUIS OF BUTE (*Vice-President*), 118 Grosvenor Road, S.W.
20 Nov. 1873.	*CAMBRIDGE UNIVERSITY LIBRARY, Cambridge (H. BRADSHAW, M.A., Librarian).
27 Mar. 1879.	H. H. SMITH CARINGTON, Brookfield House, Whaley Bridge, Stockport.
15 Mar. 1884.	R. SMITH CARINGTON, St. Cloud, near Worcester.
24 Mar. 1883.	*Major TANKERVILLE J. CHAMBERLAIN, 80th Reg., Government House, Natal (care of V. Holt and Co., 17 Whitehall Place, S.W.).
1 Sept. 1884.	*W. H. C. CHAMBERLAINE, Blagden House, Keevil, Trowbridge, Wilts.
12 Apr. 1882.	*JOHN H. CHAPMAN, M.A., F.S.A., 38 St. Charles Square, North Kensington, W.
21 May, 1878.	*THOMAS WILLIAM CHARLTON, Chilwell Hall, Nottingham.
18 Oct. 1870.	*CHETHAM'S LIBRARY, Hunt's Bank, Manchester.
6 Oct. 1881.	J. W. CLAY, Rastrick House, near Brighouse.
11 Sept. 1880.	H. T. COGHLAN, 14 Hyde Park Gardens, W.
23 June, 1869.	*G. E. COKAYNE, F.S.A., Norroy King-at-Arms, College of Arms, Queen Victoria Street, E.C.
1 June, 1869.	The Rev. FREDERIC T. COLBY, D.D., F.S.A. (*Council*), Litton Cheney Rectory, Dorchester, Dorset.
4 Dec. 1883.	CHARLES F. COLE, Flintfield, Caterham, Surrey.
6 Dec. 1870.	Major J. KYRLE COLLINS, Wiltondale, Ross, Herefordshire.
22 Mar. 1883.	EDWARD CONDER, Elmhurst, Romford, Essex.
16 Mar. 1874.	EDWARD COODE, Polapit Tamar, Launceston.
10 Mar. 1871.	His Honour Judge W. H. COOKE, 42 Wimpole Street, W.
21 Feb. 1882.	*Colonel EDWARD H. COOPER, 42 Portman Square, W.

26 May, 1885.   W. A. COPINGER, The Priory, Greenheys, Manchester.
28 July, 1869. W. H. COTTELL, Yeolmbridge, Wood Vale, Forest Hill, S.E.
18 May, 1870.   *W. PRIDEAUX COURTNEY (Council), Ecclesiastical Commission, 10 Whitehall Place, S.W.
20 July, 1873. *J. C. CRABB, Clifton Lodge, Fallowfield, near Manchester.
24 June, 1878. *E. B. CRANE, Worcester, Massachusetts, U.S.A.
10 July, 1884. WILFRID CRIPPS, Farleigh House, Sandgate, Kent.
12 Aug. 1881.   *F. A. CRISP, Inglewood House, Grove Park, Denmark Hill, S.E.
8 Dec. 1883.   *TALBOT K. CROSSFIELD, 354 Hackney Road, E.
25 Nov. 1882.   *GERY MILNER-GIBSON CULLUM, Hardwick House, Bury St. Edmund's.
28 Apr. 1869.   *The Hon. HENRY ROPER-CURZON (Vice-President), The Ants' Nest, Tonbridge.
15 May, 1874.   J. E. CUSSANS, 4 Wyndham Crescent, Junction Road, N.
18 May, 1875.   *Lady ELIZABETH CUST, 13 Eccleston Square, S.W.
8 Oct. 1874.   *Miss CUST, 20 Thurloe Place, South Kensington, S.W.
2 Dec. 1884.   J. EDWARD K. CUTTS, 28 Southampton Street, Strand, W.C.

20 Nov. 1883.   *Mrs. DALISON, Hamptons, Tunbridge.
5 May, 1874.   The Rev. JOHN NEALE DALTON, M.A., F.S.A., Marlborough House, S.W.
29 May, 1869.   R. S. LONGWORTH-DAMES, M.A., 21 Herbert Street, Dublin.
18 Mar. 1874.   *The Rev. G. H. DAVENPORT, Stanford Hall, Loughborough.
28 July, 1869. *GORDON DAYMAN, St. Giles's, Oxford.
4 Nov. 1870.   The Rev. JOHN BATHURST DEANE, M.A., F.S.A., Sion Hill, Bath.
27 Dec. 1876.   *DE BERNARDY BROTHERS, 28 John Street, Bedford Row, W.C.
25 Aug. 1883.   *JOHN T. DICKINSON, Eastbourne, Prince's Park, Liverpool.
31 Dec. 1875.   The Hon. HAROLD A. DILLON, F.S.A., 3 Swan Walk, Chelsea, S.W.
18 Apr. 1878.   JOSEPH DODGSON, 33 Park Row, Leeds.
1 Jan. 1879.   THOMAS DORMAN, Sandwich, Kent.
22 Sept. 1869. *ROBERT DOWMAN, 29 Shakspeare Street, Ardwick, Manchester.
12 June, 1874. WILLIAM DOWNING, Springfield House, Olton, Acock's Green, Birmingham.
4 Oct. 1872.   *Sir WILLIAM DRAKE, F.S.A., 46 Parliament Street, S.W.
9 Nov. 1875.   *The Rev. JOHN INGLE DREDGE, Buckland Brewer, Bideford.
10 Jan. 1878.   *Mrs. DUGDALE, Yewden, Henley-on-Thames.
1 Nov. 1882.   *The Rev. R. E. H. DUKE, Monk Fryston, South Milford, Yorkshire.
22 June, 1870. GEORGE F. DUNCOMBE, 17 St. Stephen's Road, Bayswater, W.
17 June, 1878. *The Dean and Chapter of DURHAM, Chapter Offices, Durham.
12 Jan. 1872.   ROBERT DYMOND, F.S.A., 1 St. Leonard Road, Exeter.

18 Apr. 1878.   JOHN PARSONS EARWAKER, M.A., F.S.A., Pensarn, Abergele, North Wales.
10 Feb. 1883.   *The Hon. DANIEL C. EATON, New Haven, Connecticut, U.S.A. (Hon. Local Secretary for Connecticut, U.S.A.).
18 May, 1870.   The EARL OF EGMONT, 26 St. James's Place, S.W.
15 Apr. 1869.   *DUDLEY G. CARY ELWES, F.S.A. (Council), 9 The Crescent, Bedford.
22 June, 1870. *V. CARY ELWES, F.S.A., Billing Hall, Billing-road Station, Northampton.
18 Oct. 1870.   WILLIAM ROBERT EMERIS, M.A., F.S.A., Louth, Lincolnshire.

19 May, 1869.	J. G. FANSHAWE, 2 Halkin Street West, Belgrave Square, S.W.
27 Feb. 1885.	EDWARD GARTHWAITE FABISH, 24 Coleman Street, E.C.
19 Jan. 1878.	HENRY ST. CLAIR FEILDEN, Corpus Christi College, Oxford.
22 Sept. 1869.	WILLIAM FENNELL, Wakefield.
3 Nov. 1873.	Miss FFARINGTON, Worden, Preston.
16 June, 1872.	J. LEWIS FFYTCHE, M.A., F.S.A., The Terrace, Freshwater, Isle of Wight.
8 Dec. 1877.	*Colonel THOMAS WM. FLETCHER, M.A., F.R.S., F.S.A., Lawneswood House, Stourbridge.
31 Dec. 1875.	*CECIL G. S. FOLJAMBE, M.P., F.S.A., 2 Carlton House Terrace, S.W.
29 Jan. 1879.	JOHN FOSTER, Town Head, Horton in Ribblesdale, Settle.
31 Dec. 1875.	*JOSEPH FOSTER, 21 Boundary Road, St. John's Wood, N.W.
28 Nov. 1870.	*CHARLES H. FOX, M.D., The Beeches, Brislington, Bristol.
11 June, 1884.	A. W. FRANKS, M.A., F.S.A., British Museum, W.C.
16 Jan. 1884.	*EDWIN FRESHFIELD, LL.D., F.S.A., 5 Bank Buildings, Old Jewry, E.C.
27 Apr. 1871.	CLEMENT S. BEST-GARDNER, Eaglesbush, Neath.
5 Feb. 1883.	CHARLES W. GEORGE, 24 Aberdeen Terrace, Clifton.
17 Apr. 1871.	*HENRY H. GIBBS, St. Dunstan's Villa, Outer Circle, Regent's Park, N.W.
27 Mar. 1872.	*JAMES GIBSON, Salem, Washington County, New York, U.S.A.
12 May, 1878.	*JOSEPH GILLOW, 19 Northwood Road, Highgate. N.
8 Sept. 1871.	CHARLES GOLDING, 73 High Street, Colchester.
25 Jan. 1870.	*HENRY GOUGH, Sandcroft, Redhill.
12 Apr. 1869.	*GRANVILLE LEVESON GOWER, F.S.A. (*Council*), Titsey Place, Limpsfield, Surrey.
7 Oct. 1882.	HENRY GRAY, 25 Cathedral Yard, Manchester.
22 Sept. 1869.	*HENRY SYDNEY GRAZEBROOK, Treasury Chambers, Whitehall, S.W.
31 Dec. 1881.	*JOSEPH J. GREEN, Stansted Montfitchet, Bishop's Stortford.
16 Dec. 1870.	BENJAMIN WYATT GREENFIELD, 4 Cranbury Terrace, Southampton.
24 Nov. 1869.	The Rev. HENRY THOMAS GRIFFITH, B.A., Smallburgh Rectory, Norwich.
26 May, 1883.	Sir WILLIAM GUISE, Bart., Elmore Park, Gloucester.
26 July, 1878.	*RICHARD H. J. GURNEY, North Repps Hall, Norwich.
29 Dec. 1872.	J. E. A. GWYNNE, F.S.A., F.R.G.S., 97 Harley Street, W.
29 Apr. 1869.	EDWARD HAILSTONE, F.S.A., Walton Hall, Wakefield.
12 June, 1882.	Mrs. HALLIDAY, West View, Torquay, South Devon.
10 Aug. 1874.	*Captain PHILIP HAMOND, care of C. A. Hamond, Twyford Hall, Guist, Norfolk.
11 Apr. 1883.	*Sir REGINALD HANSON, M.A., F.S.A., 4 Bryanston Square, W.
29 Sept. 1880.	*THEODORE J. HARE, Crook Hall, Chorley.
1 Jan. 1884.	HENRY SEATON HARLAND, F.S.A., Stanbridge, Staplefield, Crawley, Sussex.
30 Apr. 1869.	*WILLIAM MARSH HARVEY, Goldington Hall, Bedford.
23 Jan. 1885.	*W. J. HARVEY, 14 Vicarage Road, Camberwell, S.E.
17 Apr. 1869.	*The Rev. SAMUEL HAYMAN, M.A., The Rectory, Douglas, Cork.
22 Feb. 1883.	C. ARTHUR HEAD, Hartburn Hall, Stockton-on-Tees.
3 June, 1873.	*WILLIAM C. HEANE, M.R.C.S., The Lawn, Cinderford, Gloucestershire.
14 May, 1869.	Lady HEATHCOTE, Hursley Park, Winchester.
28 Feb. 1885.	*J. D. HEMSWORTH, Monk Fryston Hall, South Milford, Yorkshire.
10 Mar. 1885.	The Rev. T. HERVEY, M.A., Colmer Rectory, Alton, Hants.

18 May, 1876.   Miss FRANCES MARGERY HEXT, Lostwithiel, Cornwall.
22 Sept. 1869. JOHN HIRST, Dobcross, Saddleworth.
27 Dec. 1879.   *HISTORICAL SOCIETY OF PENNSYLVANIA (care of B. F. Stevens, 4 Trafalgar Square, W.C.).
10 Dec. 1885.   JOHN HITCHMAN, Oak Villa, Sherborne Road, Acock's Green, Birmingham.
1 Jan. 1883.   RICHARD A. HOBLYN, 2 Sussex Place, Regent's Park, N.W.
24 Apr. 1869.   The Ven. Archdeacon HOLBECH, Farnborough, Banbury.
31 Dec. 1879.   WILLIAM J. HOLLWAY, Woodrising, Pinner, Watford.
2 Nov. 1877.   CHARLES G. HORNYOLD, Blackmore Park, Great Malvern.
16 June, 1872. *ROBERT HOVENDEN, Heathcote, Park Hill Road, Croydon.
27 Mar. 1869.   *JOSEPH JACKSON HOWARD, LL.D., F.S.A. (*Hon. Treasurer*), 3 Dartmouth Row, Blackheath, S.E.
4 Nov. 1870.   *THOMAS HUGHES, F.S.A., The Groves, Chester.
20 Feb. 1874.   W. ESSINGTON HUGHES, 89 Alexandra Road, South Hampstead, N.W.
20 Feb. 1879.   HULL SUBSCRIPTION LIBRARY, Albion Street, Hull (ALFRED MILNER, Librarian).

11 Dec. 1871.   *INNER TEMPLE LIBRARY, The Librarian, E.C.

29 Dec. 1877.   W. F. MARSH JACKSON, Smethwick, near Birmingham.
23 Sept. 1872. *WILLIAM JACKSON, F.S.A., care of Granville Kershaw, Holly Bank, 21 Roe Lane, Southport.
22 July, 1872. *T. E. JACOBSON, M.D., Sleaford, Lincolnshire.
9 Feb. 1880.   *FRANCIS JAMES, 190 Cromwell Road, S.W.
1 July, 1869.   *The Rev. EDMUND JERMYN, M.A., Forbescourt, Dundee, N.B.
2 Nov. 1877.   ARTHUR J. JEWERS, F.S.A., Chester Place, Mutley, Plymouth.
20 Mar. 1881.   *JOHN JOSEPH JONES, Abberley Hall, Stourport.
6 Mar. 1871.   MORRIS C. JONES, F.S.A., Gungrog, Welshpool.

3 June, 1873.   The Rev. EDWARD KING, B.A., F.S.A. Scot., Werrington Vicarage, near Launceston.
17 Apr. 1880.   KING'S INNS LIBRARY, Dublin (J. M. LA BARTE, Librarian).
1 Jan. 1879.   *Mrs. HENRY KINGSLEY, 10 Ridgway Place, Wimbledon.
31 Dec. 1870.   *THOMAS C. SNEYD KYNNERSLEY, Moor Green, Moseley, Birmingham.

30 Dec. 1882.   FREDERIC DE HOCHEPIED LARPENT, Barrackpore, Bombay.
13 Dec. 1883.   C. MILLER LAYTON, F.S.A., Shortlands, Castle Hill Avenue, Folkestone.
4 Nov. 1870.   *THOMAS LAYTON, F.S.A., Kew Bridge, Middlesex.
2 Jan. 1871.   Sir EDMUND A. H. LECHMERE, Bart., M.P., 13 Bolton Row, Mayfair, W.
22 Sept. 1869. The Rev. F. G. LEE, D.C.L., F.S.A., All Saints' Vicarage, York Road, Lambeth, S.E.
27 Dec. 1882.   *JOSEPH LEETE, Eversden, South Norwood Park, S.E.
24 Nov. 1883.   *LEHIGH UNIVERSITY, South Bethlehem, Pennsylvania, U.S.A. (per H. Sotheran and Co., 136 Strand, W.C.).
27 Apr. 1874.   *STANLEY LEIGHTON, M.P., Athenæum Club, 107 Pall Mall, S.W.
3 Apr. 1869.   *Mrs. LITTLEDALE, 26 Cranley Gardens, S.W.
2 Sept. 1872.   *LIVERPOOL FREE PUBLIC LIBRARY, William Brown Street, Liverpool (PETER COWELL, Librarian).
8 Sept. 1871.   The Rev. W. J. LOFTIE, F.S.A., 3a Sheffield Terrace, Campden Hill, Kensington, W.

9 May, 1873.	*LIBRARY COMMITTEE OF THE CORPORATION OF THE CITY OF LONDON, Guildhall Library, E.C. (W. H. OVERALL, Librarian).
20 Dec. 1877.	LONDON LIBRARY, 12 St. James's Square, S.W. (ROBERT HARRISON, Librarian).
2 Nov. 1877.	*WILLIAM LONG, F.S.A., West Hay, Wrington, Somerset.
24 June, 1881.	*G. B. LONGSTAFF, Southfield Grange, Wandsworth, S.W.
7 Apr. 1869.	*WILLIAM H. DYER LONGSTAFFE, Gateshead.
31 Dec. 1878.	B. DE BERTODANO LOPEZ, 22 Chester Terrace, Regent's Park, N.W.
14 May, 1869.	Sir JOHN MACLEAN, F.S.A. (*Council*), Glasbury House, Richmond Hill, Clifton, Bristol.
28 Nov. 1870.	*The Rev. A. R. MADDISON, Vicars' Court, Lincoln.
1 Feb. 1879.	Mrs. MANBY, care of Charles Jenser, Esq., Oakhill, Bath.
16 Mar. 1874.	*MANCHESTER FREE LIBRARY, Manchester (CHARLES W. SUTTON, Librarian).
23 June, 1869.	His Grace the DUKE OF MANCHESTER (*President*), 1 Great Stanhope Street, W.
10 Apr. 1869.	*GEORGE W. MARSHALL, LL.D., F.S.A. (*Council*), 60 Onslow Gardens, S.W.
12 Mar. 1885.	*Hon. ROBERT MARSHAM, 5 Chesterfield Street, Mayfair, W.
7 Oct. 1882.	EDMUND STORY-MASKELYNE, Hatt House, Box, Wilts.
7 June, 1877.	The Rev. G. S. MASTER, West Dean Rectory, Salisbury.
20 May, 1869.	*WALTER C. METCALFE, F.S.A., 10 Lupus Street, St. George's Square, S.W.
7 May, 1878.	*THOMAS TINDAL METHOLD, 7 Ashburn Place, Cromwell Road, South Kensington, S.W.
24 May, 1869.	The Right Hon. VISCOUNT MIDLETON (*Vice-President*), Eaton Square, S.W.
20 July, 1878.	SAMUEL MILNE MILNE, Calverley House, near Leeds.
24 Aug. 1870.	The Rev. JOHN MIREHOUSE, Colsterworth Rectory, Grantham.
10 Sept. 1877.	MITCHELL LIBRARY, Ingram Street East, Glasgow (F. T. BARRETT, Librarian).
1 Apr. 1879.	*W. J. C. MOENS, Tweed, near Lymington, Hants.
1 Nov. 1881.	J. B. M. LINGARD-MONK, Belmore, Craneswater Park, Southsea.
12 Apr. 1869.	*The Right Hon. LORD MONSON (*Vice-President*), 29 Belgrave Square, S.W.
18 May, 1870.	*Colonel CHARLES THOMAS JOHN MOORE, F.S.A., Frampton Hall, near Boston.
17 June, 1878.	Mrs. MOORE, Lawneswood House, Stourbridge.
20 Feb. 1880.	*JOHN MULLINGS, Cirencester.
31 Dec. 1869.	GEORGE J. MURRAY, Mytchett Place, Frimley, Surrey.
16 Apr. 1875.	*W. MARTIAL MYDDELTON, 12 Albion Grove, Stoke Newington, N.
28 May, 1884.	NATIONAL LIBRARY OF IRELAND (care of Hodges, Figgis, and Co., 104 Grafton Street, Dublin).
14 Sept. 1872.	NAVAL AND MILITARY CLUB, 94 Piccadilly, W.
4 Feb. 1884.	FRANK NEAME, Luton House, Faversham.
24 Jan. 1878.	The Rev. CHARLES NEVE, Benenden, Staplehurst.
7 Sept. 1878.	*NEW ENGLAND HISTORIC GENEALOGICAL SOCIETY, 18 Somerset Street, Boston, U.S.A. (J. WARD DEAN, Librarian), (care of E. G. Allen, 28 Henrietta Street, Covent Garden, W.C.).
15 Feb. 1879.	*NEW YORK STATE LIBRARY, Albany, U.S.A. (care of Stevens and Haynes, Bell Yard, Temple Bar, W.C.).
30 June, 1873.	FREDERICK I. NICHOLL, F.S.A., 120 Harley Street, W.
11 Aug. 1876.	G. W. NICHOLL, The Ham, Cowbridge, Glamorganshire.

8 Sept. 1871.	J. W. STRADLING NICHOLL-CARNE, D.C.L., St. Donat's Castle, Bridgend, Glamorganshire.
20 May, 1881.	J. GAMSON NICHOLSON, 8 Richmond Terrace, Cardiff.
3 Apr. 1874.	The Rev. C. B. NORCLIFFE, Langton Hall, Malton, Yorkshire.
7 June, 1875.	*NOTTINGHAM FREE PUBLIC LIBRARY (J. P. BRISCOE, Librarian).
19 June, 1874.	The Rev. T. R. O'FFLAHERTIE, Capel Vicarage, Dorking.
20 Feb. 1880.	JOHN O'HART, Ringsend, Dublin.
16 Nov. 1885.	*V. L. OLIVER, Sumner Grange, Sunninghill.
28 Feb. 1877.	*HENRY LEIGH ORMSBY, 2 Harcourt Buildings, Inner Temple, E.C.
26 July, 1869.	EVAN ORTNER, 3 St. James's Street, S.W.
6 May, 1871.	Sir CHARLES J. PALMER, Bart., Dorney Court, Windsor.
14 Feb. 1880.	*Captain JOHN W. R. PARKER, 19th Foot, The Barracks, Tralee, Kerry, Ireland.
24 Feb. 1874.	MANSFIELD PARKYNS, Woodborough Hall, near Nottingham.
7 Sept. 1877.	*THOMAS W. PARR, The Grove, Cossington, Leicester.
7 Apr. 1869.	DANIEL PARSONS, M.A., Stuart's Lodge, Malvern Wells.
28 July, 1869.	D. WILLIAMS PATERSON, Newark Valley, New York, U.S.A.
28 May, 1884.	*W. K. PAULI, Luton, Bedfordshire.
28 July, 1869.	EDWARD PEACOCK, F.S.A., Bottesford Manor, Brigg, Lincolnshire.
1 Jan. 1884.	Captain FREDERICK CLINTON PEARCE, Rockford, Illinois, U.S.A.
28 July, 1869.	The Rev. A. J. PEARMAN, Merstham, Surrey.
1 May, 1871.	IRA B. PECK, Woonsocket, Rhode Island, U.S.A.
29 Dec. 1872.	RICHARD LAWRENCE PEMBERTON, Hawthorne Tower, Seaham Harbour, co. Durham.
31 Mar. 1885.	RICHARD PETER, The Cottage, Launceston.
30 May, 1881.	WILLIAM P. W. PHILLIMORE, M.A., 124 Chancery Lane, W.C.
20 May, 1881.	Mrs. PIERCE, Sherbourne House, Leamington.
5 Apr. 1883.	*Sir LIONEL M. SWINNERTON PILKINGTON, Bart., Chevet Park, Wakefield.
15 Feb. 1873.	*W. DUNCOMBE PINK, 5 King Street, Leigh, Lancashire.
23 July, 1885.	*EDGAR POWELL, 2 Thanet Place, Temple Bar, E.C.
31 Dec. 1875.	The Rev. F. J. POYNTON, Kelston Rectory, Bath.
8 Dec. 1877.	*Lieut.-Colonel W. F. PRIDEAUX, 2 Sidlaw Terrace, Bognor.
28 May, 1879.	J. N. PYKE-NOTT, 44 Belsize Square, South Hampstead, N.W.
29 July, 1875.	*BERNARD QUARITCH, 15 Piccadilly, W.
11 May, 1869.	The Rev. Canon RAINE, York.
11 Dec. 1874.	EVELYN W. RASHLEIGH, Menabilly, Cornwall.
13 Jan. 1883.	R. NORMAN S. REDMAYNE, South Dene, Gateshead-on-Tyne.
31 Oct. 1884.	REFORM CLUB, 104 Pall Mall, S.W. (care of Mr. Ridgway, 169 Piccadilly, W.).
10 Mar. 1874.	The Rev. O. J. REICHEL, Sparsholt Vicarage, Challow Station, Great Western Railway, Berks.
29 Apr. 1871.	*SAMUEL RIGBY, Fern Bank, Liverpool Road, Chester.
11 Sept. 1880.	*BROOKE ROBINSON, Barford House, Warwick.
30 Mar. 1869.	*The Rev. C. J. ROBINSON, M.A. (*Auditor*), West Hackney Rectory, Stoke Newington, N.
12 Nov. 1883.	*W. P. ROBINSON, care of Messrs. E. and J. B. Young and Co., New York (per Trübner and Co., 57 Ludgate Hill, E.C.).

6 Jan. 1883.	ARNOLD HENRY ROBSON, The Esplanade, Sunderland.
14 Apr. 1860.	ROCHDALE FREE PUBLIC LIBRARY, Rochdale.
27 May, 1869.	*The Rev. EDWARD ROGERS, M.A., Odcombe Rectory, Ilminster.
12 Sept. 1877.	W. O. ROPER, Southfield, Lancaster.
1 Jan. 1883.	*SIMPSON ROSTRON, 1 Hare Court, Temple, E.C.
3 Dec. 1873.	J. BROOKING ROWE, F.S.A., Plympton Lodge, Plympton, South Devon.
29 Jan. 1878.	*ROYAL HISTORICAL SOCIETY (P. EDWARD DOVE, Secretary), 11 Chandos Street, Cavendish Square, W.
20 Jan. 1871.	ROYAL IRISH ACADEMY, 19 Dawson Street, Dublin.
28 May, 1869.	ROYAL LIBRARY, Windsor Castle, Windsor.
28 July, 1869.	The Rev. DAVID ROYCE, Netherswell Vicarage, Stow-on-the-Wold.
18 May, 1870.	*JAMES RUSBY, F.R.Hist.Soc., 18 Oppidans Road, Regent's Park, N.W.
12 Dec. 1874.	EDWARD RUSSELL, Boston, U.S.A.
20 Jan. 1871.	JOHN PAUL RYLANDS, F.S.A. (*Hon. Secretary*), Heather Lea, Claughton, Birkenhead.
31 Dec. 1881.	*THOMAS GLAZEBROOK RYLANDS, F.S.A., Highfields, Thelwall, near Warrington.
27 July, 1879.	*W. DE RYTHRE, Riverstown House, Monasterevan, Ireland.
24 June, 1878.	S. SUTHERLAND SAFFORD, Parkshot, Richmond, Surrey.
3 June, 1873.	*General Sir JOHN ST. GEORGE, K.C.B., 22 Cornwall Gardens, Queen's Gate, S.W.
31 Dec. 1885.	*JAMES ST. LEGER, 24 South Audley Street, W.
14 Dec. 1885.	*EDWARD ELBRIDGE SALISBURY, Lyme, Connecticut, U.S.A.
18 Aug. 1873.	JOHN EDMUND SANDBACH, Stoodley Hall, Eastwood, Todmorden.
12 July, 1881.	Mrs. LEOPOLD SCARLETT, 30 Cranley Gardens, S.W.
8 Dec. 1877.	G. D. SCULL, 2 Langland Gardens, Frognal, N.W.
15 Dec. 1883.	*WALTER H. S. SHADWELL, 21 Nottingham Place, Marylebone Road, W.
10 July, 1884.	MICHAEL SHEARD, Boothroyd, Birstall, Leeds.
8 Dec. 1885.	SHEFFIELD CENTRAL FREE PUBLIC LIBRARY, Surrey Street, Sheffield.
18 Feb. 1873.	*CONINGSBY C. SIBTHORP, Canwick Hall, Lincoln.
6 Sept. 1882.	RICHARD SIMPSON, 13 Thurlow Road, Roslyn, Hampstead, N.W.
29 Jan. 1878.	*SION COLLEGE LIBRARY, 42 Aldersgate Street, City, E.C. (Rev. W. R. MILMAN, Librarian).
5 June, 1874.	HUBERT SMITH, Belmont House, Bridgenorth.
10 Nov. 1873.	*J. C. C. SMITH, H.M. Probate Court, Somerset House, W.C.
25 Jan. 1871.	The Rev. WALTER SNEYD, 55 Portland Place, W.
22 Mar. 1871.	*SOCIETY OF ANTIQUARIES OF LONDON, Burlington House, W.
12 Nov. 1883.	SOCIETY OF ANTIQUARIES OF NEWCASTLE-UPON-TYNE, The Castle, Newcastle-upon-Tyne.
20 Jan. 1877.	*EDWARD SOLLY, F.R.S., F.S.A., Camden House, Sutton, Surrey.
7 June, 1872.	*SOMERSETSHIRE ARCHÆOLOGICAL SOCIETY, Museum, Taunton.
27 Jan. 1879.	*Rev. J. H. STANNING, Leigh Vicarage, Leigh, Lancashire.
24 Dec. 1881.	*JOHN STANSFELD, Woodville, Clarendon Road, Leeds.
30 May, 1884.	The Rev. FRANCIS STERRY, Poltimore Rectory, Exeter.
10 Oct. 1884.	EDWARD STONE, 5 Finsbury Circus, E.C.
31 Dec. 1875.	The Rev. HUGH A. STOWELL, Breadsall Rectory, Derby.
25 Nov. 1885.	*PETER STUBS, Statham Lodge, Warrington.
22 Sept. 1869.	*JOHN SYKES, M.D., F.S.A., Doncaster.
3 Apr. 1876.	Mrs. G. BLUNDELL-THOMPSON, The Grove, Allerton, Liverpool.
17 April, 1885.	JOHN J. THOMPSON, Historical Society of Pennsylvania, 1300 Locust Street, Philadelphia, U.S.A.
15 June, 1878.	*C. H. TINDAL, Platt Hall, Rusholme, Manchester.

15 Dec. 1883.	*JOHN TOLHURST, F.S.A., Glenbrook, Beckenham, Kent.
23 Dec. 1884.	GEORGE W. TOMLINSON, F.S.A., The Elms, Huddersfield.
28 Dec. 1876.	JOHN TREMAYNE, Heligan, St. Austell, Cornwall.
1 Jan. 1884.	*HENRY TRETHEWY, Silsoe, Ampthill, Bedfordshire.
16 Mar. 1871.	*JOSEPH HERBERT TRITTON, 36 Queen's Gate Gardens, S.W.
8 Mar. 1881.	H. J. TROTTER, 2 Harcourt Buildings, Temple, E.C.
1 Feb. 1876.	*STEPHEN TUCKER, Somerset Herald, College of Arms, Queen Victoria Street, E.C.
19 Jan. 1881.	WM. MURRAY TUKE, Saffron Walden.
31 Oct. 1884.	*WM. H. UPTON, Wallawalla, Washington, U.S.A. (*Hon. Local Secretary for Washington, U.S.A.*).
9 Jan. 1875.	HENRY F. J. VAUGHAN, 30 Edwardes Square, Kensington, W.
10 June,1869.	*Sir HENRY M. VAVASOUR, Bart., F.S.A. (*Vice-President*), 8 Upper Grosvenor Street, W.
3 Dec. 1874.	Colonel P. D. VIGORS, Holloden House, Bagenalstown, co. Carlow, Ireland.
18 Dec. 1874.	*HENRY WAGNER, F.S.A. (*Auditor*), 13 Half Moon Street, Piccadilly, W.
23 Feb. 1884.	*Sir HEREWALD WAKE, Bart., Courteenhall, Northampton.
26 May, 1883.	HUBERT H. WALL, P.O. Box 1737, New York, U.S.A.
18 May,1870.	*EDWARD WALTHAM, Wolsingham House, 22 Christchurch Road, Streatham Hill, S.W.
2 Jan. 1871.	The EARL OF WARWICK, 1 Stable Yard, St. James's, S.W.
28 Feb. 1877.	*WASHINGTON LIBRARY OF CONGRESS, U.S.A. (care of E. G. Allen, 28 Henrietta Street, Covent Garden, W.C.).
22 Feb. 1883.	*A. JAMES WATERLOW, Great Doods, Reigate, Surrey.
2 Sept. 1872.	*WATKINSON LIBRARY, Hartford, Connecticut, U.S.A. (care of E. G. Allen, 28 Henrietta Street, Covent Garden, W.C.).
22 June,1870.	FRANK G. WATNEY, Landmore, Aghadowey, co. Derry.
4 Nov. 1870.	*JOHN WATNEY, F.S.A., F.R.G.S., Mercers' Hall, Ironmonger Lane, Cheapside, E.C.
18 Oct. 1884.	The Rev. F. W. WEAVER, Milton Vicarage, Evercreech, Bath.
1 Mar. 1871.	ARCHIBALD WEIR, M.D., St. Mungho's, Great Malvern.
18 May, 1870.	*W. H. WELDON, College of Arms, Queen Victoria Street, E.C.
1 Dec. 1882.	His Grace the DUKE OF WESTMINSTER (*Vice - President*), Grosvenor House, Grosvenor Street, W.
22 Sept. 1869.	Lieut.-Colonel GOULD HUNTER-WESTON, F.S.A., Hunterston, West Kilbride, Ayrshire.
2 Oct. 1874.	CHARLES A. WHITE, New Haven, Connecticut, U.S.A.
1 July,1876.	Captain EDWARD ARTHUR WHITE, F.S.A. (*Council*), Old Elvet, Durham.
28 July, 1869.	WILLIAM H. WHITMORE, Boston, U.S.A.
14 Feb. 1885.	Rev. CHRISTOPHER HALES WILKIE, Kingstone Rectory, Canterbury.
12 June,1878.	J. J. GARTH WILKINSON, M.D., F.R.G.S., 4 Finchley Road, St. John's Wood, N.W.
22 Dec. 1870.	The Rev. AUGUSTIN WILLIAMS, Todenham Rectory, Moreton-in-the-Marsh.
24 Apr. 1879.	CHARLES WILLIAMS, Moseley Lodge, Birmingham.
10 April, 1885.	*Rev. J. BOWSTEAD WILSON, Knightwick Rectory, Worcester.
31 Dec. 1880.	EDWARD WINDEATT, Totnes, Devon.
13 Apr. 1880.	*BENJAMIN WINSTONE, 53 Russell Square, W.C.
13 Apr. 1871.	*The Hon. ROBERT C. WINTHROP, 90 Marlborough Street, Boston, U.S.A.

24 Nov. 1869.	R. H. WOOD, F.S.A., Penrhos House, Rugby.
18 May, 1876.	CHARLES H. L. WOODD, F.G.S., 34 New Bond Street, W.
14 Jan. 1884.	*The Rev. ADOLPHUS F. A. WOODFORD, M.A., 25A Norfolk Crescent, Hyde Park, W.
21 Feb. 1882.	*JOHN WOODGATE, Little Bentley Hall, Colchester.
18 May, 1870.	*Sir ALBERT W. WOODS, F.S.A., Garter King-of-Arms, College of Arms, Queen Victoria Street, E.C.
20 Aug. 1878.	Dr. A. E. WOOLRYCH, 20 Royal Avenue, Chelsea, S.W.
29 Dec. 1885.	*WORCESTER FREE PUBLIC LIBRARY, Worcester, Massachusetts, U.S.A. (SAMUEL S. GREEN, Librarian).
7 Oct. 1879.	*YALE COLLEGE, Lyme, Connecticut, U.S.A. (care of E. G. Allen, 28 Henrietta Street, Covent Garden, W.C.).
23 Feb. 1884.	LAMBTON YOUNG, 16 Harcourt Terrace, Radcliffe Square, S.W.

PUBLICATIONS.

VOL.
1. — The Visitation of London, in 1568, by Cooke. Edited by J. J. Howard, Esq., LL.D., F.S.A., and G. J. Armytage, Esq., F.S.A.
2. — The Visitation of Leicestershire, in 1619, by Lennard and Vincent. Edited by John Fetherston, Jun., Esq., F.S.A.
3. — The Visitation of Rutland, in 1618, by Camden. Edited by George J. Armytage, Esq., F.S.A.
4. — The Visitations of Nottingham in 1569 and 1614. Edited by Geo. W. Marshall, Esq., LL.D., F.S.A.
5. — The Visitations of Oxford, 1574 and 1634. Edited by W. H. Turner, Esq.
6. — The Visitation of Bedon in 1620. Edited by the Rev. F. T. Colby, D.D., F.S.A.
7. — The Visitation of Cumberland in 1615. Edited by John Fetherston, Esq., F.S.A.

[The preceding Seven Works are out of Print.

8. — Le Neve's Catalogue of Knights. Edited by George W. Marshall, Esq., LL.D., F.S.A. £1:1:0
9. — The Visitation of Cornwall, 1620. Edited by Col. Vivian and Dr. H. H. Drake. £1:1:0
10. — The Registers of Westminster Abbey. Edited by Colonel Chester, D.C.L., LL.D. £1:1:0
11. — The Visitation of Somersetshire in 1623. Edited by the Rev. F. T. Colby, D.D., F.S.A. £1:1:0
12. — The Visitation of Warwickshire. Edited by John Fetherston, Esq., F.S.A. £1:1:0
13. — The Visitations of Essex in 1552, 1558, 1612, and 1634. Part I. Edited by Walter C. Metcalfe, Esq., F.S.A. £1:1:0
14. — The Visitation of Essex, consisting of Miscellaneous Pedigrees, and Berry's Pedigrees. Part II. With general Index. £1:1:0
15. — The Visitation of London, 1633-4. Vol. I. Edited by J. J. Howard, Esq., LL.D., F.S.A., and Colonel Chester, D.C.L., LL.D. £1:1:0
16. — The Visitation of Yorkshire in 1564. Edited by the Rev. C. B. Norcliffe, M.A. £1:1:0
17. — The Visitation of London, 1633-4. Vol. II. Edited by J. J. Howard, Esq., LL.D., F.S.A. £1:1:0
18. — The Visitation of Cheshire in 1580. Edited by J. Paul Rylands, Esq., F.S.A. £1:1:0
19. — The Visitations of Bedfordshire in 1566, 1582, and 1634. Edited by F. A. Blaydes, Esq. £1:1:0
20. — The Visitation of Dorsetshire, in 1623, by St. George and Lennard as Deputies to Camden. Edited by J. Paul Rylands, Esq., F.S.A. £1:1:0
21. — The Visitation of Gloucestershire, in 1623, by Chitting and Phillipot as Deputies to Camden. Edited by Sir John Maclean, F.S.A., and W. C. Heane, Esq., M.R.C.S. £1:1:0
22. — The Visitations of Hertfordshire in 1572 and 1634. Edited by Walter C. Metcalfe, Esq., F.S.A. £1:1:0

PROSPECTIVE PUBLICATIONS.

Shropshire Pedigrees, comprising the Visitations of 1569, 1584, and 1623. To be Edited by J. Paul Rylands, Esq., F.S.A.

The Visitations of Norfolk in 1563, 1589, and 1613. To be Edited by Walter Rye, Esq.

The Visitations of Worcestershire in 1569 and 1634.

The Visitations of Hampshire, in 1530, 1552, 1575, and 1622, by Benolte, Hawley, Cooke, and Philipot as Deputy to Camden.

The Visitations of Sussex, in 1530, by Benolte; 1574, by Cooke; and 1633, by Philipot and Owen as Deputies to St. George and Burrough.

The Book of Heirs from 1 Edward I. to 17 Henry VI. To be Edited by Sir John Maclean, F.S.A.

The Visitation of Berkshire, in 1531, by Benolte. To be Edited by Granville Leveson Gower, Esq., F.S.A.

The Visitations of Northamptonshire, in 1566 and 1618, by Harvey and Camden.

Entrance Fee: Half-a-Guinea.   Annual Subscription: One Guinea.

Members whose Subscriptions are due are requested to forward them to J. J. Howard, Esq., LL.D., Honorary Treasurer, at 3 Dartmouth Row, Blackheath, Kent, who will also receive Subscriptions towards the publication of "Parish Registers."

Persons wishing to join the Society should apply to J. Paul Rylands, Esq., F.S.A., Hon. Sec., Heather Lea, Claughton, Birkenhead.

The Publications of the Society which are in print can be obtained, by Members *only*, at the prices above mentioned, on application to Messrs. Mitchell and Hughes, 140 Wardour Street, W.

REGISTER SECTION.

PUBLICATIONS.

Vol. I.—THE REGISTERS OF ST. PETER'S, CORNHILL, LONDON. Part I.,
A.D. 1538 to 1666. Edited by GRANVILLE LEVESON GOWER, Esq., F.S.A.   £0 : 10 : 6

Vol. II.—THE REGISTERS OF CANTERBURY CATHEDRAL. Edited by
ROBERT HOVENDEN, Esq.   £0 : 10 : 6

Vol. III.—THE REGISTERS OF ST. DIONIS BACKCHURCH, LONDON.
Edited by Colonel J. L. CHESTER, D.C.L., LL.D.   £0 : 10 : 6

Vol. IV.—THE REGISTERS OF ST. PETER'S, CORNHILL, LONDON. Part II.,
A.D. 1666 to 1754. Edited by GRANVILLE LEVESON GOWER, Esq., F.S.A.   £0 : 10 : 6

Vol. V.—THE REGISTERS OF ST. MARY ALDERMARY, LONDON.
Edited by Colonel J. L. CHESTER, D.C.L., LL.D.   £1 : 1 : 0

Vol. VI.—THE REGISTERS OF ST. THOMAS APOSTLE, LONDON.
Edited by Colonel J. L. CHESTER, D.C.L., LL.D.   £1 : 1 : 0

Vol. VII.—THE REGISTERS OF ST. MICHAEL, CORNHILL, LONDON.
Partly Edited by Colonel J. L. CHESTER, D.C.L., LL.D.   £1 : 1 : 0

Vol. VIII.—THE REGISTERS OF ST. ANTHOLIN, BUDGE ROW; AND
ST. JOHN BAPTIST ON WALLBROOK, LONDON.   £1 : 1 : 0

Vol. IX.—THE REGISTERS OF ST. JAMES, CLERKENWELL, LONDON.
Vol. I. Edited by ROBERT HOVENDEN, Esq.   £1 : 1 : 0

Vol. X.—THE REGISTERS OF ST. JAMES, CLERKENWELL, LONDON.
Vol. II. Edited by ROBERT HOVENDEN, Esq.   £1 : 1 : 0

Vol. XI.—THE MARRIAGE REGISTERS OF ST. GEORGE, HANOVER
SQUARE, LONDON. Vol. I. Edited by JOHN H. CHAPMAN, Esq., M.A., F.S.A. [*In the Press.*]

PROSPECTIVE PUBLICATIONS.

THE REGISTERS OF ST. JAMES, CLEKENWELL, LONDON. Vol. III.
To be Edited by ROBERT HOVENDEN, Esq.

THE MARRIAGE REGISTERS OF ST. GEORGE, HANOVER SQUARE,
LONDON. Vol. II. To be Edited by JOHN H. CHAPMAN, Esq., M.A., F.S.A.

THE REGISTERS OF CHRIST CHURCH, NEWGATE STREET, LONDON.

THE REGISTERS OF DURHAM CATHEDRAL. To be Edited by Captain
WHITE, F.S.A.

THE REGISTERS OF BATH ABBEY CHURCH, BATH.

THE REGISTERS OF ST. SEPULCHRE'S, LONDON.

AND MANY OTHERS.

The Publications of the Register Section will be supplied to Members on payment of an extra Subscription of One Guinea, and can be obtained, by Members *only,* from Messrs. MITCHELL and HUGHES, 140 Wardour Street, W., at the above Prices.

Forms of Application, and all other particulars, may be obtained by applying to J. PAUL RYLANDS, Esq., F.S.A., Hon. Sec., Heather Lea, Claughton, Birkenhead.

In compliance with Section 108 of the
Copyright Revision Act of 1976,
The Ohio State University Libraries
has produced this facsimile on permanent/durable
paper to replace the deteriorated original volume
owned by the Libraries. Facsimile created by
Acme Bookbinding, Charlestown, MA

2003

The paper used in this publication meets the
minimum requirements of the
American National Standard for Information
Sciences - Permanence for Printed Library
Materials,
ANSI Z39.48-1992.

www.ingramcontent.com/pod-product-compliance
Lightning Source LLC
Chambersburg PA
CBHW020911230426
43666CB00008B/1414